Edited by Stephen J. Bury

One hundred objects in the Frick Art Reference Library

Uniformbooks
in association with the Frick Art Reference Library, The Frick Collection

The Frick Collection
1 East 70th Street, New York, NY 10021
frick.org

First published 2022 by Uniformbooks in association
with the Frick Art Reference Library, The Frick Collection
Copyright © The Frick Collection
ISBN 978-1-910010-28-0

Uniformbooks
7 Hillhead Terrace, Axminster, EX13 5JL
uniformbooks.co.uk

Trade distribution by Central Books
centralbooks.com

Printed and bound in the United Kingdom by T J Books

With the support of the Eugene V. and Clare E. Thaw Charitable Trust

27 | *Kleine Kabinett*

Introduction

A conversation between Sally Brazil (Associate Chief Librarian, Archives) & Dr. Stephen J. Bury (Andrew W. Mellon Chief Librarian) about the centenary of the Frick Art Reference Library.

Sally – How did you decide the date for celebrating the centenary of the Library?

Stephen – You might think this was an easy question to answer. I started to think about a conversation I had with Sarat Maharaj years back at the Istanbul Biennial, maybe the 1995 one, about Alighiero Boetti's artist's book *Classifying the Thousand Longest Rivers in the World* (1977), where he gives the source/spring of a river and measures to where it debouches into the sea. Sarat pointed out that in Hindu philosophy the source of the river might lie in the gods making love or war in the heavens. So it is much more complex—a sliding scale of conceiving, founding and opening.

Should it be the date of the vision Helen Clay Frick had after her London visit to Robert Witt on the 30th of May 1920? But the decision that "the U.S.A. would have, in memory of Henry Clay Frick, a Frick Art Reference Library, founded by his daughter", might have been made the night of the 30th of May, the morning of the 31st or several days later. Or, the 8th of November 1920 when the handwritten Library Diary proclaimed "Library founded. Ruth Savord began work as Librarian. She and Miss Frick began cutting up [a] few things on hand and working out forms, etc."

Then there is the question of viability—when would the Library be able to have enough materials to begin to answer questions? Paul Sachs (1878–1965) at the Fogg Art Museum and an adviser to Helen had suggested 13,000 reproductions would constitute "a minimum working collection", possibly attained in February 1922: the Library Diary for 7 March 1922 notes "passed 15000 in our picture count". And the Library only surpassed 3,000 books in January 1923.

The number of visitors could be another measure: from the beginning there were individual visitors such as library staff from New York Public Library or Mr. Clifford, Librarian of the Metropolitan Museum. So perhaps the date, 27 January 1922, when a class of Princeton art students were brought to the Library by Frank Jewett Mather, Professor of Art and Archaeology, and Director of the Princeton University Art Museum 1922–46, could be the beginning. Then the opening of the first purpose-built Library 9 June 1924 could also be a good candidate.

I have gone with 27 January 1922 when student researchers were introduced to the Library: it's a date midway between 1920 and 1924, and numerical viability had almost been attained. But it will be a long centenary celebration extending into 1924.

Sally – Why have you decided to call the book 'One hundred objects'?

Stephen – 'One hundred objects' was initially a working title, and it was obvious that object was being used in the widest possible meaning. I wanted to have a sense of the people who contributed—and their being made manifest in an object e.g. a photograph, plaque, acquisition, legal agreement etc.—and create also a sense of space or place. I also wanted to tell a sort of art history for the areas the Library has covered—it's arranged chronologically, but not as, or rarely, an art historical timeline. To meet the hundred years some objects have had to be organized by date of their acquisition.

Sally – What are some of the themes?

Stephen – One leitmotif has been the use of technology. In 1920 a card catalog was innovative; systematic photography of works of art in-situ and the recording of information as oral history about the work and owners, such as in the Frick's American campaigns, beginning in Virginia in March 1922 and ending in Massachusetts in October 1950, with four field trips to Italy 1923–28; the use of agents abroad to collect photographs and printed material in London (Witt), Paris and the Netherlands (Brière), Italy (Sansoni, Offner, Mason Perkins); indexing art and archaeology periodicals from 1927 until eventually Art Index supplanted it; the dumb-waiters and telautographs in the 1935 building; microfilming the photoarchive in 1941; the Monuments Men map project 1943–44; mass and boutique digitization; the New York Art Resources Consortium; web archiving; computer vision; zoom programming; international programming e.g. PHAROS, the international consortium of photo archives; the digital art history lab.

Sally – Another one that strikes me is the role of women. Historically, the field of librarianship has been overwhelmingly populated by women and until your appointment as the Andrew W. Mellon Chief Librarian, the Frick Art Reference Library has always had a women as chief librarian. In fact, males of the species were rarely to be found

ORIG.-HOLZSCHNITT VON ELENA LUKSCH-MAKOVSKY.

employed at the library except as photographers and in security or maintenance work. Once a women married, she almost always left the library's employment, a common occurrence in many professions for decades. Now, of course, the field has expanded and although there are still more women than men choosing librarianship as a career, no one will be asked to leave if they tie the knot!

Given that historical context, it's not surprising that, beginning with our founder Helen Clay Frick, the library's focus and development have been guided by notable women. The line of librarians who headed the library, beginning with Ruth Savord in 1920, all came to the library with strong art historical backgrounds in addition to their professional training received at the most prestigious library schools of the day (shout out to Columbia University where I received my degree many years ago). Their professionalism and devotion to the library, where many of them spent decades, continue to inspire me.

Stephen – And another theme would be scholarship. From 1926 the new Library was hosting lectures: Dr. Richard Offner (1889–1965) gave twelve lectures on Florentine painting 10 February to 28 April 1926; Count Umberto Gnoli (1878–1947) three on Central Italian painting 22–24 November, and Gabriel Millet (1867–1953) on Christian Art in the East. In 1927 Offner lectured on Siena and the Marches every Wednesday 9 February–27 April, and Walter W. S. Cook (1888–1962) on Spanish Illuminated Manuscripts from October 1927 to January 1928, a New York University Extension course, which took place every Friday afternoon from four until six o'clock. The Annual Report noted: "The extension courses have brought a number of graduate students to the Library to whom we have been able to render real service." With the 1935 extension to the Frick Mansion, the creation of a lecture hall, took on some of these activities, although book launches and talks still took place in the Library. Between 2000–06 an annual series of 'Dialogues on Art' were organized by the Library, before it opened the Center for the History of Collecting from 2007, run by Dr. Inge Reist, which held symposia, lectures, book launches (for its publication program), and fellowships, who again gave presentations on their research.

From 2010 there was an increased emphasis on training researchers and the general public. We were always restricted by the size of the Small Reading Room with its large, inflexible desks. but also creating programs such as the Technological Revolutions in Art History (with the Museum of Modern Art) and Recovering Women's Legacies: Artists, Dealers, Collectors, and Patrons (with the Wildenstein Foundation) which exploited the reach of speakers and audience through being

virtual through Zoom, necessary because of the Covid-19 pandemic.
   In 2000 Louisa Wood Ruby created the Library summer internship program, which the Collection adopted in 2014. This has now moved onto paid internships, although during the stay at Frick Madison, these will largely have to be virtual. For me, one of the highlights of 2020/21 was a one week fellowship/internship for ten students from diverse backgrounds in a cohort also shared with three other member institutions of ARIAH: Center for Visual Arts at the National Gallery, Winterthur and the Archives of American Art—they all had to research an object of their choice and present at the end of the week, after workshops by Library staff on physical and virtual resource materials and techniques. What were your thoughts on this, Sally?

Sally – That is a long list of achievements! The library staff has always been proactive in their support of scholarship, including in the traditional realm of in-person reference service. With the advent of email reference, publishing our catalog on line, participating in inter-library loan programs, a recent digitize on demand initiative, joining national and international consortia to share our resources around the world, we've managed to broaden our user community significantly. I agree that the Covid-19 pandemic accelerated the library's innovative strategizing to retain and support our researchers and allowed us to reach world-wide audiences with our virtual programming. This has been a silver lining in what has been a difficult period for everyone.

Stephen – Another theme is photography. Perhaps this is not surprising with over half the library's collections being photographs, and photography being another example of a new technology being embraced and developed in the service of art history. And much of the documentation of our institutional building projects from 1912 onwards is photographic. But some of the hundred objects have other photographic sources, such as the Frank Stokes collection of albumen prints of artists in their Paris studios in the late 1880s/early 1890s, the 'Vienna Museum' catalogue which is an early use of photography in an auction catalogue, or the Edward Dossetter photographs of the rooms in Gower Lodge, Windsor.

Sally – The library was fortunate to have its own in-house photography department almost from its inception. In 1923 Miss Frick hired Ira W. Martin to establish the photography studio and shortly thereafter, in 1926, Martin hired Thurman Rotan as his assistant. These two men worked at the library in total from 1923 to 1987. Ira Martin retired in

1951 and Thurman Rotan retired in 1987, after over sixty years at the library! One exception to the "get married and leave" policy at the library was the partnership of Thurman Rotan and his wife, Mary, who was able to continue working at the library after she married Mr. Rotan.

The library photographers traveled to photograph works of art in situ in New York and in many other locations in the United States. These trips resulted in over 60,000 images that the library has digitized over the years and which are available at *digitalcollections.frick.org*. We still have some of their photographic equipment in the archives. The library's Conservation Lab opened in photo studio space in 1981 and several years later the library's Digital Lab continued to make use of portions of the original photo studio to produce and manage the library's digital photography efforts.

Alfred Cook, who worked for the Frick family, but was not a member of the library's photography staff, was hired by Helen Clay Frick to document the transformation of the Frick home into The Frick Collection from 1931 to 1935. Cook's photographs are a remarkable assemblage of photos documenting the progression from demolition to construction to completion of both The Frick Collection and the new Frick Art Reference Library. These photographs have been digitized and can be seen in our digital portal under the archives tab at *digitalcollections.frick.org*.

Stephen – Looking back at the last hundred years, I have to acknowledge standing on the shoulders of giants, to use Isaac Newton's phrase. Each of my predecessors was a professional librarian, bringing the techniques of information management to the documentation of art, a revolution in itself. Ruth Savord (Librarian, 1920–24), introduced a cataloguing system for images, and, encouraged by Sir Robert Witt, collected images with just the basic information of identification. She also established a Department of Photography 1 January 1923, with the addition of the photographer Ira. W. Martin (1886–1960)

Sally – As I mentioned earlier, the head librarians were distinguished professional librarians. Ruth Savord, our first head librarian who had so much to do with implementing Miss Frick's vision for the library, resigned from the library the day before it opened in May 1924. Apparently Miss Frick required library staff of all levels to wear smocks at work. This proved to be too much to ask for Miss Savord and she resigned rather than wear one. She went on to work in other libraries, ultimately retiring after a thirty year career, presumably smock-less, as the librarian for the Council on Foreign Relations. The smock requirement was not addressed in later memos or at least didn't cause another dust-up. The library's dress code for the public —now that's another issue! Until 1989 women (staff and researchers) were forbidden to wear pants, short skirts and stilettos at the library and men were required to wear jackets. This caused a ruckus from the 1970s onwards but the motto "My house, my rules" held firm even for a time after Helen Clay Frick's death in 1984, and was rescinded under The Frick Collection directorship of Charles Ryskamp.

Sally – While the library's dress code is now a relic and reminder of the forces of tradition, the work undertaken at the library over the decades under the six chief librarians since 1924 has been fully in step with and in many cases in advance of library trends and world events. Ethelwyn Manning (tenure 1924–47) oversaw the bulk of the library's many photographic campaigns and led the library during World War II while staff worked to prepare the maps used during the war by Allied troops to identify, and hopefully avoid the destruction of historical sites and monuments in Europe. Her successors, Hannah Johnson Howell (tenure 1947–70) and Mildred Steinbach (tenure 1970–77) oversaw the accelerated acquisition of both print and photographic library holdings.

Helen Sanger (tenure 1978–94) worked at the library for forty-seven years. Under her, the library entered the world of computers and internal cataloging systems began to change. The library kept up with evolving library technology without sacrificing the concentrated attention historically paid to scholarship and in-depth reference work. After Helen Clay Frick died in 1984, it was Miss Sanger who facilitated the merger of the library with The Frick Collection. As I mentioned earlier, it was under her leadership that the library opened its first Conservation Lab for book and paper conservation in 1981.

During Helen Sanger's tenure, the library also ventured into the world of grant-funding and fundraising. Grants for preservation and publications began to come to the library. Miss Sanger also worked closely with the Collection's director, Charles Ryskamp, to ensure the financial future of the library through a special fundraising effort (concluded after her retirement) to raise an endowment to support the library's operations. Her position was endowed and she was the library's first Andrew W. Mellon Chief Librarian. I was lucky enough to have crossed paths often with Miss Sanger after she retired and I joined the staff in 1997. She volunteered her time to the library and was a welcome sight in the library stacks.

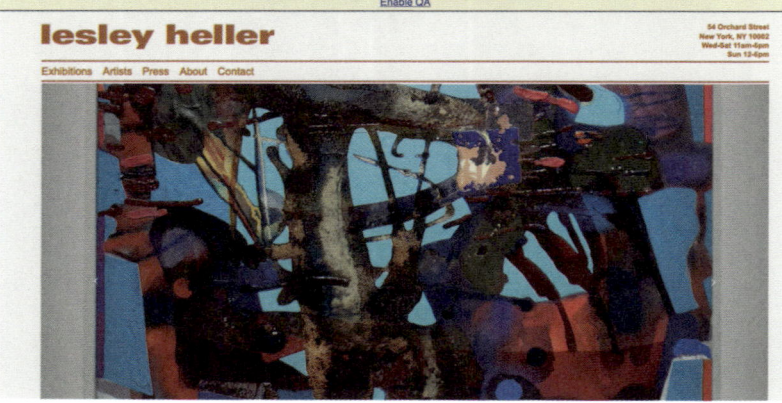

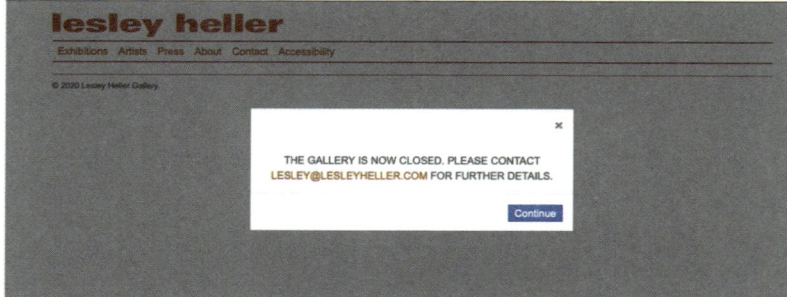

80 | Web Archiving

Patricia Barnett (tenure 1995–2008), who hired me in 1997 and established the Archives Department at The Frick Collection, oversaw and expanded many programs at the library which still exist, notably the founding of the New York Art Resources Consortium (NYARC), the Center for the History of Collecting and the creation of the library's Digital Lab. She pursued grants with gusto and under her watch the library received numerous government and private foundation grants that supported conserving and digitizing fragile library materials. From my perspective, one of the most important achievements was her successful effort to acquire the Frick Family Papers held by the Helen Clay Frick Foundation. We are fortunate to share this collection with the University of Pittsburgh and in 2015 were thrilled to have the portion of the papers we hold donated to us.

Stephen – And then I came in May 2010, after being caught up in the Icelandic volcano eruption, which disrupted transatlantic air travel: I thought I would never get here. The Library had more or less been running itself for nearly two years, and it was in a steady state: the structure I inherited from Patricia Barnett worked perfectly well—I didn't tinker with it until 2018, and it was 2019 before I did a wholesale restructure. But I did think that the Library management group needed to work better as a team, so I coupled the development of a three-year strategic plan as a team building exercise. The vision— to be at the heart of art historical research; the values of putting the needs of researchers (including the needs of future researchers) first; working collaboratively, professionally and to demonstrate leadership in our areas of expertise, have endured beyond the three-year coverage of the strategy.

Sally – How did web archiving come about?

Stephen – Very tentative steps had been taken when I started in May 2010—mainly some small auction house sites. In the UK at the British Library I had started the UK Web Archive, a permission based selective harvest of websites instances of which were made publicly available on the Web, but this was quite intensive on technological resources. I was determined to keep the costs down here by working collaboratively with the Internet Archive's Archive-It. I also saw it as a way to build a joint collection for the partners of the New York Art Resources Consortium (NYARC). It was also one of the 2010–13 Library strategic priorities.

The Andrew W. Mellon Foundation gave us a grant to explore

the issues from selection, harvesting, metadata, discovery and preservation. And then they supported our strategy with a larger implementation grant over two years. Now we have a total of 8.5 terabytes of harvested websites, with a preservation copy in Duracloud.

Sally – How did you decide on the digitization strategy?

Stephen – There was quite a lot of digitization going on around the photoarchive and archive but there was no clear plan. Some projects were grant funded but at the end of them staff had to be let go, and their expertise and experience was lost to the Library. A priority of the 2010 strategy was to increase the pace of digitization, and proposed developing a digitization strategy and to top-slice the budget to support digitization. A group of staff threshed out a framework and the clear priorities were the completion of the digitization of the Photoarchive, unique items where copyright permitted, and archival materials on demand.

Sally – What are unique items?

Stephen – The concept of unique items arose from the 2008 OCLC report on NYARC An Art Resource in New York and a follow-up exercise by OCLC Research Libraries on the Frick Art Reference Library to determine what unique holdings it had. The result of 27% of Frick holdings not being held by another Library in WorldCat. There may be other copies but they are not in major libraries and are not accessible. Knowing that there is some duplication of items through retrospective and other bulk uploads to OCLC i.e. two libraries could have two separate WorldCat entries, I had interns verify the data: the result was 25% unique materials, still an unusually high percentage for an art library, in fact for any type of library. A further study revealed that an additional 40% of our records showed that we were the only North American holding. I was proud of this distinctive feature of our collection, but I awakened in the middle of the night, worrying that a fire might destroy the only copy of an item. We decided on two workflows—the identification of unique items bought or given on arrival, and their routing to the Digital Lab; and the identification on request through inter-library loan. This material suits a boutique digitization approach, rather than a mass digitization one, but I'm sure if someone was to provide the funding we could come up with a methodology for mass digitization of this material.

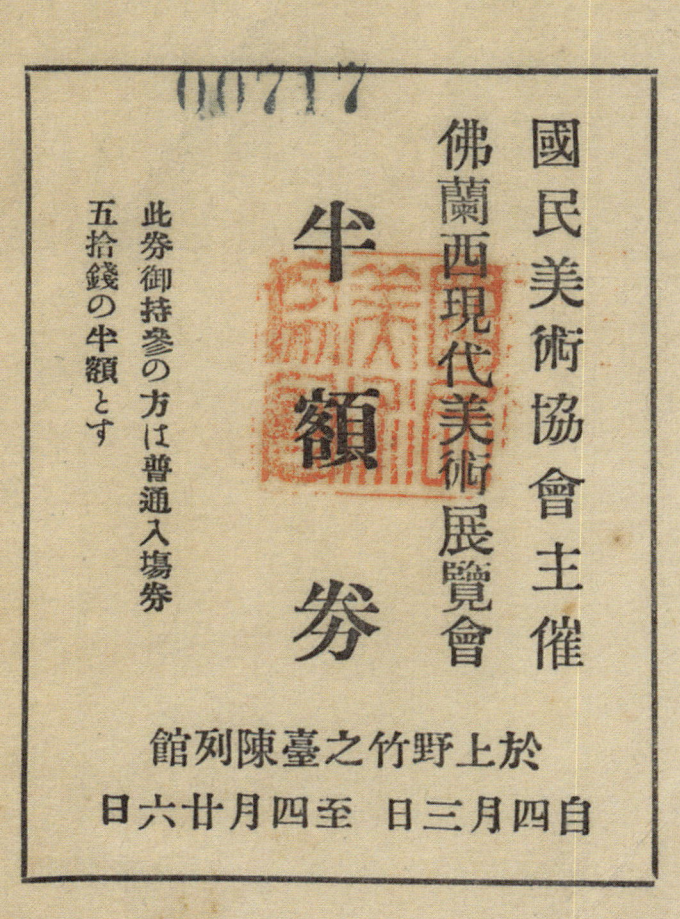

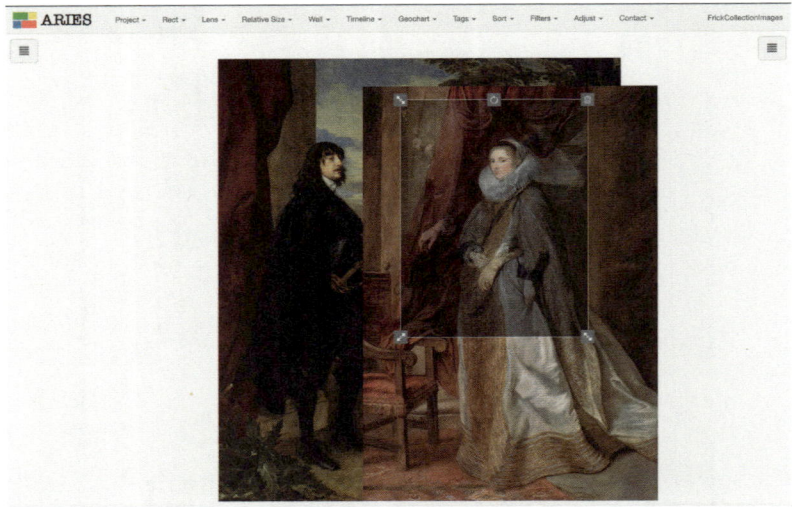

Incidentally, a good or bad by-product of the unique item study is that, in acquiring antiquarian materials, we prefer that there is no other library holding: it's not just maintaining or increasing the statistic, but about the best use of our resources for a better documentation of art history. The size of a collection is less important than its uniqueness.

Sally – I know you have been interested on the new ways we could exploit digital content. Is this how we entered the field of digital art history?

Stephen – That was the context but it went back further in my past. At the British Library I was asked to lead the 21st Century Curator Project, looking at maintaining and enhancing skillsets to bridge the physical and virtual. The Andrew W. Mellon Foundation funded a project, called the 21st Century Curator Project, with me as the Principal Investigator, and partnering with the New York Public Library in a conference and series of staff exchanges—I think this later contributed to me being proposed as a candidate for the Frick position in 2009. Anyway, part of the British Library earlier remit was to represent the Library on the Digital Humanities Conference Committee—I think my first conference was in Edinburgh. I soon became a little disenchanted: scholars were merely translating their existing project into a digital form, whereas I was looking for something more—yes digital substitution is allowed, but I came to a harder definition: the use of computational tools or methods with digital data to answer digital humanities questions. Digital art history would then be the use of digital methods on digital data to answer art historical questions. The predominance of digital images and conservation data, in my eyes at least, making it distinctive from digital humanities.

Sally – What was the precipitating moment at the Library?

Stephen – The main impetus came from the digitization of the Photoarchive and the possibilities, which we could see from its exploitation through computer vision. Samantha Deutch at the Center for the History of Collecting, Louisa Wood-Ruby and Ellen Prokop from the Photoarchive easily convinced me that we should start a virtual Digital Art History Lab to promote digital art history within and without the institution: we embarked on a series of pop-up events or roadshows. Samantha also raised the money to develop a replacement of the analogue light box with the digital ARIES (Art Image Exploration Space). It also demonstrated our philosophy of collaboration as we worked with the New York University Tandon School of Engineering. We went on to work with Stanford-Cornell and the University of Pennsylvania—Helen Clay Frick would have loved that connection—and in these cases we are using Artificial Intelligence (AI) with the data of the Photoarchive.

Sally – To refer back to your notion of the Library as bridging the physical and the digital, your support for digital art history has not been at the expense of a series of important archival and book collections. What have been your favorite acquisitions?

Stephen – That's a bit like the question I always get asked—what's your favorite painting or object in The Frick: my answer is normally: "Well today it's…" And the satisfaction of acquisition often lies in the process: from understanding what an item or collection is, evaluating the usefulness for the Library's audience, negotiating the gift or sale, and making it available—a whole range of skills you don't get taught at library school. But I am avoiding the subject.

One important archive for the Library and the Collection is the Frick Family Papers, which Pat Barnett, Andrew W. Mellon Chief Librarian and Don Swanson, the library's conservator, secured as a deposit/loan in 2001. While the Helen Clay Frick Foundation partially funded conserving and processing the collection, it is difficult, impossible even, to raise money to conserve, process or digitize a collection that you don't own. So in 2015 I was pleased to be able to convert this into an outright gift.

But in terms of an archive acquisition, I would rate the Loewi-Robertson Archive very highly—in fact so highly we actually we paid for this, a rare thing for us to do, as I think hosting—storing, conservation and making available—in perpetuity is so expensive that a Library should be paid to do so, rather than pay for its acquisition. Sally, you describe it as one of the objects. Do you want to say anything else about it?

Sally – I absolutely love this collection. Dating roughly from the later 1930s to the early 2000s, the records provide first hand evidence of the internal workings of a gallery, located first in Venice, Italy, and finally in Los Angeles, California, which played a significant role in providing museums and private clients all over the world, and particularly in the United States, with textiles, from small scraps of

91 | *French Fashion at the End of the Ancien Regime*

ancient fabrics to complete ensembles, furniture, paintings and entire room interiors. The stock books and correspondence files alone will give future scholars so much new material to explore. I am looking forward to completing the rehousing and organizing of this collection in advance of what I think will be loads of thoughtful scholarship on collecting in America, taste trends, gallery relationships with private clients and institutions, provenance research and World War II gallery operations.

Stephen – I like the Hollywood names turning up in the sales ledgers— Mrs. Humphrey Bogart etc. And in terms of printed materials it would hard to choose between the Starr-Wolfe Wedgwood Library gift (2018) or adding to the Heim Gallery sale catalogs purchase of 2005 over the last ten years. I know you are going to ask me to choose one— in which case it would be the 2016 gift of the *Gallerie des modes et costumes français* (1778–1787), where you can almost trace the causes of the French Revolution in the extravagant dresses and hairstyles. Again, this is one of our hundred objects.

But acquisitions are not just a one-person activity—archive and acquisition staff may be involved in the decision to accept a gift or purchase an item or collection, but there are also conservators, cataloguers, and not least the staff to retrieve items for the public. And digital staff to make them available to the whole world.

Good staff, relevant services and excellent collections is a winning formula.

Sally – Where is the Frick Art Reference Library in the league of art libraries worldwide?

Stephen – I got into ranking in a rather invidious way in order to try and convey the importance of support for—and indeed the continued existence of—the Library. So what are or could be the criteria for any sort of ranking?

I think access is important. There are huge copyright constraints to digitization and the cost of conservation, photography, quality control, metadata, access and preservation are so enormous which means that a lot of materials will—sadly, always—have to be consulted in person. This for me means that easy access for the public is a very important criterion. The Frick Art Reference Library's ready availability compared to restrictive (because of policy or extremely limited public hours) museum or research libraries requiring recommendations or proof of need and some university libraries even requesting a fee, and where some electronic resources might still be unavailable to the visitor. Does any other museum library recall an item from a curator if a member of the public needs to use it? Can the visitor request an inter-library loan? I think the Frick does very well on this—and we are not publicly funded in any way.

The size and quality of the collections are important too. But I would qualify this by the uniqueness of the collections. We have over half a million printed items (25% unique etc.), but we have 1.2 million photographs of works of art (perhaps 15% unique), and 8.5 terabytes of web archives (100% unique), not to mention our 7000 linear feet of paper-based archives.

Involvement in national and international initiative is both a mark of respect and a means of engagement with new ideas. The Frick conceived of PHAROS and brought fourteen photo archives from Europe and America together to work on bringing our digitized materials together with computer vision so that one can search by image alone, and see our common holdings and metadata. By December 2021 we will have a fully working prototype and an infrastructure for it to continue into the future. We are partners in the Getty Portal, the Digital Cigonara project, an ARLIS/North America digital sales catalogue project and working with the Internet Archive to create a US-wide web archiving of art resources.

The conception, design and implementation of online research tools is a significant criteria. The Frick Art Periodicals Index was digitized and is now an EBSCO service. The Spanish Dictionary of Artists was also digitized and is freely available on the website. The Center for the History of Collecting created an archives directory which is again freely available on the website. We took in and house the Montias database of seventeenth-century Dutch inventories. I take pride that we replaced the art historians light-box with ARIES, an open-source tool for manipulating art images. We are trying to create an API for it to work with PHAROS.

And every good Library needs public programming, which in the Frick's case cover workshops on using WorldCat and Zotero, provenance research and digital art history, not to mention the Center for the History of Collecting's fourteen years of symposia, lectures, book launches and publications. Our symposia on Computer Vision and Technological Revolutions and Art History attracted full participation, now amplified through virtual technologies.

I'm happy that the Frick Art Reference Library is at the top table. For me, that is mission accomplished.

CHARLES R. HULBECK

Oilpaintings, Watercolors, Drawings

January 3 - January 24
1945

FEIGL GALLERY

601 MADISON AVENUE (AT 57th ST.)

NEW YORK CITY

Acknowledgements

First of all, I would like to thank Kathleen Flanagan and the Eugene V. and Clare E. Thaw Charitable Trust for their support.

My thanks and appreciation are due to Payton Goad who has helped organize the project and contributed entries. Her predecessor, Eliza Graham, marshaled several cohorts of interns working on the book, including Payton.

I am very grateful to my Library colleagues who contributed entries to the book: Ralph Baylor, Cynthia Biber, Sarah Bigler, Sally Brazil, Susan Chore, Samantha Deutch, Sumitra Duncan, Payton Goad, Julie Ludwig, Suz Massen, Michelle McCarthy-Behler, John McQuaid, Kerri Pfister, Mikhail Shklyarevsky, and Louisa Wood Ruby.

Sally Brazil, Susan Chore and Julie Ludwig also advised on the archival context of the entries. Sonia Agnew, Mark Bresnan and John McQuaid helped with the dates of acquisition.

A series of interns have contributed research, blogposts, a magazine and audio recordings about the entries: Alexandra Binnie, Nicole Boyd, Suna Cha, Caroline Chang, Payton Goad, Miriam Hunt, Iman Khako, Ingrid Kottke, Rose Sheehan, and Muyon Zhou.

Michael Bodycomb, Susan Chore, George Koelle, Kylie Schmitt and Cris Sunwoo helped with the photography and sourcing of images. Lissette Nunez and Anthony Redding retrieved the items from offsite.

Colin Sackett of Uniformbooks designed and published the book.

How to Use this Book

The objects are arranged chronologically by a date, which might be the date of an event, its creation, publication, acquisition or donation. Other relevant dates are provided in round brackets. For example, object 2, *The Bowling Alley* is filed under 1920 when it was first used as a library, but the other dates 1916, 1924, 1934, 1997 relate to its construction in 1916, its change of use in 1924 when the first purpose-built library opened, the re-use of some of its wood paneling in 1934 in the second purpose-built library, and finally the restoration of the bowling alley in 1997.

The index allows the reader to track how the object relates to other entries, and to create their own stories. An asterisk* after the title indicates a colour illustration in the introduction.

41 | *Frick Art Reference Library Façade*

1	*In the Beginning*
	1920 (2001, 2015)

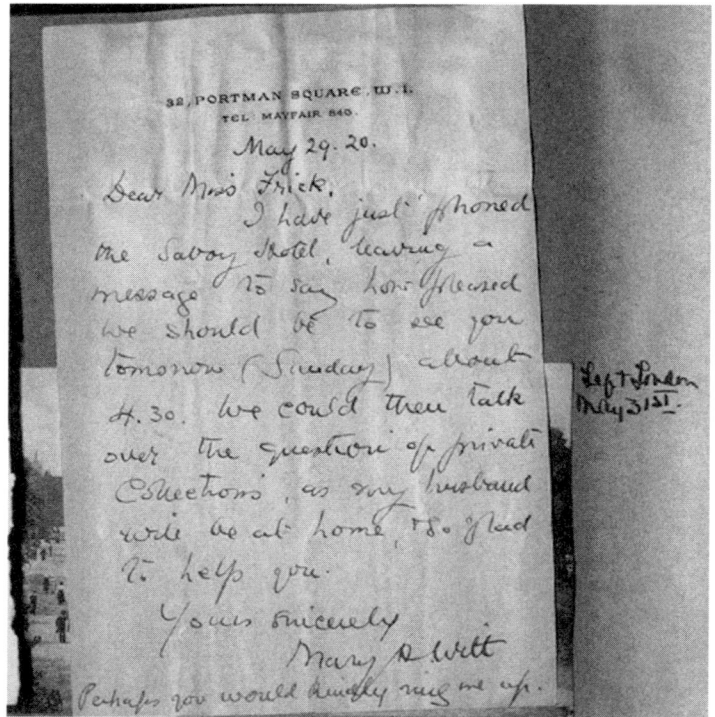

In May of 1920, five months after her father's death, Helen Clay Frick sailed for Europe aboard the S.S. Celtic with her cousin, Karl F. Overholt. She would remain abroad for the duration of the summer, visiting England, France, Switzerland, and Belgium. This marked her first trip back to Europe since her Red Cross service in France near the end of World War I, and she seems to have had several aims in mind. First, she was interested in researching some aspects of her father's collection, including visiting landscapes and buildings depicted among his masterpieces, as well as the houses in which some of them had formerly hung. As a newly-appointed trustee of The Frick Collection, she was also keen to familiarize herself with the management of museums and educational institutions. On a more personal note, she reconnected with families she had met during her wartime service, visited her former governess, Marika Ogiz, in Switzerland, and toured areas ravaged by the war, pasting images of ruins at St. Quentin and Ypres next to their pre-war versions in her scrapbook.

This scrapbook, one of three compiled from that trip, covers her crossing from New York to Liverpool and travel throughout England. Filled with postcards, snapshots, pressed flowers, clippings, and ephemera, the volume also contains correspondence regarding visits to the British Museum, Apsley House, Lansdowne House, Holland House, Knole, the State Apartments at Windsor Castle, and Castle Howard. During her stay in England, Helen Clay Frick also toured Carlyle House, Sir John Soane's Museum, the Tower of London (at night, no less), Oxford, Hampton Court, Leighton House, Warwick Castle, Stratford-on-Avon, Lord Northbrook's Collection, the National Portrait Gallery, and York. She paid a final visit to the National Gallery before departing for France in mid-June.

On 29 May, two days before leaving London for Oxford, Helen Clay Frick received an invitation from Mary Witt to visit her and her husband, Robert Witt, at their home the following day. Mary Witt wrote: "We could then talk over the question of private collections, as my husband will be at home, and so glad to help you." At either this meeting or one shortly thereafter, Robert Witt related to Miss Frick his role in the National Gallery's 1909 purchase of *Christina, Duchess of Milan* by Holbein, which Henry Clay Frick believed he had secured for his own collection. As Witt recounted, the necessary funds were wired at the last minute from an anonymous female donor in Wiesbaden. This was probably just the sort of insight Miss Frick was hoping to gain about her father's collecting, just as she did when she visited a copy of Velazquez's *Philip IV* at the Dulwich Picture Gallery, or when she took in the views at Salisbury Cathedral and Mortlake Terrace.

More consequentially, however, Miss Frick's visit to the Witt home at 32 Portman Square changed the trajectory of her adult life. The Witts' impressive collection of photographs and reproductions of works of art was well known, but upon seeing it Miss Frick was inspired to form a library of her own, asking Robert Witt if she could create a version of it in New York. Miss Frick now had an idea for something she could build and nurture as a memorial to her father. Moreover, it would serve as an essential resource for art historians and directly align with the aims of The Frick Collection, defined in her father's will as "encouraging and developing the study of the fine arts, and of advancing the general knowledge of kindred subjects". Miss Frick began planning her library almost immediately, her contacts and experiences from this trip playing a critical role in its early days.

—*Julie Ludwig*

The Bowling Alley
1920 (1916, 1924, 1934, 1997)

The Frick Mansion was constructed between 1912–14 by Thomas Hastings of Carrère and Hastings Architects. At some point Mr. Frick decided to have a bowling alley and billiard room installed in the large sub-basement of the new mansion for the recreational use of his children and guests. In the Frick Art Reference Library's archives there is a series of correspondence between Carrère and Hastings Architects and The Brunswick-Balke-Collender Co. discussing the bowling alley, and agreeing the installation of a two-lane pine and maple bowling alley, complete with ten-pin spots, gutters, foul lines, and composition mineralite bowling balls of varying size.

The construction and installation of the bowling alley took place in the summer of 1916, sadly leaving only three years of enjoyment before Mr. Frick died in 1919. Devastated by the loss of her father, Helen Clay Frick sought a way to honor him and his love of art and art history. The Frick Art Reference Library was born a mere year later upon Helen's return to New York after traveling to Europe and being inspired by Robert Witt's collection of photographs of works of art in London. Without wanting to dismantle any room at 1 East 70th Street, Helen decided to make use of the sub-basement bowling alley and billiard room, neither having seen much activity recently. Stacks were erected first in the billiard room and then extended into the bowling alley until a purpose-built library replaced it. Even when the 1924 Library was built, the initial and temporary home

of the Frick Art Reference Library still housed back-of-house library activities, such as storage, photo-mounting and indexing.

Perhaps from sentimentality or from economy, when it came to construct the second library in 1934, Helen re-purposed wood paneling from the bowling alley in the Small Reading Room of the new library. Amongst numerous construction special orders for Carrère

and Hastings Architects, there is a 1914 special order for the ornate wood paneling for the bowling alley's walls and its freestanding columns. Another special order came twenty years later in January 1934 to the office of John Russell Pope, the architect of the new library building and the conversion of the house to a museum: this was the confirmation that some of the wood-panels lining the bowling alley could be safely removed and transferred to the walls of the 1934 Small Reading Room.

The bowling alley was restored in 1997. It, along with the billiard table nearby, is enjoyed by staff members of The Frick on Staff Education Day, and by special guests of the Director.

—*Payton Goad*

3 First Photoarchive Acquisition
1920

Almost immediately after the 'founding' of the Library on 8 November 1920, Helen Clay Frick began collecting photographs of works of art. Drawing inspiration (and in the beginning assistance) from Robert Witt, she set out to build a collection, among the first of its kind in the United States, which would allow American scholars of the relatively new discipline of the history of art to study European art from home.

The first photographs acquired for the Library were purchased through Witt from the London photographer A. C. Cooper. Founded in 1918, by Augustus Charles Cooper (1873–1960), A. C. Cooper was one of the first firms in London to specialize in fine art photography. Cooper was commissioned by the Library from the 1920s through the 1980s to document works of art offered for sale on the London art market, primarily at Christie's and Sotheby's.

The first batch of photographs purchased from Cooper by Witt for the Library are shown on the receipt below. The lots correspond to the 19 November 1920 Christie's sale of the collection of Paul Jean Cels, Esq. and others. The Library also owns an annotated copy of the catalog for this sale, which records both buyer names and prices. Not only do these photographs serve as illustrations for unillustrated auction catalogues, but they also allow researchers to study works of art that have since disappeared into private collections.

In the early days of the Library, all the A. C. Cooper purchases came through Witt. He is listed as the buyer on receipts through the 1930s. However, starting in 1921, Helen was coordinating directly with photographers and agents in Europe, such as Mario Sansoni and Clotilde Misme (later Brière) to purchase photographs from dealers, museums, and private collections.

This first documented purchase for the Library's Photoarchive marks the beginning of what is still a constantly evolving collection. The Photoarchive, now comprising over 1.2 million reproductions of works of art, is still growing through gifts and purchases and documentation is continuously updated with information from museums, scholars, dealers, and collectors. In the last ten years the digitization of the Photoarchive has been a priority for the Library.

—Sarah Bigler

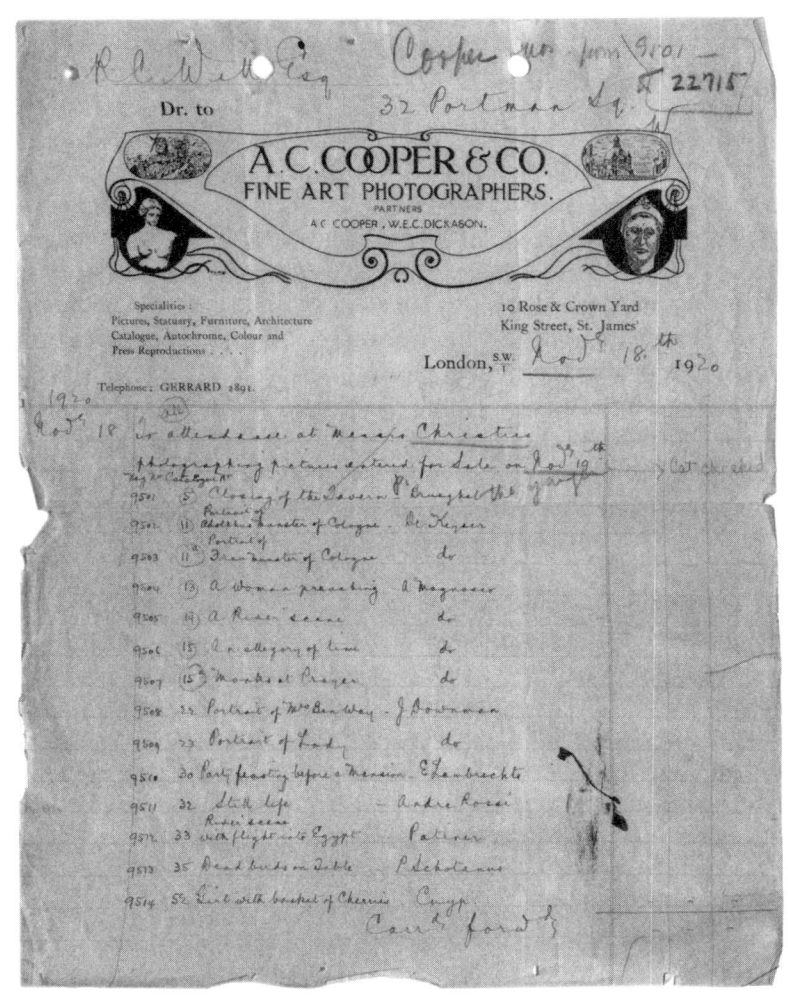

4 The Witt Catalog
1920

Robert Witt (1872–1952) was born in London and attended Clifton College, Bristol and New College, Oxford. He ultimately was certified to practice law, and eventually became a partner in the historic firm of Stephenson, Harwood and Tatham. Witt became an art connoisseur; he helped to found the National Art Collections Fund, and was a Trustee of the National Gallery and the Tate Gallery and the chairman of the National Loan Collections Trust. He was appointed C.B.E. in 1918 and knighted in 1922. In 1899 Witt married Mary Helene (1870–1952) who also studied at Oxford and shared Witt's collecting interests. Together they founded the Witt Library of Reproductions in their London home at 32 Portman Square. Mary's contribution has probably been underestimated.

In 1920, while traveling through London, Helen Clay Frick received a letter of introduction from John R. Van Derlip (1860–1935), lawyer and founding president of the Minneapolis Institute of Art, introducing her to Robert Witt. Helen spent three days with Robert and Mary Witt, inspecting their archive of photographs and reproductions of works of art, and decided to found the Frick Art Reference Library. Helen adopted many of the organizational systems in her Photoarchive that the Witts used in their library, from mounting photographs on cardboard, to filing artists alphabetically with in their national schools and further organizing the works by artists by a classification schema by subject, all designed to assist with easy and rapid reference.

In December 1920, the Witts privately printed an introduction to their Library of Reproductions, *Catalogue of painters and draughtsmen represented in the Library of Reproductions of Pictures & Drawings formed by Robert and Mary Witt*. By this time, the library had more than 150,000 reproductions representing more than 8,000 painters and draftsmen, from the twelfth century until the 1920s, though the bulk of the collection were artists born before 1800, with works held in public and private collections. In the catalog, Robert Witt explained that the library was formed to create a comprehensive, systematically arranged, and classified collection of photographs and illustrations from books and catalogues to facilitate easy and rapid reference and research to be used by scholars, critics, writers, collectors, dealers, and anyone interested in paintings. Witt's goal was aimed at completeness, to collect reproductions of every painter and draftsman of any repute, up until the middle of the nineteenth century. For more contemporary artists, due to volume of their artistic output, he restricted inclusion to

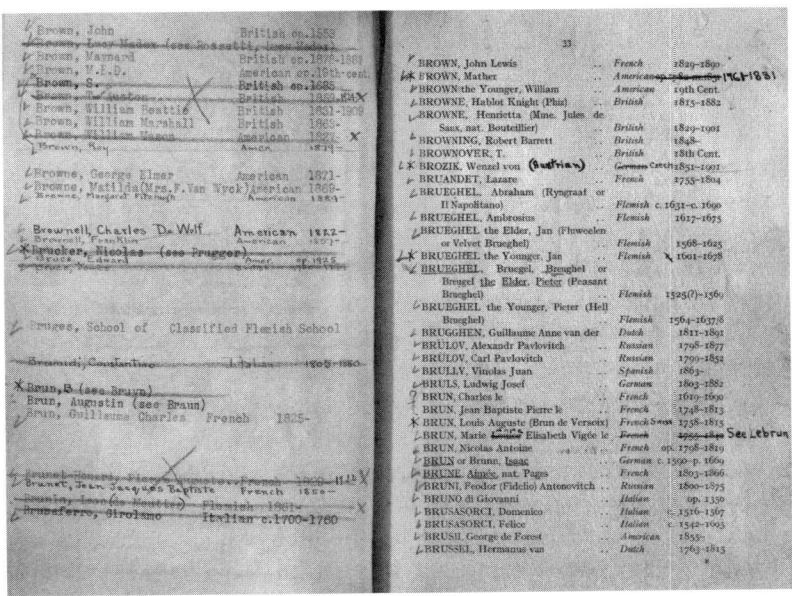

Catalogue of painters and draughtsmen represented in the Library of Reproductions of Pictures & Drawings formed by Robert and Mary Witt. London: Privately printed, 1920.

artists that were included in national collections or frequently asked for in his library.

In addition, Witt explained how his library was organized. The primary classification was by national schools: British, American, Dutch, etc. Secondly they were arranged by subject: Old Testament, New Testament, Historical, Mythological, Portraits, etc. The Catalog included a page devoted to his Subject Index. Following the Subject Index were instructions for using the library and following that a list of the artists contained in the library, with their national school and life or activity dates.

Robert Witt sent Helen an inscribed copy of his catalog, shortly after its printing, "To / Helen Frick / from / Robert Witt / in hope that it will prove / of help / in her / great undertaking. / 'Possunt, quia posse videntur' / Virgil / Dec. 1920 London". Helen and her staff did use the Witts' publication to great effect, ticking off artists and adding pages of additional artists collected by Helen and her staff for the Frick Art Reference Library.

—Kerri A. Pfister

From Modern to Old Masters
1920 (1908)

Henry Clay Frick (1849–1919) made his Gilded Age fortune in the coke and steel industries of Pittsburgh, Pennsylvania. In 1871, he founded a coke manufactory with a cousin that would later be known as H. C. Frick & Company. Frick eventually controlled almost eighty percent of the coke used to produce iron and steel in the area, making him a millionaire by the age of thirty. In 1882, he partnered with Andrew Carnegie to form the Carnegie Steel Co., Ltd. After Frick became chairman of the board in 1895, his acquisition of pictures became more focused than the prints and sketches he acquired when he was a young man. His friend, the art dealer Roland Knoedler, influenced his collecting, and between 1895 and 1900, he acquired more than ninety pictures of mostly modern works. Frick resigned from his duties at Carnegie Steel Co., Ltd. in 1899. This was the same year that he purchased his first Rembrandt painting, *Portrait of a Young Artist* (now attributed to Rembrandt's studio), and he turned away from modern and towards old master pictures. Frick and his family relocated to New York City in 1905 while still maintaining residences in Pittsburgh and Prides Crossing, Massachusetts. Until his mansion at 1 East 70th Street was completed in 1914, he rented an opulent mansion built by William H. Vanderbilt located at 640 Fifth Avenue.

In 1908, while living in the Vanderbilt mansion, Frick privately printed a catalog of forty-nine paintings in his collection. The self-publication of collection catalogs was common during the time of Frick. Knoedler & Co. handled the printing of the catalog through The Gillis Press. Most entries in this un-illustrated catalog include artist, title, description, dimensions, and provenance. Some entries also include exhibition and publication history as well as signature information. It is unclear if Knoedler is responsible for its text, but since the firm organized the printing of the catalog, it is a possibility. Eight of the thirty-two artists represented were active in the second half of the nineteenth century. Artists such as Jean Baptiste Camille Corot and Jean François Millet are seen alongside George Romney and El Greco. Several of the works in the catalog are not found in The Frick Collection today, and there are several works in The Frick Collection that do not appear in the catalog since they were acquired by Frick after 1908. An example of a painting no longer associated with Frick is *The Family Party* by David Teniers. It appears in the 1908 catalog of Frick's collection and was returned to Knoedler for credit in 1909. It now is in the collection of the Fine Arts Museums of San Francisco. Murillo's self-portrait is in

Catalogue of the Henry C. Frick Collection of Paintings. New York: Privately printed, 1908.

the 1908 catalogue but was not part of the 1919 bequest: it was given to The Frick by Dr. and Mrs. Henry Clay Frick II in 2014. A notable work in The Frick Collection not found in the catalog is *St. Francis in the Dessert* by Giovanni Bellini, which Frick acquired in 1915.

The importance of libraries acquiring multiple iterations of catalogs for a collection over time in order to track provenance and changes in taste becomes apparent when examining this catalog, which is now also available digitally.

—Suz Massen

6. Frick Art Reference Library Scrapbooks
1920–99

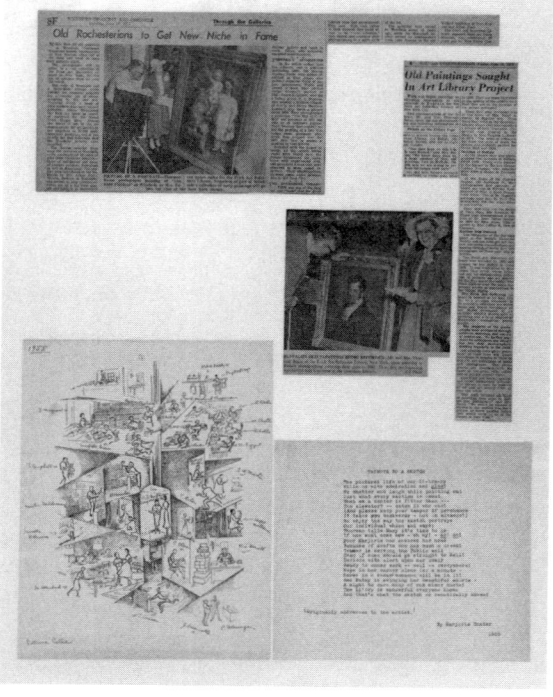

The five volumes of Frick Art Reference Library Scrapbooks, 1920–99, informally document the history of the Library over its first seventy years: they follow the Library's accomplishments and historic moments, highlight connections to other institutions and art scholars, and offer details of staff events and activities.

The contents also reflect the professional and personal interests of Library founder and director Helen Clay Frick (1888–1984), including news of family members, Pittsburgh connections, lawsuits, loans of her personal art collection, and most prominently, The Frick Collection. As the daughter of the museum's founder, and a Board of Trustees member until 1961, Miss Frick included clippings about The Frick Collection side-by-side with Library items. In fact, even though a separate Frick Collection scrapbook, dated 1931–43, was compiled by Library staff, clippings about the museum appear in both volumes.

Based on handwritten notes in the scrapbooks, it is clear that Helen Clay Frick made selections for the volumes, but little is known about which staff members were responsible for their continued growth. According to a note written by Miss Frick in the 1960–69 scrapbook, Grace Nedley, who joined the staff as a typist on 29 November 1920, started and kept the first Library scrapbook, but no other information on compilers has been found.

Newspaper and magazine clippings form a large portion of the contents of the volumes, but the scrapbooks also contain letters, telegrams, poems, greeting cards, photographs, original drawings by staff members, brochures, maps, and event ephemera, including invitations, menus, seating charts and speeches.

Clippings, letters, and cablegrams about the founding of the Frick Art Reference Library, the construction and opening of its original building in 1924, and the connection to Robert Witt, whose own Witt Library was the inspiration for the Frick Art Reference Library, are among the highlights of the earliest volume. Also of note in the first scrapbook is a collection of sixty-five bookplates, gathered as inspiration for the design of a Frick Art Reference Library bookplate: a sketch of the proposed bookplate and a list of possible mottos show the initial ideas considered, but the project was unrealized.

Other topics that receive substantial coverage include the opening of the new Frick Art Reference Library building and The Frick Collection in 1935, the Library staff's work with the Committee for the Protection of Cultural Treasures in War Areas during World War II, and the death of Helen Clay Frick in 1984. Throughout the volumes are articles about art scholars connected to the Library, and local news stories about Library photography expeditions.

The scrapbooks also contain items about Library staff, including speeches and poems read at anniversary and retirement parties; clippings about exhibitions and public appearances; and wedding announcements, baby pictures, greeting cards and obituaries, all following the lives of current and former staff members.

In the 1990s, the Library's Conservation Department sought to treat, stabilize, and rehouse the scrapbook items in new volumes that would both protect the contents and allow the scrapbooks to be consulted without fear of damage. Each item was cleaned and de-acidified, adhesives were removed, and items were safely mounted on special paper—Kelmscott handmade paper that was left over from the production of *The Frick Collection: An Illustrated Catalogue of the Works of Art in the Collection of Henry Clay Frick, 1949–1956*. The pages were then encased in mylar, the volumes were bound in buckram cloth, and the titles were stamped in gold on the front and spines, transforming the scrapbooks into volumes that can be safely presented and viewed at talks, tours and special events highlighting the history of the Frick Art Reference Library.

—Susan Chore

7 Classifying Photographs of Works of Art
1921

After her inspirational visit to the Witts and their collection of photographs of works of art in 1920, Helen began acquiring photographs and reproductions from Europe and the United States, but she knew that without a system to sort, store, and recall these photographs they would not be of use to the art historical community. Helen looked again to the Witts for the best means to make the Photoarchive beneficial to researchers and so dispatched Ruth Savord, the first Chief Librarian of the Frick Library, to London in 1921 to study the classification system the Witts used and to develop a structure for the Photoarchive. The resulting classification system is the backbone of the Photoarchive and continues to play a vital role today.

The Frick Photoarchive Classification Headings are an ingenious method to catalog an ever-growing collection of photographs while also allowing for adaptation that would be necessary in the future. Since the Photoarchive is a growing collection the classification had to be formulated so that reproductions could be easily discovered but flexible enough to allow for thousands of new photographs each year.

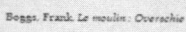

Boggs, Frank Myers
118-10b
100 = American School
18 = Landscapes with water
18-10 = Landscapes with water: With windmills and watermills

The alphanumeric system is easy to understand once the structure is broken down. The first digit refers to the national school of the artist (1 for American, 2 for British, 7 for Italian, etc.). The next two digits refer to the subject matter of the work (17 for Landscapes, 22 for female portraits, 36 for animals, etc.). The subject matter can be further broken down by numbers following a dash allowing for further descriptions of a landscape (with people, with animals, with buildings), portrait (full-length, with hats, direction of the head), or type of animal. In total there are almost 600 classifications for paintings and drawings with an additional 150 classifications for sculpture and architecture. Upon reviewing the Frick's system, Sir Robert Witt wrote that his system was "amateurish and arbitrary". And later in 1927 when Witt was looking for photographs of paintings of Christian saints, the Frick was able to reply immediately with their inventory because of the classification system.

The Photoarchive classification system continues to be at the forefront of art historical research one hundred years after its implementation. In collaboration with Stanford, Cornell, and the University of Toronto the Photoarchive is developing a machine-learning program to use artificial intelligence to assign the classification headings to uncataloged photographs. After processing hundreds of thousands of photographs with classifications assigned by Photoarchive staff, the computer has learned to assign the accurate Photoarchive headings at an error rate on par with a human expert. Assigning one of the 600 classification headings is often the most time consuming task in the cataloging processing, so with this new technology, Photoarchivists will be able to devote time and energy to other projects.

The Photoarchive classification headings have been at the heart of the Frick Art Reference Library since its inception. Its forward thinking structure allowed for easy searching and recall of Photoarchive material while also leaving room for the collection to grow to its current state of 1.4 million reproductions. And it continues to be at the cutting edge of art historical research as it represents a move forward to machine learning and more efficient cataloging.

—John McQuaid

8 Madame Brière
1921 (1970)

Clotilde Brière-Misme (1889–1970) was the daughter of the Lyons architect, Louis Misme, and Jeanne Maurice, the feminist editor of *La Française*. Between 1911–13, she was educated at the École du Louvre under André Michel and Gaston Brière, Conservateur du Musée de Versailles, whom she married in 1925. From 1918 she was a librarian of the Bibliothèque d'art et d'archéologie, which had been given Jacques Doucet's library of rare books in the history of art. She was in charge of prints and photographs there from 1928. She contributed the section, 'La chronique des arts' for the *Gazette des Beaux-Arts*. She was a specialist in Dutch painting, and the Frick Art Reference Library has many of her books, containing a dedication.

She came to Helen Clay Frick's attention through Robert Witt who had used her to supply French and Dutch materials. Helen asked her to provide, where possible, for the same areas, duplicate or triplicate (so one or two could be cut up leaving one uncut item) copies of sales catalogs, exhibition catalogs, monographs as well as photographs. Madame Brière was especially attentive to French regional museums and collections. Over 7,400 photographs for the Photoarchive were acquired up to 1956, and they covered not only Old Masters but also modern and contemporary artists.

But she was also attentive to antiquarian materials, and was responsible for the acquisition of the historic auction catalog collection of the Amsterdam dealer and owner of Frederick Muller & Cie, Anton Mensing (1866–1936), a foundation of the Library's strength in this area. She also collected for Helen under the German occupation of Paris, until the U.S.A. entered World War II.

Geographically-based agents were used elsewhere. In Italy, photographs were made, commissioned or acquired by or through Sansoni & Nesti, F. Mason Perkins (Siena), Count Umberto Gnoli (Umbria, the Marches and Sicily), Richard Offner (Florence), and Gabriel Millet (Byzantine Art).

Helen recognized the important role Madame Brière played in building the Library's collection over forty years; the only plaque on the Main Reading Room walls reads:

'In loving and grateful memory of Clotilde Brière-Misme, whose knowledge and constant help during the first twenty years of The Frick Art Reference Library were responsible for its growth and efficiency'.

—Stephen Bury

Copy of cable received March 26, 1941 from Vichy Office of
Guaranty Trust Company:

CAMPBELL HAS COMMUNICATED WITH MR. AND MRS. GASTON BRIERE WHO
SEND FOLLOWING MESSAGE TO MISS HELEN FRICK QUOTE WE ARE DEEPLY
GRATEFUL FOR YOUR KIND OFFER BUT ARE UNFORTUNATELY UNABLE ACCEPT.
STOP. NATIONAL MUSEUMS STILL NEED MY HUSBAND WHO CANNOT LEAVE
TASK HE HAS UNDERTAKEN. STOP. ON OTHER HAND OUR INTERESTS HAVE
MUCH SUFFERED SINCE BEGINNING OF WAR AND OUR DEPARTURE FROM
FRANCE NOW WOULD RUIN THEM. STOP. LIFE HERE HAS NOT BEEN VERY
HARD UNTIL NOW AND WE OFTEN THINK OF YOU.

9 The Braamcamp Sale
1921 (1771)

Over the past one hundred years, the Library has made a consistent effort to collect not only current auction catalogs, but also older and more rare catalogs dating back as early as the seventeenth century. One of the stars of this effort is the catalog of the famous Braamcamp sale that took place on 31 July 1771, in Amsterdam, acquired via Madame Brière in 1921 as part of the Anton Mensing collection of sales catalogs.

Gerrit Braamcamp (1699–1771) began his career as a wine merchant but quickly realized that his fortune would better and quicker be made in the lumber business. Once he had acquired some wealth, he became aware of the booming art trade in eighteenth-century Amsterdam and began buying Dutch pictures of the highest caliber at a fast pace. In order to house his collection as well as to establish himself as one of Amsterdam's most important men of business, he purchased the Sweedenrijck, a mansion on 'The Golden Bend'—the most prestigious part of the wealthy Herengracht. A generous man by nature, he opened his collection, which he called the 'Temple of Arts', to the public. His collection became so well known that it was one of the premier attractions for guests and foreign rulers visiting the city.

When Gerrit died after a long illness on 17 June 1771, he had already

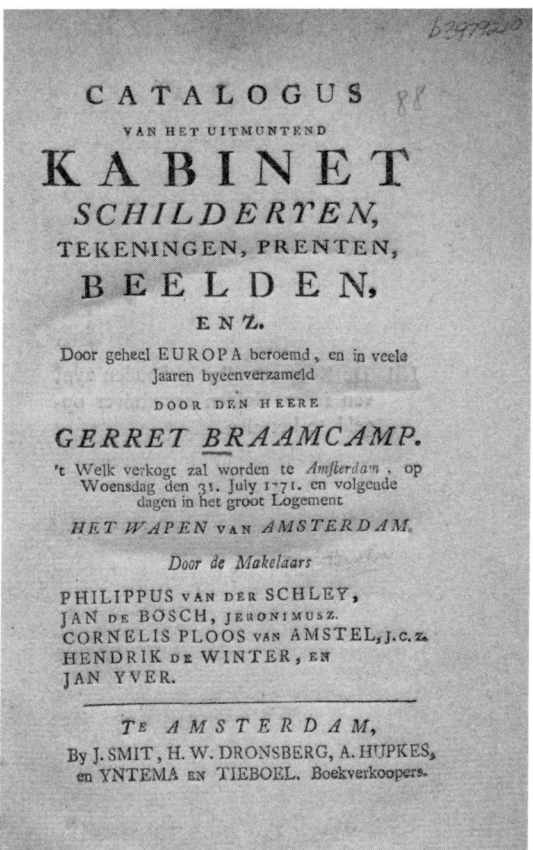

stipulated that the sale of his works would take place on 31st July. Well aware that the auction would attract a great deal of attention, he had arranged for an exhibition of the works to take place at a nearby hotel of which he was the proprietor. 12,000 tickets were printed for the event, but eventually over 20,000 visitors made their way through the incredible collection. Works by Rubens, Rembrandt, Peter de Hooch, Gerard Dou, Jan van Huysum, Gerard Terborch, Gabriel Metsu, and Paulus Potter were among the prestigious offerings. In all, 313 paintings, 282 drawings, 240 prints in volumes, and 82 sculptures were sold, for a grand total of 290,448.10 guilders, an astounding amount for the time that reflects the high caliber of the collection. The copy of the catalog the Library owns has prices and buyers written in by hand, as well as a printed price list tipped in at a later date. After the auction the catalog was republished with the printed names of buyers and prices as *Musaeum Braamcampianum*.

While a large portion of the paintings that were in the sale have by now ended up in renowned collections around the world—the Louvre, the Rijksmuseum, the Metropolitan Museum of Art, the Los Angeles County Museum, and the National Gallery of Ireland to name a few, one of the most famous at the time, a *Triptych* by Gerard Dou, was almost immediately lost at sea on the way to its new owner, Catherine the Great of Russia. More recently, a Rembrandt, *Christ in the Storm on the Sea of Galilee*, was stolen from the Isabella Stewart Gardner Museum in the infamous heist of 1990.

In addition to the Braamcamp auction sale catalog, the Frick Photoarchive contains images of over fifty works from the collection.

—*Louisa Wood Ruby*

Changing Taste
1921 (1784, 1787)

Joseph-Hyacinthe-François de Paule de Rigaud, comte de Vaudreuil (1740–1817), was born in Saint-Domingue and his money came from his creole mother's sugar plantations there. He embarked on a glittering aristocratic career in Paris and Versailles. However, because the wars with England jeopardized the West Indian sources of his wealth, he was in search of court appointments, initially through the comte d'Artois, and then through his distant cousin Gabrielle-Yolande de Polastron, who had married the comte de Polignac: she became Marie-Antoinette's favorite in 1775. It is likely that Vaudreuil, *L'Enchanteur*, was a lover of the comtesse, and possibly the father of Jules de Polignac. He certainly used her to intrigue in ministerial appointments, but there was opposition to his own promotion, only securing in December 1780 the post of *grand fauconnier du roi*, which is used on the title page of the 24–25 November 1784 auction catalogue.

The first and second auctions have been seen as marking a swerve in collecting from Italian and Low Countries work to the French school (and especially contemporary works). The first auction in 1784 certainly sees the sale of the former. Acting through the dealer and auctioneer Alexandre Joseph Paillet, the Comte d'Angiviller, *surintendant des bâtiments du roi* (1774–89)—a post that Vaudreuil would have liked himself—spent around 300,000 livres on Low Countries work: Metsu *The Chemist*, Rubens *Hélène Fourment with Two of her Children*, Jordaens *The Four Evangelists*, Rembrandt *Hendrickje Stoffels* and *The Philosopher Meditating* were just some of the thirty-six works that joined the Royal Collection, now the Louvre.

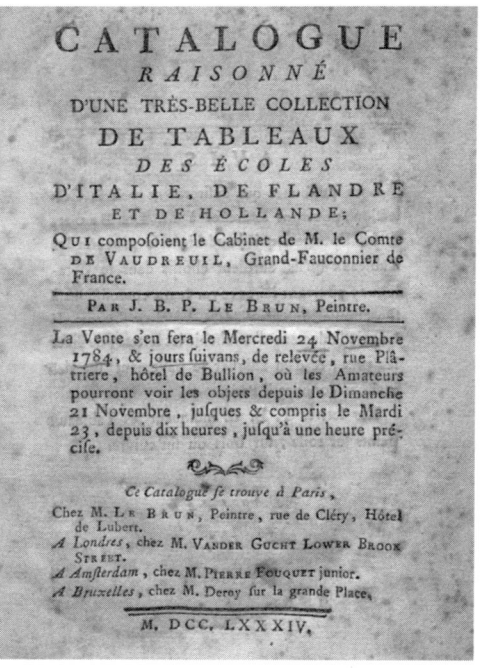

But there were also two French works by Bourdon and Vernet for sale, despite Le Brun's preface to the catalogue, which talked about Vaudreuil's inability to deprive himself of his French paintings.

Jean-Baptiste-Pierre Le Brun (1748–1813) acted as an agent for Vaudreuil, who may have had an affair with his wife, the painter Elisabeth Vigée Le Brun. Vaudreuil frequented their home, the hotel de Lubert, rue de Cléry, which was also a space to entertain, exhibit and meet with artists: Vaudreuil sometimes bought directly from artists.

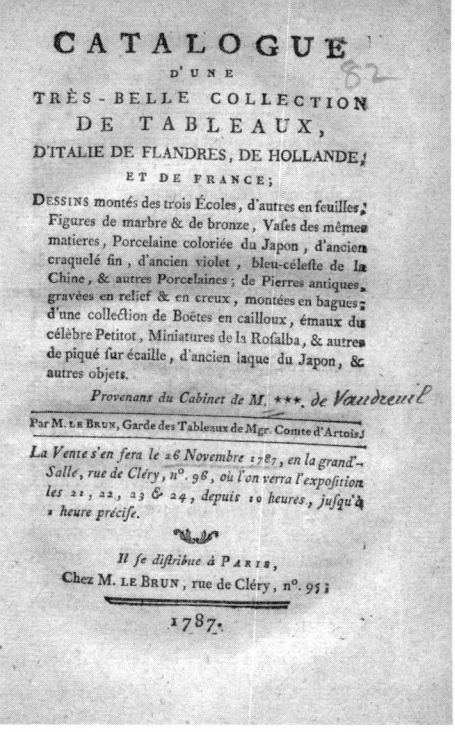

Increasing indebtedness and pursuit by creditors, meant that that the second sale on 26 November 1787 was more likely involuntary and included decorative work specifically made for his home in the rue de la Chaise, where he had supported French writers and artists. But the catalogue also suggests that there were still works by Low Countries artists—Berchem, Rubens, Van Dyck, Wouwermans etc.— remaining in the collection, although Luc Vincent's *Guide des amateurs et des étrangers voyageurs à Paris*, published in January 1787 describes Vaudreuil's home as reflecting a love for French art.

—Stephen Bury

11 The Orléans Sale
1921 (1800)

The bulk or the surviving collection of paintings amassed by Philippe d'Orléans was dispersed in London at a series of exhibitions, private sales and auctions from 1798–1811. But previously, in 1792, 147 Flemish, Dutch and German paintings from the Orléans, or, as it was then called the Palais Royal collection, had been bought by the dealer Thomas Moore Slade (1749–1831), working with Lord Kinnaird, and bankers, Mr. Morland and Mr. Hammersley, for 350,000 livres. Exhibited in April 1793 at 125 Pall Mall, with admission costing one shilling, they were sold to various buyers, including the Earls of Carlisle (Van Dyck), Darnley (Rubens) and Warwick (Van Dyck): The Frick Collection's Snyders husband and wife portraits by Van Dyck and Holbein's *Sir Thomas More* were sold at this point.

The Italian and French paintings had been sold in 1792 by Louise Philippe d'Orléans (now Philippe Égalité) to the Brussels banker, Édouard Walkiers, who then sold them to Count Laborde-Méréville, who moved the collection to London in 1793, looking for a sale. The intermediary for the sale to the Bridgewater syndicate was Michael Bryan (1757–1821), a dealer and agent, who later composed the *Biographical and Critical Dictionary of Painters and Engravers* (1813–1816). His gallery was at 88 Pall Mall, where in December 1798 he showed the smaller Italian paintings nos.1–138. The larger paintings nos.139–296 were shown at the Lyceum on the Strand. Admission (through the purchase of a catalogue) for both venues was two shillings and six pence (as opposed to a shilling for the Slade exhibition): at least there was one happy visitor in the form of the writer William Hazlitt (1778–1830) who wrote that "a new heaven and a new earth stood before me". Sales were by private contract, and the remaining part was sold by auction by Peter Coxe, Burrell and Foster on 14 February 1800 at Bryan's Gallery, Pall Mall. Despite the title page of the sale catalog they were not all Italian—it included a single Watteau, which went for a miserly eleven guineas. William Buchanan (1777–1864), a lawyer and somewhat shady dealer, provides the prices attained for the Coxe sale at the beginning of the first volume of his *Memoirs of Painting...* (1824), although the complete list has discrepancies with his body text: Veronese *Mercury and Herse*, sold to Viscount Fitzwilliam, went for 105 guineas in the former, and 200 in the latter. Lord Darnley acquired, amongst others, Veronese *Happiness* and *Scorn* for 200 and 150 guineas respectively.

There were later sales in 1802 and 1811 of what did not sell and what was now being resold. And although the 'better' pictures sold

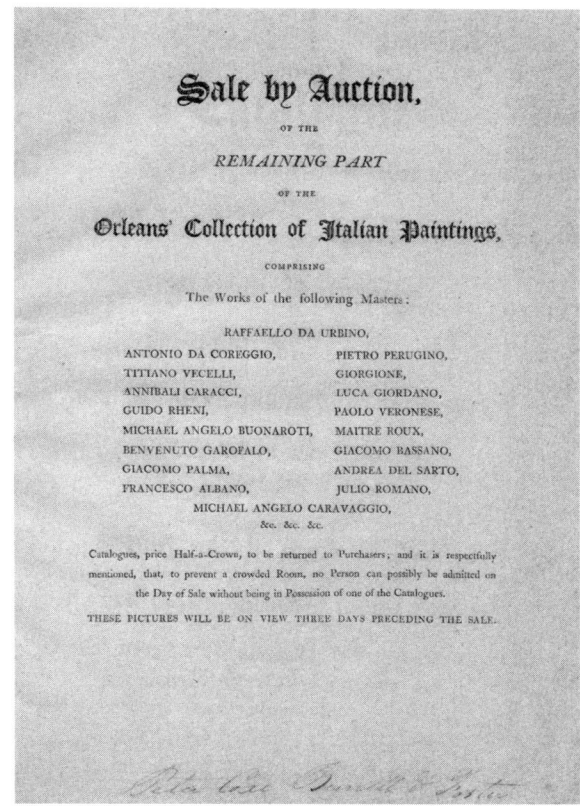

The Catalogue of the remaining part of the Orleans' collection of Italian paintings, which were exhibited last year at Bryan's Gallery, in Pall Mall, and at the Lyceum in the Strand, for sale by private contract, and which will be sold by auction by Peter Cox, Burrell and Foster, at Mr. Bryan's Gallery, in Pall Mall, on Friday the 14th of February, 1800. London: Coxe, Burrell and Foster, 1800.

well, many went at low prices. But the Bridgewater syndicate still had covered its costs and secured 94 of the 305 paintings for their own collections, which still exist in some form.

—Stephen Bury

12 A Deadly Auction
1921 (1833)

John Clerk, Lord Eldin (1757–1832) was a very successful Scottish barrister and Whig appointee as the Solicitor General of Scotland in 1806 and as a Lord of Session in 1823. He, like his father and uncle, were friends of the geologist James Hutton (1726–97), who proposed the theory of uniformitarianism i.e. that the present causes of geological change—earthquakes, volcanic eruptions, erosion and aggregation, landslips etc.—had also been present in the past. Clerk was a member—elected a fellow in 1784—of the Royal Society of Edinburgh.

His home at 16 Picardy Place, Calton Hill, Edinburgh contained a substantial library and a large collection of paintings and prints, china, bronzes, casts and terra-cottas, and fifty-five books of architectural drawings by Robert Adam (1728–92), inherited from Clerk's mother, Susannah Adam. Entrance to the auction was through purchase of a catalog only.

One hundred and seventy-three pictures were for sale over the first three days, including works supposedly by Raphael, Titian, Tintoretto, Veronese, Parmigiano, Rubens, Van Dyck etc. Many of these are misattributed, copies or "workshop of". Lot 113, the last lot of the second day, titled *Adoration of the Shepherds* but elsewhere in the catalog as *Adoration of the Wise Men/Magi*, was supposedly by Titian. Described as a "capital picture" with a note giving its provenance as "formerly in the Balbi Palace, Genoa", in fact it was *Adoration of the Magi* by Jacopo Bassano. It sold for £262–10 shillings. By 1856 it was part of the collection of the Royal Scottish Academy, and is now in the National Gallery of Scotland.

It included British art too—for example, Alexander Runciman (1736–85) is listed as the artist of no.62 with *A Landscape, with a Friar sitting on the foreground*, which is his *Italian River Landscape with a Hermit*, again now in the collection of the National Gallery of Art, Scotland. It sold for five guineas.

The sale of Clerk's library had already taken place in 1832. But the posthumous sale of the art was to take place on 14 March 1833 and the thirteen following days (Sundays excluded) at John Clerk's house, conducted by the Liverpool auctioneer Thomas Winstanley (1768–1845). Winstanley, as dealer, might have been the source of some of Clerk's collection, although this is unlikely as the sale catalog was drawn up by W. & S. Woodburn, St. Martin's Lane, London, and not by Winstanley.

It was on the third day of the sale that the floor in Clerk's house, where the auction was taking place, gave way—whether through poor maintenance of the property or overcrowding, or both. One person was killed and others injured. Researchers have examined surviving copies for physical traces of the calamity but have found none. And the sale must have gone ahead—somewhere at least—as the printed price supplement attests.

—*Stephen Bury*

13 Building the Spanish Photograph Collection
1922

In order to build the Photoarchive, the founding collection of the Frick Art Reference Library, Helen Clay Frick and her staff acquired photographs from multiple sources in the United States and Europe. To maximize Library resources, instead of sending staff on expensive trips to Europe, the Library employed agents who were experts in their fields to obtain or commission photographs for the Photoarchive. One immensely productive relationship developed between the Library and Walter W. S. Cook, professor at New York University specializing in Spanish Art.

Walter W. S. Cook was born in 1888 in Orange, Massachusetts. Upon his return from World War I in 1919, Cook enrolled in Harvard University and received his PhD in 1924. His thirty-year relationship with the Library began in 1922 while he was conducting research for his dissertation, 'Romanesque Panel Painting in Catalonia', and only ended after his retirement from New York University in 1953. While engaged as an agent for the Library, Cook acquired over 40,000 photographs of paintings, sculpture, and illuminated manuscripts, most originating from Spain, his area of expertise.

Obtaining high-quality photographs of works of art in the first half of the twentieth century was not as straightforward as it is today. Due to cost, most art historical texts did not have pictorial representation of the works of art discussed within. A scholar, books in hand, would often consult a photoarchive to provide the visual element lacking in the text. Cook's expertise in Spanish art and his connections on the Iberian Peninsula allowed him to obtain photographs that would not have been available to most researchers at that time.

Cook's work for the Library is documented in fifty years of correspondence retained in the Frick Archives. These letters from Cook (and the responses from Library Staff) offer insight into a scholar travelling across the Atlantic for the sake of his field. Handwritten letters written on hotel stationery in Barcelona, Madrid, Paris, and even from his cabin on trans-Atlantic ships, tell of new batches of photographs the Library should purchase (as well as new books and journals to be considered and letters of introduction for scholars visiting New York). His discerning eye is also evident as he makes sure to exclude photographs that are not of good quality or are duplicates of reproductions already in the Library.

These letters also give a contemporary look at the field of art history from the 1920s to early 1950s. Cook's early complaints about the lack

Alonso Sánchez Coello. *Don Carlos, Son of Philip II.* 1555–1559. Museo del Prado, Madrid. (Archivo Mas photograph obtained from W. W. S. Cook, 27 February, 1946).

of paper for his correspondence and notes are almost unthinkable to the modern reader. He also makes technical recommendations such as in 1934 recommending a side-by-side slide projector to the Library to better illustrate lectures as well as encouraging the Library to partly fund the building of scaffolding at some sites in Spain that would allow for better photographs of large frescos and sculpture. As the thirty-year relationship between Cook and the Library developed, so too did the level of familiarity in the correspondence. Early letters consisted of obtainable photographs and the prices they were available for. But over time formal salutations and signatures become first names, the weather in New York and Europe is noted, travel recommendations from both sides are included, and even Cook's handwriting becomes looser and less precise.

Walter Cook passed away in 1962, fittingly on an ocean liner making the journey across the Atlantic. His travels to Europe and work for the Frick Art Reference Library greatly enhanced the Frick Photoarchive and these photographs continued to be consulted and to advance the field of Spanish art history today.

—*John McQuaid*

14 A Field Trip to Virginia
1922

Shortly after the founding of the Frick Art Reference Library in 1920, Helen Clay Frick embarked on a mission to organize a series of trips throughout the United States (and later in Italy) to document little-known works of art in private collections, small public collections, libraries, and museums.

The first of these trips took place in Virginia from March to April of 1922. On this first trip, Helen was accompanied by Dr. Sidney Fiske Kimbell, Lawrence Park, and Miss Gertrude Hill. Dr. Sidney Fiske Kimbell (1888–1925) was an architectural historian and head of the Department of Art and Architecture at the University of Virginia. Lawrence Park (1873–1924) was an art historian and architect, specializing in early American portraiture, specifically the work of Gilbert Stuart and Joseph Badger (c.1707–65). Gertrude Hill (1888–1972) was a friend of Miss Frick, they served in the same Red Cross unit in France during World War I, and she accompanied Miss Frick on her first trip back to Europe after the war in 1920. She was the sister of the tobacco tycoon George Washington Hill. Miss Julia Sully (1870–1955), a descendant of the artist Thomas Sully, also joined the party in Richmond. Driven by their chauffeur, the group traveled throughout Virginia visiting private homes, museums, and historical sites, inquiring about and recording works of art.

This scrapbook, compiled by Helen chronicles the group's adventures on the muddy back roads of Virginia, visiting stately colonial homes and local landmarks. The scrapbook is full of snapshots of the exteriors of the homes they visited and information about the history and architecture. On the pages dedicated to their visit to the Brandon Estate owned by the Byrd family in Prince George County, Helen mentions the owner showing the party the original 1635 land grant from the governor of the Virginia colony. She has also attached a detailed family tree for the family, dating back to the tenth century.

Inside the homes, Frick photographer William McKillop documented paintings, while Helen and the others recorded information from the owners about the sitters, their families, and the origins of the paintings. Lawrence Park estimated that approximately 750 paintings were seen on the expedition and 557 of those were measured, described, and photographed. These recorded descriptions of the works photographed form the basis of the Photoarchive's vast documentation of works of art, and often include unpublished information. Park records that among the highlights were the discovery of five previously unrecorded paintings by Stuart, a number of drawings by Saint-Mémin (1770–1852), and pastels by Sharples (1751 or 1752–1811).

In her book, *The Story of the Frick Art Reference Library: The Early Years* published in 1979, Katharine McCook Knox notes the first paintings photographed on the Virginia trip were from the home of Mrs. William G. Stanard. The portraits painted c.1828 and now attributed to James W. Ford depict Colonial Robert Page (1764–1840), Sarah Walker (1766–1843), and their son, John Page (1792–). The first of the 'FARL negatives', these three photographs taken in Richmond in 1922 mark the beginning of a project which lasted over forty years and resulted in a collection of 57,000 original negatives, many of which document works of art that have subsequently been altered, lost, or destroyed.

—*Sarah Bigler*

15 The Düsseldorf Galerie
1922 (1778)

Johann Wilhelm, Elector Palatine (1658–1716) was restored to many of his possessions after the Peace of Rijswijk (1697). Heidelberg had been devastated in the Nine Years' War, so Johann Wilhelm resided in Düsseldorf, where he had been born. The Galerie, built 1709–14, was the first free-standing gallery in German-speaking lands—previously princes and nobles had displayed their art as a demonstration of power within their palaces, and with little concern for the appreciation (or viewing) of works of art. The Baroque brick building was designed by the Venetian architect Matteo Alberti (1647–1735), but executed by the court architect, Jacob du Bois: only some of the east wing now survives. It housed a substantial collection of 360 paintings with an emphasis on the Netherlands—forty-six by Rubens (including *The Adoration of the Shepherds*), ten by Rembrandt (including *The Ascension*) and twenty-five by Van Dyck.

When Karl Theodor (1724–99) succeeded Johann Wilhelm, he appointed the painter Wilhelm Lambert Krahe (1712–90) as head of the Galerie. He took the opportunity of having had to store the paintings during the Seven Years War (1756–63) to rehang the Galerie completely. Paintings were hung in the five galleries by school: Italian, Flemish, Dutch; and comparisons were invited to be made between works—Van der Werff and Rembrandt to illustrate Karel van Mander's dichotomy between smooth and rough (*net oft rouw*), objects receding or advancing, or classicism and realism. And although the pictures still seem to us close together, there was more space between them than in any previous installations.

Karl Theodor's architect, Nicolas de Pigage (1723–96), and the Basel art dealer and printmaker, Christian von Mechel (1737–1817) worked together on this monumental work of copperplate engraving: the plates are dated 1775–77 and four engravers were involved—Mechel himself, Hübner, Pintz and Eichler. The typographer was Guillaume Haas and it was printed by Jean Schweighauser.

When Karl Theodor became the Duke of Bavaria (1777) and moved to Munich, the collection was relocated there, and eventually became part of the Alte Pinakothek.

The Library's copy was acquired (with other items) in 1922 from Robert Witt, who bought it at the sale of the recently deceased Algernon Graves (1845–1922), one of the founders of provenance research.

—Stephen Bury

La Galerie électorale de Düsseldorff: ou Catalogue raisonné et figuré de ses tableaux dans lequel on donne une connoissance exacte de cette fameuse collection, & de son local, par des descriptions détaillées... / contenant 365 petites estampes redigées & gravées d'après ces memes tableaux, par Chretien de Michel... Ouvrage composé dans un gout nouveau, par Nicolas de Pigage... Basel: C. de Michel, 1778. Two volumes, bookplate of Algernon Graves. Acquired through Robert Witt, 1922.

16 Hope Hanging
1922 (1810)

One of the earliest library acquisitions *Pictures of H. Hope, Esq., Cavendish Square* was a gift from Sir Robert Witt to the library in 1922. It is likely Sir Robert presented the volume to the library in honor of Helen Clay Frick and her project, the Frick Art Reference Library, which she modeled on Witt's Library of Reproductions after she visited him in London in 1920. There is no record located to date that would indicate how Sir Robert came into possession of this item. The manuscript has been rebound in a sedate, brown library binding and it is unknown what the original binding looked like. Likewise, the contents consist of simple ink drawings of picture frames on cream paper all placed according to their location in individual rooms in Mr. Hope's Cavendish Square, London mansion.

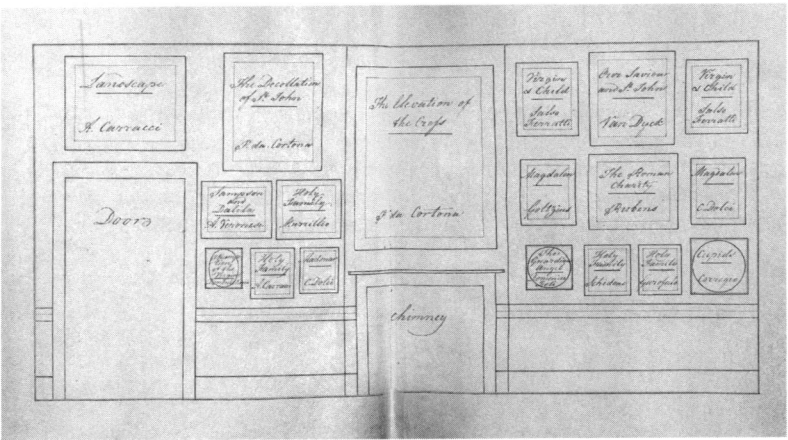

First Floor Cabinet, *Pictures of H. Hope, Esq., Cavendish Square*, 1810.

The simplicity of the book belies the opulence suggested by the artists' names written within the empty picture frames. Henry Hope and other family members going back at least two generations collected hundreds of paintings that Henry Hope assumed responsibility for after the death of others in his generation. The paintings hung first in his county estate, Welgelegen, on the outskirts of Haarlem as well as his home in Amsterdam. Hope, his relatives and ancestors collected Old Master paintings, with definite preferences for religious and mythological scenes. He also owned paintings depicting scenes reflective of his long tenure in Holland, especially landscapes. Hope also commissioned portraits of himself and his family. One well-known painting, *The Hope Family of Sydenham, Kent* by Benjamin West is now at the Museum of Fine Arts, Boston.

Henry Hope was a fantastically wealthy man who joined the family business (Hope & Co., during his tenure) a global merchant trading and financial company with global interests in commodities and finance. In a business of great risk and reward, he managed to stay (very much) on the reward side of the balance sheet.

In 1794, because of the French Revolution, Henry Hope moved to England, in what turned out to be a permanent relocation. It is known that Hope bought two Veronese allegories, now in The Frick Collection, privately from the Bridgewater syndicate handling the sale of the Orléans collection. In 1895 Hope prepared an inventory for insurance purposes of the paintings in his possession. While it has not yet been done, a close review of the inventory in comparison with the Library's manuscript would perhaps flesh out some of the generic titles in the Frick's volume.

The volume housed at the Library dates from 1810, just a year prior to Henry Hope's death in 1811. It is not known why the paintings of the house were inventoried room by room and wall by wall but given the proximity to his death, it seems safe to assume that the inventory may have been in aid of estate planning. Hope had no direct heirs and his effects were passed to nieces and nephews upon his death. In 1898 83 paintings from the Hope family were sold to Asher Wertheimer, a London art dealer, for 122,000 pounds. Many of those paintings can be found in museum collections in the United States, including the Museum of Fine Arts, Boston and the National Gallery of Art in Washington, D.C. (two at least come from the Widener bequest).

—*Sally Brazil*

17 Helen's Italian Scrapbooks
1923 (1924, 1925, 1927–28)

Helen Clay Frick compiled seven scrapbooks of her comprehensive trips to Italy in 1923–24, 1925, and 1927–28 to discover and photograph early Italian paintings and frescoes for the Library's Photoarchive collection. The scrapbooks document each trip as Helen filled them with snapshots of the cities, towns and countryside she visited. She bought and included postcards of monuments as well as prints of artworks from Italian photography firms such as Alinari, Brogi, and Lombardi. Helen annotated the pages with personal observations, discoveries, and lists of artworks she had seen in each location.

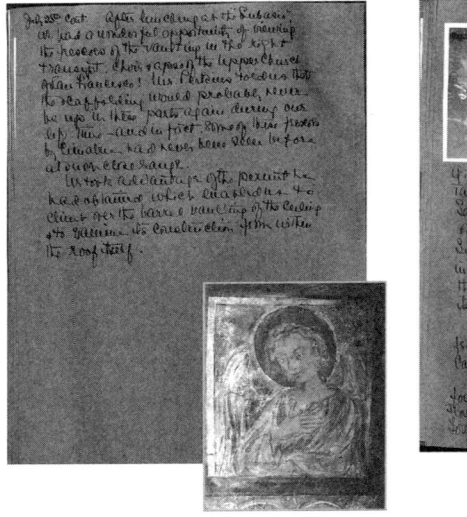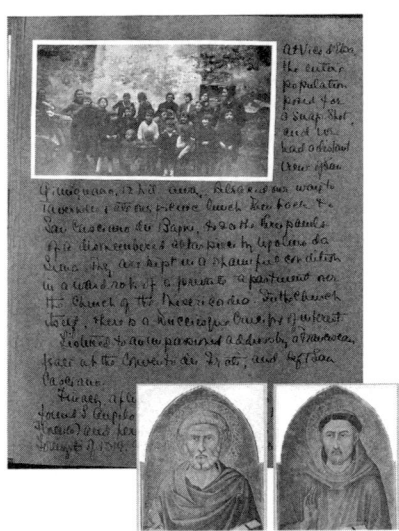

Helen Clay Frick, *Italy 1923–1924*, three volumes. *Italy 1925*, three volumes. *Italy 1927*, one volume.

On the second trip in 1925, Helen was accompanied by her friend Pauline (Polly) Wells, and art historian and critic, F. Mason Perkins (1874–1955). On 25 July Helen, Perkins and their party visited San Francesco in Assisi. Scaffolding had been erected in the Upper Church and Helen recorded her excitement in the scrapbook: "…we had a wonderful opportunity of viewing the frescoes of the vaulting in the right transept, choir & apse of the Upper Church of San Francesco! Mr. Perkins told us that the scaffolding would probably never be up in these parts again during our life-times—and in fact, some of these frescoes by Cimabue had never been seen before at such close range.

We took advantage of the permit he had obtained which enabled us to climb over the barrel vaulting of the ceiling & to examine its construction from within the roof itself." In 1926 the photographer Mario Sansoni (1882–1975) used the scaffolding to take photographs for the Frick Art Reference Library "from temporary scaffolding".

In January 1928, on their third trip to Italy, Helen and Pauline traveled to San Casciano dei Bagni, a town some seventy kilometers south of Siena, to see three panels of a dismembered altarpiece by Ugolino da Siena (Ugolino di Nerio, active 1317–27) which were being stored in a wardrobe in an apartment over the church of the Misericordia. The scrapbook does not mention any details about the altarpiece, but Pauline identified them elsewhere. On the back of the mounts in the Photoarchive, Pauline noted that the panels depicted St. Peter and St. Paul, and that they were stored together in the cupboard with another painting of a Madonna and Child with Donor also by Ugolino da Siena from the same church. She also noted that the paintings were damaged—the paint had flaked off revealing the white gesso underneath. Each of the three panels were photographed by Sansoni in 1929. Through research and with the help of Perkins and Sansoni, Helen was able to acquire and commission photographs of previously unpublished and little known works of art throughout Italy for the library.

—*Kerri A. Pfister*

Library Staff Photograph
1923

This photograph shows members of the Frick Art Reference Library staff posing in the exterior courtyard of the Frick residence, an area that was later enclosed and transformed into the Garden Court of The Frick Collection during the 1933–35 John Russell Pope construction project. Just to the north of the courtyard, the construction of the Frick Art Reference Library building at 6 East 71st Street was underway. The staff, housed in the bowling alley of the Frick residence, would move in to the new Library on 1 May 1924.

Photograph of Frick Art Reference Library staff, Summer 1923. Ira W. Martin, photographer.

The staff members shown in the photograph, from left to right, are Helen Robbins, Lavinia Buckler, Elsie Brusselas, Pauline P. Wells, Muriel Baldwin, Marjorie Chater, Mary Wooley, Grace Nedley, Maybelle Morgan (Brown), Ruth Savord, Dagmar Holmes, Margaret Stillman (Rood), Hope Mathewson, Gilberta Rose, and Anna Flichtner (Barretto). They held positions of Librarian, reference assistant, typist, and cataloger, although titles were less rigid in the early days of the Library, and seemed to vary with each listing. Missing from the photograph, most notably, is Helen Clay Frick, the Library's founder and director. There is only one known formal staff photo in which she appears during her sixty-three year tenure as Director.

Head Librarian Ruth Savord (1894–1966), engaged as the first Library staff member on 8 November 1920, established classification systems and procedures for the new library, managed the overflowing acquisitions, and supervised the growing staff. Ms. Savord resigned on 22 May 1924, the day before the new Library building opened. While no written documentation has been found, the story survives that she resigned because of a dress code established by Helen Clay Frick—all staff members, including the Head Librarian, were required to wear lab coats while at work. Ms. Savord went on to a distinguished career as the organizer and Head Librarian of the Council on Foreign Relations library from 1930 to 1960.

Hope Mathewson (1899–1985) worked at the Library from 1922–71 as a reference worker, Head of Reference, and Head Indexer, and was responsible for both planning photographing expeditions and accompanying the photographer on trips during the 1920s and 1930s.

Pauline P. Wells (1888–1976), a reference worker, became a lifelong friend of Helen Clay Frick's and traveled with her on European trips. Ms. Wells is responsible for many of the meticulously illustrated Italian travel journals from the 1920s that documented the location and placement of works of art in churches and cathedrals, and helped to identify works that the Library wanted to include in its photograph collection.

Other 1923 staff members went on to success elsewhere. Muriel Baldwin (1890–1960) became Chief of the New York Public Library Art and Architecture Division. Grace Nedley (later Bamford) (1899–1960) became the first policewoman in Greenwich, Connecticut in February 1947 and was decorated for her service.

The Library has been known throughout its history for its long-tenured staff. Among those pictured, Dagmar Holmes worked at the Library for twenty-one years, Anna Flichtner Barretto for twenty-six years, Marjorie Chater for forty-two years, and Maybelle Morgan Brown for forty-four years.

The photographer, Ira W. Martin (1886–1960), began on 1 January 1923 and founded the Library's Photographic Department. While Mr. Martin worked at the Library until his death in 1960, he also had a successful photography career outside of the Library.

The Archives contains hundreds of additional photographs of staff, from 1923 to the present, including all-staff photos, individual portraits, snapshots, and event photos of picnics, dinners, and holiday and retirement parties.

—*Susan Chore*

19 Nichi futsu geijutsu sha*
1923 (1922, 1924, 1932, 1936, 2021)

Until 2010 the Frick Art Reference Library generally avoided acquiring what were thought to be just translations of English, French, German, Italian or Spanish texts. But a realization of the importance of such works for the study of the reception of art led the Library to look more closely at such works, emanating from Estonia to Japan, where the period 1900–37 has become a focus.

It is often assumed that the interest in and collecting of modern art in Japan was a post-World War II phenomenon, associated with the economic boom, industrial success and high property prices. But the interest in modern European art began much earlier. In the 1920s many Japanese artists had studied or worked in Paris or Europe, e.g. Key Sato (1906–78); critics, who did not leave Japan, corresponded with French, German and Italian critics and artists, e.g. Tai Kanbara (1898–1997), who was in touch with Marinetti. However, the role of the Franco-Japan Fine Arts Company (*Nichi futsu geijutsu sha*), which operated 1922–36, has been overlooked, and the Frick Art Reference Library's acquisition in 2021 of a collection of fifty-four items relating to its activities, makes possible research on this almost unknown organization.

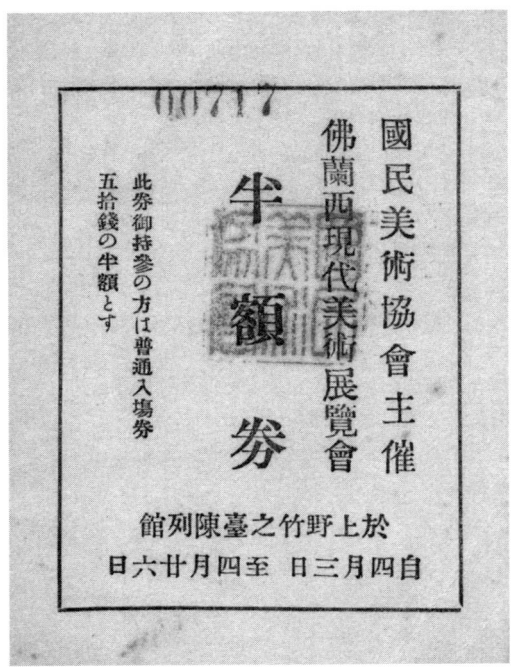

Exposition d'art francais contemporain au Japan 1923 = Furansu gendai bijutsu tenrankai. Tokyo: Kokumin bijutsu kyokai shusai, 1923. Entry ticket for the exhibition.

It seems to have been the idea of the French art dealer Herman d'Oelsnitz (1892–1941), supported by the French Ambassador, Robert de Billy. It also involved Hoshin Kuroda (1895–1967), an art historian, who in 1922 worked in the publicity section of the Mitsukoshi department store, which specialized in kimonos. After collaborating on three French exhibitions, d'Oelsnitz and Kuroda founded the Franco-Japan Fine Arts Company in 1924: some 4,300 paintings, 540 sculptures and thousands of decorative art objects were shown, exposing French impressionism, post-impressionism, modern art and design to Japan: many of these objects remain in Japanese museums and private collections. Economic difficulties—related to the exchange rate—reduced the scale of activities and the company was dissolved in 1932, although some activity continued. Kuroda's 1956 autobiography, 'Memory of Paris', (*Pari no omiode*) is another important source of information on these activities.

In its heyday the Company held annual exhibitions, now described as 'Buddha' exhibitions, in Tokyo and Osaka: in modified forms they toured elsewhere. Color postcards of works of art supplemented large and small exhibition catalogues. The Company also ran a gallery on the sixth floor of the Sankyo Building in Tokyo, where it held small exhibitions and published *Le bulletin de l'art français et japonais*, 1925–28. This collection is a treasure-trove for the history of collecting of modern French art in Japan in the first half of the twentieth century.

—*Stephen Bury*

20 Colour Reproduction*
1923 (1821)

[Jacob] Cornelis Ploos van Amstel (1726–98) was an Amsterdam based art dealer, collector, engraver and publisher. The Frick Art Reference Library has an annotated copy of his posthumous sale catalogue, four volumes in two, 3 March 1800 and following days, at Philippe van der Schley, Amsterdam. The Photoarchive allows the researcher to discover where some of these items now are—for example, Adriaen van Ostade's drawing *Strolling Violinist at an Ale House Door* (1673) is now at the Morgan Library.

His collection also included scientific instruments and it is interesting to speculate what, if any, role they played in his discovery of his technique of color reproduction. The publication in 1770 of a series of forty-six plates called for a demonstration of the process in Haarlem, after which he was granted a privilege engrossed with the text "his figures were neither engraved, nor etched, nor hammered on copper, but were produced by means of ground varnishes, powders and liquids". The prints were not colored by hand "but printed… entirely… with oil-colors". However, later analysis has suggested than the plates reveal marks made by hand.

His apprentice, Christian Josi (1768–1826), who had married Jan Chalon's daughter, Carolina Susanna, acquired most of Ploos's prints in 1800. He had also studied mezzotint with John Raphael Smith (1751–1812) in London, where he set up as a print dealer in Gerrard Street, Soho in 1818. He then began to enlarge Ploos's series of "imitations" of Dutch and Flemish master drawings from forty-six to one hundred prints 1821–27/28. After his death his own collection of the drawings and prints of Rembrandt, Hollar and others was auctioned at Christie's 18 March to 1 April 1829: the Frick Art Reference Library has a priced copy of this sale with name annotations.

The preface to this work, *Collection d'imitations de dessins d'après les principaux maîtres hollandaise et flamands, commence par Ploos van Amstel*, includes fascinating anecdotes on eighteenth-century collecting.

—Stephen Bury

Reproduction of a drawing of a Dutch church interior. The album caption attributes it to Pieter Jansz. Saenredam (1597–1665), but it has been ascribed to Hendrick Cornelisz Vliet (c.1611–75) from *Collection d'imitations de dessins d'après les principaux maîtres hollandaise et flamands, commence par Ploos van Amstel, continue et portée au nombre de cent morceaux, avec des renseignements historiques et détaillés sur ces maîtres et sur leurs ouvrages. Precedés d'un discours sur l'état ancien et modern des arts dans les Pays Bas / par C. Josi.* London: C. Josi; Mannheim: Artaria et Fontaine; Amsterdam: Frères van Cleef, 1821–27.

21 Itinerant Turner
1923 (1799)

Romanticism, the interest in the picturesque and the difficulties of foreign travel, created an almost insatiable demand for topographical prints—of castles, churches, bridges, and general views of the British Isles—as engravings and then aquatints, creating demand for artists' watercolors and sketches necessary to make them.

The Royal Academy Schools did not teach landscape painting, and topography was likened by Henry Fuseli (1741-1825), professor of painting from 1799, as akin to mapmaking. William Turner (1775-1851), later known as Joseph Mallord William Turner, attended the academy at age fourteen, but sought perspective and topography lessons from Thomas Malton (1748-1804) at his evening drawing class in Conduit Street, London, where Thomas Girtin (1775-1802) also studied.

By 1794 the engraver and print-seller John Walker of Rosomans Street, Clerkenwell, near Spa Fields, had employed Turner to make watercolors of picturesque sites to be engraved for the *The Copper Plate Magazine, or, Monthly Cabinet of Picturesque Prints*, no.1 (February 1792)–no.125 (June 1802), which the Frick Art Reference Library also possesses. Turner contributed sixteen scenes from his travels in the Midlands and Wales in 1794, and the Lake District, Yorkshire and Northumberland in 1797, including views of Westminster Bridge, Rochester, Matlock, Nottingham, Ely, Sheffield, Bridgnorth, and Chepstow.

In 1799 Walker decided to issue a selection of these views not as a serial but in one volume, *The Itinerant: A Select Collection of Interesting*

Chepstow Bridge, engraving by James Storer after an original drawing by William Turner. The old bridge, primarily made of wood on a sole-plate design, across the Wye, between Gloucestershire and Monmouthshire, had been there since the middle ages. In 1785 four arches on the Monmouth side were replaced by stone. The bridge was rebuilt in 1816. It is telling how much the transport infrastructure during the Industrial Revolution still depended on medieval bridges.

and *Picturesque Views in Great Britain and Ireland*. Turner contributed fifteen views. Other artists besides Turner (and Walker) included W. Brand, Charles Catton (1756–1819), Edward Dayes (1763–1804), Thomas Girtin, Thomas Hearne (1744–1817), J. Hornesey, Henry Jeayes, William Marlow (1740–1813), Francis Nicholson (1753–1844), John Nixon, Amelia Noel (1759–1818), William Orme (1771–1854), Philip Reinagle (1749–1833), George Samuel, Paul Sandby (1731–1809) and William Tayleure. The engravings were made mainly by Walker, but some plates were signed by James Baily, N. Burnwhite, James Fittler (1758–1835), John Roffe (1769–1850), James Storer (1771–1853), Thomas Tagg and J. Widnell. The plates were also available individually. The Frick's copy has the armorial bookplate of the cricketer, Liberal politician and collector, William Fuller-Maitland (1844–1932), Stansted Hall, Essex.

—*Stephen Bury*

22 Blueprint of 1924 Library
1923

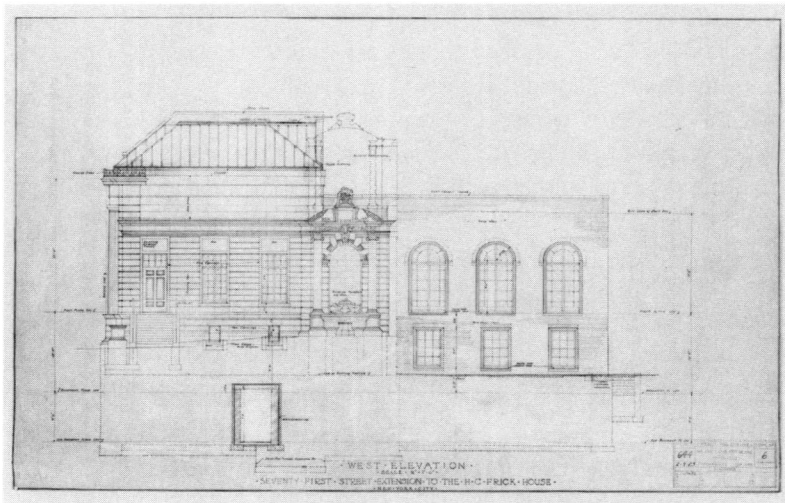

The west elevation of the first Frick Art Reference Library building, located at 6 East 71st Street, is depicted in this architectural drawing, dated 9 February 1923. The Library was designed by architects Carrère & Hastings and Shreve, Lamb & Blake, and the general contractor was Thomas O'Reilly & Son. The one story building, constructed of Indiana limestone, featured an entrance just off of East 71st Street, facing the Frick residence to the east.

The Library building, referred to as the Seventy-First Street Extension to the H. C. Frick House on the plan, was built on property that was part of the original land purchase made by Henry Clay Frick in 1912 for his residence at 1 East 70th Street. The Frick Collection Trustees agreed both to the use of The Frick Collection property for the Library building, and to pay for approximately 60% of the cost of construction, with the remaining amount to be footed by the Library's founder and director, Helen Clay Frick.

When construction of the Library building began on 14 May 1923, the Library was housed in the bowling alley and billiard room of the Frick residence, and staff, photographs, and books were spilling into other areas of the house, from the basement to the third floor. Although the staff answered inquiries, and allowed for the occasional special visitor, it was impossible for researchers to consult photographs and other library materials in person as long as the Library remained in the Frick residence, where it had been housed since November 1920. The construction of the new one-story building with a Reading Room and stack space would be an important step in the growth and significance of the Frick Art Reference Library.

Thomas Hastings (1860–1929) of Carrère & Hastings, had also been the architect of the New York Frick residence, constructed in 1913, and had designed a sculpture gallery for Henry Clay Frick in 1916. The sculpture gallery had connected to the residence, and extended across East 71st Street to the edge of the property. Although the sculpture gallery was never built, Mr. Hastings realized the westernmost building from this project could be redesigned as the new library building. In fact, the 1916 and 1923 south elevations of these buildings are virtually identical.

Another instance of repurposing for this construction project is documented by notes on this architectural drawing: the front exterior wall, including three decorative pediments above the windows, the fountain, lattice work and the wall extending beyond the building all were "existing" at the time the drawing was made. Construction photographs from 1923 indicate that these walls and decorative features were already part of the stonework in the Frick residence's exterior courtyard and driveway and were reused in the Library's construction.

The Library opening was held on 23 May 1924, and students were welcomed on June 9th of the same year. The interior of the new Library building included a spacious Reading Room, the Librarian's Office, the Owner's [Helen Clay Frick's] Room, three stack areas, staff work areas, and a staff lounge.

Even with the reuse of existing materials, the cost of the Library, originally estimated at $140,000, was $215,529. The Frick Collection Trustees contributed $91,601, and Miss Frick paid the remainder of $123,928.

The original Library building was demolished in December 1934, and became the site of The Frick Collection's East Gallery, Oval Room and Music Room as part of the conversion of the Frick residence into a museum. The current Frick Art Reference Library, designed by John Russell Pope, was constructed as part of the same project in newly-acquired lots next to the original building.

—*Susan Chore*

Truly Yours, Helen
1924

The Archives houses voluminous correspondence, diaries, and photographs related to the opening of the new 1924 Library, especially through the perspective of staff.

Katharine "Kitty" Knox was a close friend to Helen, as well as an art historian and author specializing in early American art. Miss Knox worked with the Frick Art Reference Library as a researcher, consultant, and special staff member for over fifty years. A Western Union Telegram dated 22 May 1924, confirms a simple message of Miss Knox's attendance for the opening of the Frick Art Reference Library which took place that upcoming Friday. 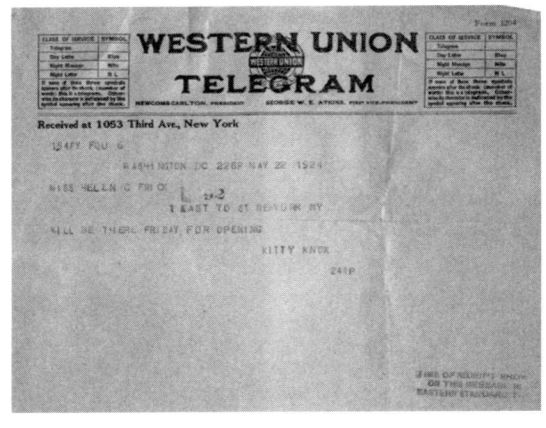 Miss Knox was a vital character in the creation of the Library and she would eventually go on to write a book about this time: *The Story of the Frick Art Reference Library: The Early Years* (1979).

There are a few other names to mention in the creation of the Library such as second Head Librarian, Ethelwyn Manning who worked there 1924–47. During this period she assisted with expansion, staff growth, and overseeing the Frick Art Reference Library's participation in the Protection of Cultural Treasures in War Areas (later known as the Monuments, Fine Arts, and Archives program). Miss Manning eventually stepped down in December of 1947 and it was during her retirement party that Miss Frick wrote a sentimental speech expressing her gratitude towards all Miss Manning had done throughout her time at the Frick Art Reference Library: "Under your generalship (crossed out to read 'guidance') the FARL has grown from a puny infant into an important adult whose place in the world of art is undisputed." During Miss Manning's tenure, the staff of the library more than doubled and she helped create its reputation.

Amongst the many letters to and from Miss Frick is a 1932 recommendation she wrote for Miss Nedley, a typist. Scrawled in pencil on

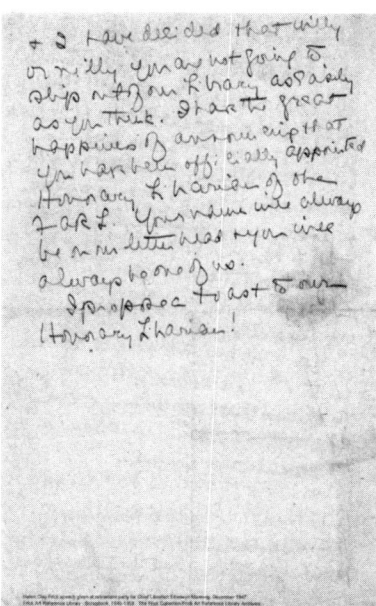

paper, Miss Frick states that Miss Nedley came to the library in the fall of 1920 as a stenographer and eventually worked her way up to secretary of the Head Librarian where she remained until 1929. She writes, "In that time, she proved herself to be very reliable, loyal, efficient and willing. I am glad to give her the highest recommendation".

Miss Frick was always direct and honest in her references—which led in the same year to an unsuccessful libel suit by James Howard Bridge.

—Payton Goad

24 *Madonna and Child*
1925 (1984)

At the first part of the sale of the large collection of Achillito Chiesa, the son of a Milan businessman, at the American Art Galleries, New York, 27 November 1925, an agent for Helen Clay Frick bought Andrea di Bartolo *Madonna and Child* for $3200. It was at the Frick Art Museum, Pittsburgh until it was bequeathed to The Frick Collection at Helen Clay Frick's death in 1984. It was also photographed by the Frick Art Reference Library photographer, Ira W. Martin (1886–1960), who worked for the Photoarchive from 1932.

Housed in a later, 'modern', tabernacle frame, in the Venetian style, the painting, tempera and gold leaf on panel, is 21 x 13 inches in dimensions. The sales catalogue describes the image: "The Madonna is seated on a cushion in a flowering meadow, holding the Child at her left. On high against a gold background, two angels praying."

Andrea di Bartolo or Andrea di Bartolo Cini (1358/64–1428) studied with his father, Bartolo di Fredi Cini and perhaps worked on the latter's *Massacre of the Innocents*, now at the Walters Art Museum, Baltimore. By 1390 he had set up his own studio producing work in the conventional Siennese style, influenced by Duccio and Simone Martini. He worked in the Veneto as well as the Sienna area, and received commissions from the Dominicans and Franciscans. This Madonna and Child may owe something to Simone's Madonna of Humility and to manuscript illumination of the *hortus conclusus* or enclosed garden: Andrea di Bartolo also executed such illuminations for manuscripts. A distinguishing feature of this type of image is that Child did not suckle, but sits or stands on the Madonna's lap. The American art historian, Millard Meiss (1904–75) identified four possible versions of this image by Andrea di Bartolo.

To visitors to the wood-paneled office of the Chief Librarian on the Third Floor, it may seem that Andrea di Bartolo's *Madonna and Child* has been there since the new Library opened in 1935. However, it has been only from 1984 that they have overseen the meetings taking place in that room.

—Stephen Bury

Andrea di Bartolo
(Italian, 1358/64–1428)
Madonna and Child.
Gift of Helen Clay Frick,
1984.

25 Third Post-Impressionist Exhibition
1923 (1913)

Roger Fry (1866–1934) organized the exhibition *Manet and the Post-Impressionists* at the Grafton Galleries, 8 Grafton Street, London, 8 November 1910–11 January 1911—the "first" Post-Impressionist exhibition. The *Second Post-Impressionist Exhibition* took place at the same venue 5 October–31 December 1912. These were important events in the reception of modern art in England. Less well known is the "second second" or third Post-Impressionist exhibition.

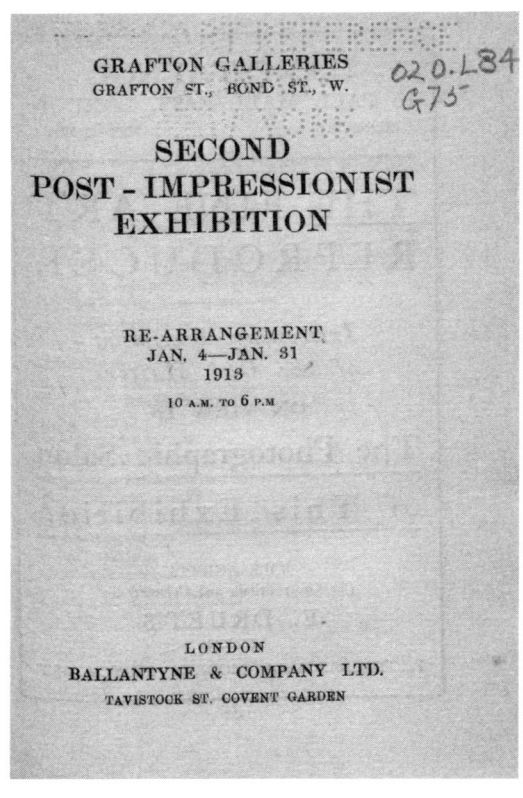

The second and third catalogs share a decorated cover, designed by Fry and Vanessa Bell (1879–1961), but drawn by Duncan Grant (1885–1978): it has a quasi-cubist face of a woman with a hand raised in possible horror at the announcement of the exhibition. The title page of the third exhibition has the additional text "re-arrangement Jan. 4–Jan. 31 1913". The three introductory essays are identical in both catalogs—'The English Group' by Clive Bell (1881–1964), husband of Vanessa Bell (née Stephen), in which he introduced the concept of "significant form"; 'The French Group' by Roger Fry; and, 'The Russian Group' by Boris von Arep (1883–1969). There were 242 numbered entries in the October 1912 catalogue, compared to 252 in the January 1913 version.

While both exhibitions began with Russian prints in the staircase, the 1913 exhibition lacked Matisse's plaster *Le Dos* in the entrance landing. Next upon entering the Octagon Room, the 1913 visitor was confronted with a Cézanne solo exhibition of thirty-three works, lent on consignment from Bernheim-Jeune et Cie, whereas the 1912 visitor would have seen five Cézannes, two lent or consigned by Vollard, and three lent by Gaston Bernheim-Jeune, accompanied by two paintings by Matisse (in 1913, relocated to the Large Gallery), three by Vlaminck (two relocated to the Large Gallery), five by Derain (one relocated to the Large Gallery and one to the End Gallery), one by Lhote (relocated to the Large Gallery), one by Marchand (relocated to the Large Gallery), one by Picasso (relocated to the Large Gallery), and one by Duncan Grant (relocated to the Large Gallery). Eric Gill's sculpture, *The Golden Calf*, concluded the Octagon Room section.

The 1912 exhibition had sixteen Matisse paintings and concluded with Matisse's plaster sculpture, *L'araignée*. The 1913 version had eight Matisse paintings: *L'araignée* had been moved to the end of the Centre Gallery, joining there the third state of Matisse's *Buste de femme*. Of the works by Matisse originally in the Large Gallery, *Nu au bord de la mer*; *Cyclamens*; *Conversation* (owned by the Russian tea merchant Sergei Tschoukine); *Poissons rouges; Les aubergines*; and *Coucous sur le tapis bleu et rose* (these last three lent by Bernheim-Jeune et Cie) remained.

Seven Picassos (six lent by Kahnweiler and one by Vollard) were in both the 1912 and 1913 arrangements; a still life, lent by Clive Bell, appeared in 1913. Braque and Flandrin were only in the 1912 exhibition, whilst Goncharova, Marchand, Marval, Ottman, Picart, Sarian, Thiesson, Von Arep, and Wadsworth were added to the 1913 Large Gallery. The paintings and sculpture in the 1912 and 1913 versions of the Centre Gallery were very similar, but with Rousseau's *Scene de forêt*, lent by Leonce Rosenberg, notably absent in 1913. The End or North Gallery was mostly unchanged.

Many of the changes between the two shows occurred because a number of the 1912 works were on consignment from dealers such as Kahnweiler, Bernheim-Jeune and Vollard, and some had been sold during the 1912 show.

—*Stephen Bury*

26 Not Art Deco
1925 (1959)

The French title of the 1925 International Exhibition of Modern Decorative and Industrial Arts, Exposition Internationale des Arts Décoratifs et Industriels, gave rise to the term Art Deco, but there was little in the Soviet contribution to the exhibition that reflected this movement.

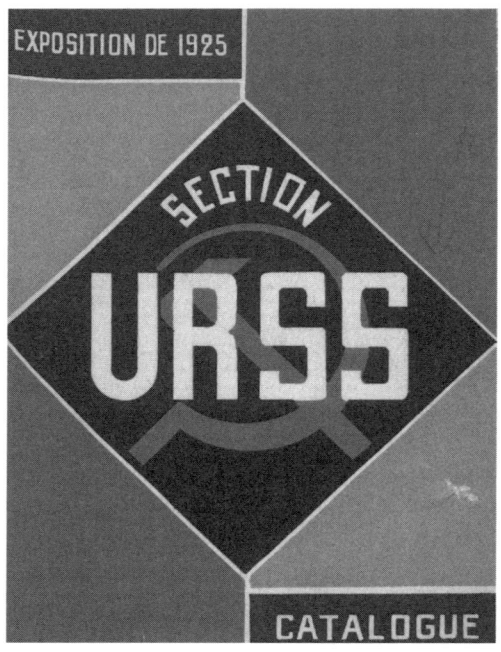

Catalogue des oeuvres d'art decorative et d'industrie artistique: exposées dans le Pavilion de l'U.R.S.S. au Grand Palais et dans les Galleries de L'Esplanade des Invalides. Paris, 1925. Gift of Rhode Island School of Design, 1959.

In fact the participation of the Soviets had come very late—France only recognized the U.S.S.R. on 28 October 1924 and the invitation only came on 1 November 1924: the exhibition was to open in April 1925. Given the lateness of the invitation, the Soviets had some idea of what was being planned for the rest of the exhibition, and could plan to be deliberately different. The Soviet organizing committee, chaired by the literary critic, Petr Semenovich Kogan, opted to promote Soviet utopianism and innovation while selling traditional folk art for hard currency, as policy shifted from war communism to the New Economic Policy (NEP). The constructivist Aleksandr Rodchenko (1891–1956) was appointed to curate and supervise the installation in Paris, from where, in an interesting series of letters to his wife Varvara Stepanova (1894–1958), he described the Parisian world of commodities—bidets, cameras, socks, suspenders, collars etc.

The exhibition was in three separate locations. The Soviet Pavilion, designed by architect Konstantin Melnikov (1890–1974), made in a month from flat-pack wood and glass, opened on 4 June rather than in April. It contained crafts on the first floor and publications of the State Publishing House (*Gosizdat*) on the second. Rodchenko's minimal and hygienic workers' club interior was in a gallery on the Esplanade des Invalides. After the exhibition, it was given to the French Communist Party. The rest of the Soviet displays took place in six halls of the Grand Palais, which had itself been erected for the 1900 (11th) World Exhibition: handicrafts were shown alongside Soviet graphics, advertisements, theater designs, work from the Higher State Artistic and Technical Workshops (VKhUTEMAS) and a model of Vladimir Tatlin's *Monument to the Third International* at the top of the central stairway, behind a conventional bust of Lenin, who had died relatively recently on 21 January 1924. To the left were advertisements for Mossel'prom products, designed by Mayakovsky and Rodchenko. Indeed, Mayakovsky, who had come to Paris en route to the United States via Mexico, won a silver medal for these advertising posters.

The catalogue had texts by Petr Kogan, Anatole Lunacharsky, Nikolai Dokuchaev, Abram Efross, and O. D. Kameneva (the sister of Trotsky). There were (at least) two editions with a variant title and cover after designs by Aleksandr Rodchenko.

—*Stephen Bury*

27 Kleine Kabinett*
1926 (1782)

The pursuit of high quality reproductions of works of art has seen such expenditures on specialized printmaking, photography and imaging which in some cases might have been more than the cost of buying the actual item. This may well be the case of print reproductions of master drawings. Vasari, one of the earliest collectors of prints, praised the chiaroscuro woodcut reproduction of a Parmigianino drawing, *Diogenes*, by Ugo da Carpi, active in Venice, Rome and Bologna 1502–32. The difficult process involved using two or more differently inked woodblocks. By the eighteenth century printmakers were experimenting with stipple engraving (also known as the "crayon manner") and aquatint.

Johann Gottlieb Prestel (1739–1808) was an engraver and painter who had travelled to Venice and Rome in the 1760s. He developed a variation of the aquatint process to achieve the effect of the original drawing, improvising double plates, the use of extremely thin gold leaf, as well as using oil paint as ink. Prestel produced three portfolios published between 1779 and 1782, by which time Prestel went bankrupt and needed the new patronage of the Frankfurt-based collector H. S. Hüsgren and further plates were issued. However, financial difficulties continued, and his wife, a former pupil, Maria Katharina Höll (1747–94) whom Prestel had married in 1769, had had enough, and moved with their children to London in 1786, setting up her own print enterprise, specializing in aquatint landscapes.

The 1779 portfolio of thirty prints is known as the *Schmidtsche Kabinett*, because the drawings were from the collection of Hamburg merchant, Gerhard Joachim Schmidt (1742–1801), consisting of 136 works, including drawings by Raphael and Van Dyck, which was auctioned on 28 May 1791. The second portfolio, known as the *Braunsche Kabinett*, consisted of forty-eight plates, from the collection of Paul le Praun of Nuremberg, the Museo Prauniano. The Frick Art Reference Library has the third portfolio of thirty-six prints, known as the *Kleine Kabinett*, the drawings coming from several collections.

The identification of who printed what is difficult as multiple plates were used and there was much collaboration, but art historians are re-assigning many to Maria Katharina Prestel and to their pupil Regina Katharina Schönecker (1760/2–1818).

—Stephen Bury

Plate 24: *Good Triumphant over Evil*, drawing by Jacques Ligozzi from the Museo Prauniano. Etching and acquatint printed in brown with gold leaf, by Maria Katharina Prestel. Dated 1781. from: *Dessins des meilleurs peintres d'Italie, d'Allemagne et des Pays-Bas: tires de divers célebres cabinet: graves d'après les orignaux de meme grandeur / par Jean Théophile Prestel.* [Frankfurt am Main: Sturm, 1782]. Purchased through Sir Robert Witt, June 1926.

Smith in Venice
1926 (1749, 1954)

Joseph Smith (c.1682–1770) was in Venice by 1700 where he worked as a trader before joining the merchant-banking house of Thomas Williams, which soon became Williams and Smith. From 1744 to 1761 he was George II's consul in Venice, hence the name 'Consul Smith'. This was not renewed by George III and, because in anticipation of continuing, he had acquired and started to renovate the Palazzo Balbi (now the Palazzo Smith Mangilli Valmarana) on the Grand Canal, he suffered financial difficulties.

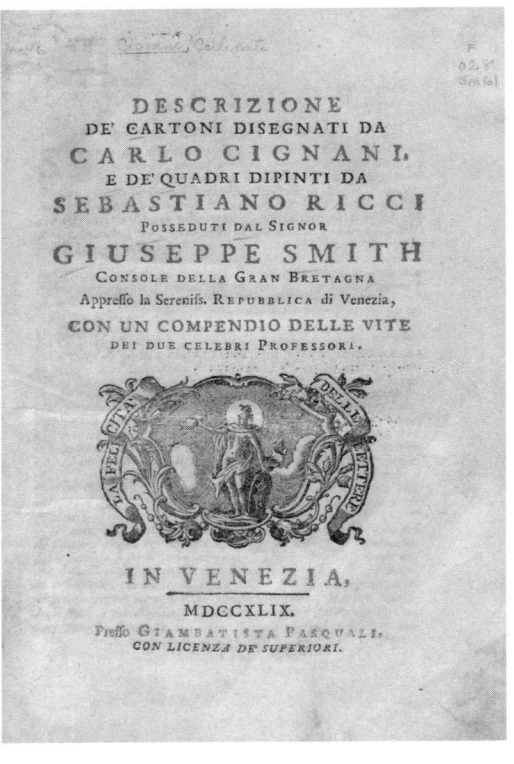

His interests were manifold and included contemporary art, incunabula, gems, Palladian architecture and Italian opera—his first wife was the literal and figurative *prima donna*, Catherine Tofts (c.1685–1756). And he had a mania for collecting, but that was often combined with dealing. In the 1720s he collected Sebastiano Ricci, by 1723 Rosalba Carriera and by 1728 Canaletto. He was considered to be an agent for the latter two: Horace Walpole disparagingly called him "the merchant of Venice". But the collection of paintings—including many *vedute* and *capricci* by Canaletto—and drawings was bought in 1762 by George III through the agency of Lord Bute's brother, James Stuart Mackenzie.

At the same time George III bought Consul Smith's substantial library, including 260 incunabula, as a founding collection for his new King's Library, now part of the British Library. His bookplate has the arms of the Smith Family of Essex and Suffolk (to which he never established a legal title), which also appears on the title page of his

1755 library catalogue, *Bibliotheca Smithiana: seu catalogus librorum D. Josephi Smithii Angli per cognomina authorum dispositus*.

This was published by the Pasquali Press, which Smith had set up with Giovanni Battista Pasquali before 1732. They published editions of Ariosto, Dante, Tasso but also print and drawing albums and rivaled the other main presses of Albrizzi and Zatta. Pasquali ran a bookshop, La Felicità delle Lettere, which became a place to discuss Enlightenment issues and to obtain books banned for import into Venice—its title appears on some of the Pasquali press title pages.

The Frick Art Reference Library has two Pasquali Press titles, on the pictures of Pellegrino Tibaldi, engraved by Bartolomeo Crivellari, acquired in 1926, and the designs of Carlo Cignani and Sebastiano Ricci from Smith's collection, acquired through Sansoni in 1954.

—Stephen Bury

29 The Orléans Collection
1927 (1727)

It would be interesting to tease out a comparison between the Orléans and the Walpole collections. The Regency of Orléans (1715–23) overlapped with Walpole's hegemony (1721–42), and their power attracted gifts of paintings as a means of influence, but Walpole was obviously not a royal, and out of the circle for courtly exchanges. And there was a marked difference in wealth between a prince at the top of a feudal and absolutist system, where nobility and clerics paid no tax, and a parliamentary system and where the propertied paid tax. Consequently, there was a discrepancy in the size (Orléans's five hundred compared to Walpole's four hundred—despite Walpole collecting over a longer period) and quality of the two collections.

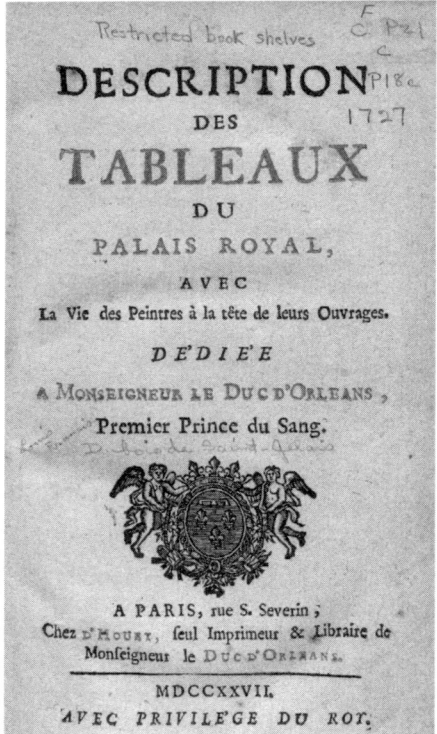

Description des tableaux du Palais royal: avec la vie des peintres à la tête de leurs ouvrages: dédiée a Monseigneur le Duc d'Orleans, premier prince du Sang / Louis François Dubois de Saint-Gelais. Paris: Chez d'Houry, seul imprimeur & libraire de Monseigneur le Duc d'Orleans, 1727. Acquired through Madame Brière, 1927.

That quality derived from Orléans absorption of major pre-existing collections. He had inherited a small collection from his father, Philippe de France, "Monsieur", Louis XIV's brother, and his mother, Henrietta Anne Stuart. Except for diplomatic gifts (such as Philip II's three poesies by Titian) and other 'bribes', much of his collection, began in earnest when he became the Regent for Louis XV, was acquired in Paris from the collections, amongst others, of Richelieu, Mazarin, and the Marquis de Seignelay (Colbert's heir). Queen Christina's collection—itself incorporating some of Rudolf II's collection from the 1648 Swedish assault on Prague, besides her substantial acquisitions in Rome—was a late addition to the Orléans collection in 1721. Negotiations had begun in 1714 with the heirs of Don Livio Odescalchi, head of the Papal army, who had bought it from the Azzolino family. The agents were the financier and collector, Pierre Crozat (1665-1740) and, until his death in 1719, his friend the sculptor Pierre Le Gros the Younger. At this point Christina's collection consisted of 275 paintings, over half of them Italian, with particular highlights the series by Titian and Veronese.

Housed in the west wing of the Palais-Royal, the pictures were arranged according to the mixed-school approach, championed by André Félibien (1619-95) and Roger de Piles (1635-1709), and followed by Crozat himself. The mixture of the religious and the mythological disturbed some viewers—the galleries of the Palais-Royal were open to the public. And even family members disapproved—Orléans son, Louis, slashed Correggio *Leda and the Swan*, and ordered Coypel to cut up the three other works by Correggio, *Danäe*, *Jupiter and Io*, and *Leda*.

Louis Français Dubois de Saint-Gelais (1669-1737), a future Secretary of the Académie royale compiled a guide, *Description des tableaux du Palais royal* in 1727: at this point there were 495 paintings, and, of course, attributions have changed over time. Engravings were also available, published 1729-42 (which also covered the Royal Collection) and from 1786-1808.

—*Stephen Bury*

30 On the Death of a Woman Artist
1928 (1666)

The Bolognese painter and printmaker Elisabetta Sirani (1638–65) died suddenly at the early age of twenty-seven, probably of peritonitis, although her servant, Lucia Tolomelli, was initially accused of poisoning her. She produced over two hundred paintings (with an unusually high proportion signed) in her short lifetime. Count Carlo Cesare Malvasia (1616–93) described in his *Felsina pittrice: vite de'pittori bolognesi* (1678) how rapidly she could actually paint.

She worked not only in portraiture, the then usual genre for a woman artist, but also in religious (e.g. several *Judith and Holofernes*) and history painting (*Portia Wounding Her Thigh*). Stylistically she is close to Guido Reni (1575–1642) but with heightened color and chiaroscuro. Reni had taught her father and Sirani was interred in the same tomb as Reni in the Basilica San Domenico. Horace Walpole in the inventory in *Aedes Walpolianae* (1752) lists *Cupid burning Armour* "by Elisabetta Sirani, Guido's favourite scholar"—although she would have been at most four years old when he was alive.

Sirani also set up in Bologna one of the earliest art schools for women: her pupils included Lucretia Forni, Veronica Franchi and Caterina Pepoli.

Her death on 28 August 1665 provoked a great outpouring of grief in Bologna as she had become a very popular figure, and her studio attracted many visitors to the city. In *Felsina pittrice* Malvasia described her large-scale funeral procession.

The Library's copy of *La poesia muta celebrate della pittura loquace, o vero lodi al pennello d'E. S., pittrice Bolognese*, a series of valedictory poems in Italian and Latin, has a preface by the poet Giovanni Luigi Picinardi (spelled Piccinardi). It was dedicated to Margherita de Medici (1612–79), the former Duchess and Regent of Parma. It was published in 1666 by Evangelista Dozza in Bologna.

Picinardi's funeral oration for Sirani, *Il pennello lacrimato*, was also published separately in the same year by the printer Giacomo Monti. An engraving of Sirani's head appears at the top of the title page and the volume contains a plan for a memorial to her (which Malvasia also illustrates). Both publications are associated with the Accademia degli Apatisti, founded in 1635, and one of the six hundred or so academies in Italy from the late renaissance to 1800, which discussed (and published on) linguistics, literature, music, politics, science and art.

—Stephen Bury

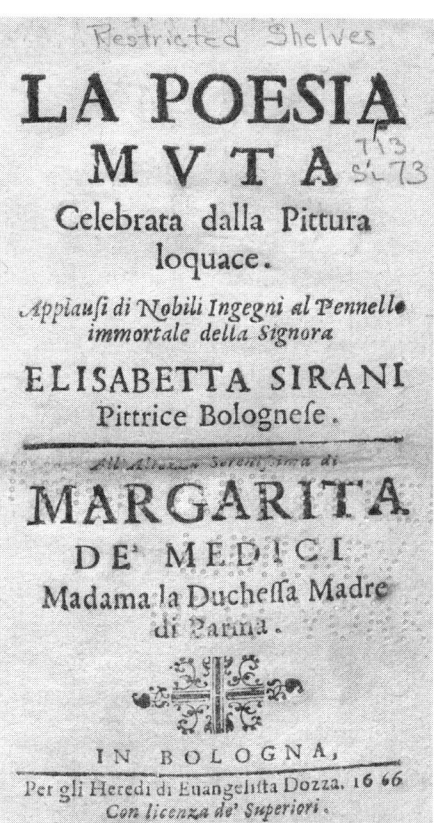

La poesia muta celebrate della pittura loquace, o vero lodi al pennello d'E. S., pittrice Bolognese / Giovanni Luigi Picinardi. Bologna: Dozza, 1666. Acquired through Richard Offner, 1928.

31 Fresco
1928 (1930, 1984)

The Virgin and Child with Saints Francis and John has looked over the researchers at the Thomas Hastings Reading Room (1930–34) and then at the John Russell Pope Reading Room (1935–). Helen Clay Frick probably met Nicholas Lochoff (1872–1948) through Mary and Bernard Berenson. Writing to Ethelwyn Manning, Chief Librarian, she wrote in January 1928: "I gave an order to the great Russian copyist Lokhoff... for Piero Lorenzetti's beautiful fresco of the Virgin and Child, in the Lower Church [of San Francisco in Assisi], for our Reading-Room! I think it will be a tremendously beautiful thing there..." Because of problems with poor light and church services, the fresco was not finished and delivered to New York until May 1930. It was mounted in the Hastings Reading Room that November.

Nicholas Lochoff (1872–1948) *Madonna and Child with Saint Francis and Saint John*. Gift of Helen Clay Frick, 1984.

In a letter dated 5 September 1930, Lochoff insisted that Lorenzetti had not painted a pure fresco, but that gilding and *tempera al secco* were also involved. He also described his own technique: "Being done at first with all the splendor of gold and bright colours, it had to undergo all the phases of being destroyed and made dirty and therefore it now reacts on all the changing of lighting just the same as the original."

Lochoff had hoped that the Soviet government would acquire a series of copies he had made since his move to Italy in 1907. On his death on 7 July 1948, his family made the Soviet government an offer of these works, but this was turned down. In 1959 Helen Clay Frick acquired twenty-three of his copies to be mounted in the Henry Clay Frick Fine Arts Library and Gallery, Pittsburgh.

What Helen Clay Frick did not know was Lochoff's revolutionary political background. He had to flee Tsarist Russia for Switzerland, where he met with Lenin whom he already knew from Pskov, and in 1901 made the drawing *The Social Pyramid*, much copied in print. In 1903 he also attended the Second Congress of the Russian Social Democratic Labor Party (RSDLP), which took place in Brussels, and where the split between Mensheviks and Bolsheviks took place. Lochoff was expelled from Belgium.

—*Stephen Bury*

Exile in New Jersey
1930 (1845)

Joseph Bonaparte (1768-1844) was a French lawyer and diplomat. His younger brother Napoléon created him King of Naples (1806-08) and King of Spain (1808-13). After the defeat of Napoléon at the Battle of Waterloo (1815), Joseph Bonaparte referred to himself as the Count of Survilliers and moved to the United States where he lived until 1839. Bonaparte purchased property near Bordertown, New Jersey, on the Delaware River with its focus being the 125 acres Point Breeze farm previously owned by the American diplomat Stephen Sayre (1736-1818). He replaced the original Georgian house with a mansion and acquired additional land. After fire destroyed his first mansion at Point Breeze, he constructed a larger mansion. Point Breeze, also known as Bonaparte's Park, grew to 1,800 acres. Bonaparte welcomed the public as well as high society and dignitaries to see his gardens, art collection, and library.

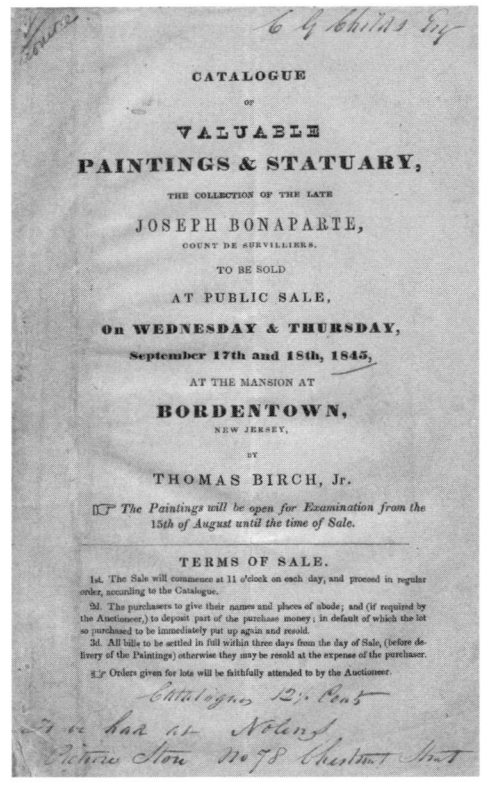

After his death in 1844, the contents of Point Breeze and the estate itself was sold by his grandson Joseph Lucien Bonaparte. The Frick Art Reference Library holds the 17-18 September 1845, catalog for an auction held at Point Breeze of paintings and statuary for his collections. The title page is annotated "C. G. Childs Esq... Catalogues 12½ Cents To be had at Nolen's Picture Store no 78 Chestnut Street". It is likely that the annotation was written by the owner of the catalog with his name being in the top, right corner. "C. G. Childs" probably refers to Cephas Grier Childs, a well-known Philadelphia lithographer who later went into publishing and became the president of the New Creek Coal Company. He also served as a director of the Pennsylvania Academy of Fine Arts. If he did write the annotation, it would predate his death in 1871.

There were three other major auctions associated with Point Breeze held in 1845, 1846, and 1847. Thomas Birch, Jr., oversaw the 1845 sales of works of art and books: the catalog of artworks is arranged by room with listings of available lots. Artist, title, and dimensions are the only information given for most lots with some including a few lines of description in their entries. Artists such as Antonio Canova, Nicolas Poussin, Salomon van Ruysdael, Claude-Josephe Vernet, and Rembrandt appear in the auction. *Two Lions and a Fawn* by Peter Paul Rubens captured the highest price, selling for $2,300 (approximately $80,819 today).

It is unclear how the Frick acquired this particular copy of the catalog, but it could have formed part of the Daniel Fellows Pratt gift of auction catalogs in 1930, mentioned in the Library's Annual Report.

—*Suz Massen*

33 *At the top of my voice*
1930 (2016)

When the retrospective exhibition of Mayakovsky's work opened in Moscow on 1 February 1930, the futurist poet and artist Vladimir Mayakovsky (1893–1930) had hit the lowest point in his short but brilliant career. His play 'The Bathhouse', both in Leningrad and at Meyerhold's theatre in Moscow, had been very poorly received, and he had not been allowed to travel abroad. At the opening, boycotted by the political, literary and artistic establishments, such as the Soviet Writers Federation, Moscow, Mayakovsky read his most recent poem 'At the top of my voice', the equivalent of his own funeral oration, "setting my heel on the throat of my own song".

The catalog of the *20 Years of Mayakovsky's Work* exhibition is strikingly simple: a typed list of 364 items, sorted into groups—books, journal articles, posters, drawings, advertisements, etc., presented as a pamphlet of twenty-seven pages, reproduced by stencil, as the printers, under political pressure, had refused to print the planned catalogue. This thorough and detailed list, compiled by the artist himself, is the most complete documentation of Mayakovsky's work (1909–29), just a few months before his suicide on 14 April 1930.

Despite its widely recognized importance, the original 1930 publication is, currently, in no other United States library. This ephemeral, fraying pamphlet with contemporary annotations in pencil is an invaluable, unique document of the history of Russian avant-garde and of the work of its major artist.

The Library has collected Russian materials since its foundation, including books on Tsarist iconography and symbolist art magazines, but it is now particularly strong in documentation of the Russian and Eastern European modernist movements.

—Stephen Bury

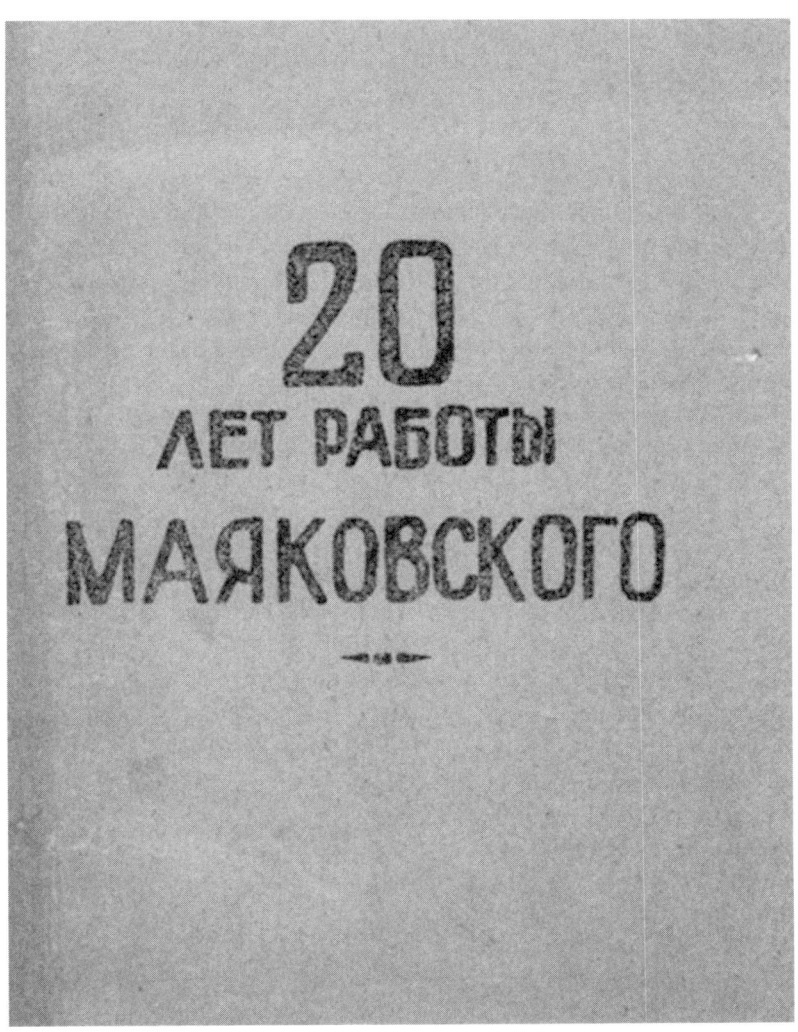

Vladimir Mayakovsky *20 let raboty Maiakovskogo*. [Moscou]: [s.n.], [1930].

34 The White Horse
1930 (1838)

The painter John Constable (1776–1837), who made the case that landscape painting should have the same status as history painting, did not sell well in his own lifetime—and in fact he sold better in France than in England, primarily through the Anglo-French dealer, John Arrowsmith. His work was so influential on French art that he can be seen as a precursor of plein-air painting, the Barbizon School and impressionism.

No.77 in the Foster & Sons catalogue of 15–16 May 1838 is entitled *View of the River Stour, with White Horse in a Barge*, now known as *The White Horse*, which we have at The Frick Collection. It was the first of the six so-called "six-footers" and was exhibited at the Royal Academy in 1819. It was bought by Constable's friend, Archdeacon John Fisher for one hundred guineas. In

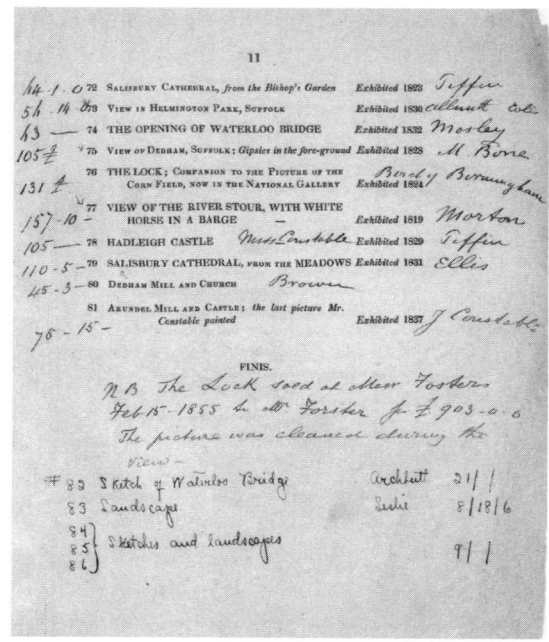

dire financial straits, Fisher sold it back to Constable for the same sum in 1829. And there is an understandable impression that Constable liked to buy his paintings back when he could. In fact, only his death on 31 March 1837, led to the dispersal of many of his works. Foster & Sons at 54 Pall Mall, London, noted in their catalogue: "among the finished pictures will be found the following grand subjects, all of which have been exhibited at the Royal Academy, and afford abundant evidence of the great genius and unwearied application of this distinguished and lamented artist: viz. Salisbury Cathedral, from the Meadows; Hadleigh Castle; View on the River Stour; The Lock; View of Dedham, Suffolk; The Opening of a Waterloo Bridge; Helmington Park; Salisbury Cathedral, from the Bishop's Garden; The Glebe Farm; Flatford Mills; Brighton

Chain Pier; The Lock at Flatford Mills." Perhaps Constable's daughters had inherited his reluctance to let go of his art: a Miss Constable—either Maria Louisa (Minna) or Isabel—bought items 70–71, 78 and perhaps a share in 54. Eventually the last heir Isabel (1823–88) gave much of the family Constables away, primarily to the Victoria & Albert Museum, including ninety-two oil sketches and three easel paintings, in 1888, with other gifts to the British Museum, National Gallery and the Royal Academy.

Morton, probably a dealer, acquired *The White Horse* for £157–10 shillings, as it made its convoluted way to The Frick Collection in 1943. Our copy of the sale catalog is obviously annotated like many of our other sale catalogs, but one needs always to be cautious as to whether the prices and purchasers' names are contemporaneous (to the sale) or retrospective additions (even copies). This copy seems to have both.

—*Stephen Bury*

35 *The Painted Pig*
1930 (2018)

Twentieth century European writers and intellectuals were fascinated by Mexico—perhaps more so than the contiguous Americans. To André Breton, Graham Greene, Aldous Huxley and Malcolm Lowry, the name of René d'Harnoncourt (1901–68), could be added. In 1924 the family property the aristocratic Austrian had inherited was expropriated by the newly-independent Czechoslovakia, and d'Harnoncourt, selling works on paper by Durer and Holbein to raise the fare, immigrated to Mexico. He worked as a freelance designer and began buying Mexican artifacts for American collectors, lecturing, and writing on the subject. In 1933 he moved to the U.S., and joined the staff of the Museum of Modern Art—knowing and having worked for Nelson Rockefeller might have helped. He had a great talent for exhibition design and installation, ranging from folk art to Picasso.

The Painted Pig was written by Elizabeth Cutter Morrow (1873–1955), wife of Dwight Morrow, U.S. Ambassador to Mexico (1927–30). There she developed a great love of Mexican folk art and built up a collection at their retreat Casa Manana (a pun on their family name), in Cuernavaca, incidentally the setting for Lowry's *Under the Volcano*. In 1929 her husband commissioned Diego Rivera to paint the mural *History of Morelos, conquest and revolution* for the Palacio de Cortes there.

The story is about Pedro, an eight-year old Mexican boy, who wants a piggy bank like the yellow one his older sister Pita has—with a blue rose as a tail, if also with an empty stomach. The market toymaker Pancho promises to make another one but forgets, and Pedro tries unsuccessfully to make his own from clay: it looks nothing like a pig, and more like an elephant. Finally, the toymaker, having offered other toys—a donkey, lion, straw horse, blue bird and jumping jacks—at his monthly visits to the market, makes Pedro his own yellow pig. Morrow was inspired by d'Harnoncourt's own collection of Mexican toys—and Pancho's multiple toy offerings to Pedro are no doubt based on this—an interesting source for the history of collecting.

In 1931 Alfred A. Knopf, New York also published *The Hole in the Wall*, a children's book both written and illustrated by d'Harnoncourt.

—Stephen Bury

The Painted pig: a Mexican picture book, text by Elizabeth Morrow, pictures by René d'Harnoncourt. New York: A. A. Knopf, 1930. Dedication from d'Harnoncourt to Miss Lucy M. Clark. Gift of Dr. Stephen J. Bury, 2018.

36 Commissar for Enlightenment
1930 (1932)

In 1930, Anatoly Lunacharsky (1875–1933), the Soviet Union's first People's Commissar for Education, published *Selected Works of Art from Fine Art Museums of the U.S.S.R.*, a catalog showcasing great works of art in the collections of leading Soviet museums, such as the State Hermitage Museum in Leningrad (what is today St. Petersburg) and the Tretyakov Gallery in Moscow. The catalog was acquired by the Frick Art Reference Library on 11 February 1932, an interesting, almost contemporaneous acquisition of a Soviet art book by the Library.

Lunacharsky, a playwright, writer and critic, as well as a Bolshevik revolutionary, was a very influential political and cultural figure in early twentieth-century Russia. He was passionate about preserving Russia's cultural heritage and used his influence and position to do so. Among other things, he was instrumental in saving many historic buildings and works of art from destruction and in defending Russia's tradition of classical ballet from those who felt it was too much a part of a decadent bourgeois past.

In addition to showing important works of art, Lunacharsky's catalog is also interesting historically, as he most likely published it with the goal of using these works of art to improve the Soviet Union's negative image abroad in the aftermath of the Russian Revolutions, Civil War, and other violent upheavals and events of the preceding three decades. He believed that the great works of art in Soviet museums demonstrated the richness of Soviet culture, and the catalog could be an effective way of convincing international readers that the U.S.S.R. also accommodated and valued non-socialist culture.

It is thus also a form of propaganda, published to appeal to foreign audiences in an effort to improve the Soviet Union's international diplomatic and trade relations; foreign trade was of particularly great importance to the floundering Soviet economy of the time. Lunacharsky shrewdly used the appeal of Russian culture and art to market the new Soviet Union to the world. The Soviets called this "cultural diplomacy".

At the same time, paradoxically, the catalog may have had the dual purpose of marketing some of the paintings to the world. The U.S.S.R. was in such dire need of hard currency in the 1920s and early 1930s that the Soviet government was also secretly engaged in selling many of the country's great works of art to foreign buyers; a few of the paintings in the catalog were indeed later sold and twenty-one paintings bought by Andrew W. Mellon (1855–1937) in 1931 formed the foundational collection of the National Gallery of Art, Washington D.C. in 1937.

Valentin Serov *Girl with Peaches* (1887), oil on canvas. Tretyakov Gallery, Moscow. From *Selected works of art from fine art museums of the U.S.S.R*, with notes edited and an introduction written by A. V. Lunacharsky. Moscow: Association of Painters of the Revolution, 1930.

The catalog contains some of the most famous works by the greatest artists of many countries, eras, and schools, including El Greco *Apostles Peter and Paul*, Frans Hals the Elder *Portrait of A Young Man*, Rembrandt *The Prodigal Son*, *Portrait of an Old Man* and *Ahasuerus and Haman at the Feast of Esther*, Velasquez *Portrait of Pope Innocent X* etc. It also included the work of Russian painters, such as Ilya Repin *The Unexpected Return* and Valentin Serov *Girl with Peaches*: the latter shows Vera the eleven-year old daughter of the entrepreneur Savva Mamontov at his Abramtsevo estate. Each of the fifty color plates is accompanied by notes edited by Lunacharsky.

Consequently, the catalog provides an interesting look at some of the holdings of major art museums in contemporary Russia and offers insight into the early Soviet Union and one of its leading political and cultural figures.

—Mikhail Shklyarevsky

37 Read / Don't Read
1931 (1930, 2019)

José Corti or Corticchiato (1895–1984) was a Paris-based writer, editor, journalist, bookseller, and publisher. In 1925, at a challenging time for the finances of the Surrealists, he set up Éditions Surréalistes, which published their works on a subscription basis or, where possible, at the author's expense. He came to the rescue of *La Révolution surréaliste* after Gaston Gallimard withdrew his support, and published what was to be its last issue, no.12 (December 1929) and which contains Breton's 'Second manifesto'. The Librarie José Corti was a bookshop specializing in Surrealist books (and books on cinema) at 6 rue de Clichy, which moved to 11 rue de Médicis in 1935. Two catalogues with prices survive, and the Frick Art Reference Library has copies of both. The first is probably dated 1929/30: a publication in the list bears the date 1930 and the Magritte collage on the cover has the title "Paris in 1930". It consists of a single sheet folded to make six pages. There are fifty-seven titles for sale: these include eleven Breton books and manifestos, including *Nadja* and *Les Champs magnétiques* (although there is no credit for the co-author, Philippe Soupault), but there are additional joint or edited publications; Aragon has twelve and Eluard eleven publications. Char is next with one—so there is no alphabetical order in the Surrealist hierarchy. There are *éditions de luxe, éditions numerotée, éditions originale, tirage limité*—all aimed to maximize the revenue from a publication.

The second catalogue of 1931 is more conventional in format—a fifteen-page sewn pamphlet. However, it has tipped-in photographs of twelve of the authors—now in alphabetical order: Maxime Alexandre, Aragon, Breton, René Char, René Crevel, Salvador Dali, Paul Éluard, Max Ernst, Benjamin Péret, Tristan Tzara and Pierre Unik, with filmmaker Luis Buñuel at the end. Its front cover has a steel-engraved collage by Max Ernst. Reviews of the books are included and whether they are sold out (*épuisé*) is noted.

The back cover has the first published appearance of the author approval chart, "Lisez"/"Ne Lisez Pas": the public is urged to read Swift, Sade, Hegel, Marx, Baudelaire, Jarry, Hamsun, Freud, Apollinaire, Mayakovsky etc., but not Plato, Voltaire, Balzac, Verlaine, Bergson, Proust etc. This sort of exercise was a frequent Surrealist game—*Littérature* no.18 (March 1921) has a weighted table of great authors. But it also owes much to the avant-garde manifesto formula of dichotomy—this is good, this is bad.

—Stephen Bury

LISEZ :	NE LISEZ PAS :	LISEZ :	NE LISEZ PAS :
Heraclite.	Platon.	Lautréamont.	Kraft-Ebbing.
	Virgile.		Taine.
Lulle.	St Thom. d'Aquin.	Rimbaud.	Verlaine.
Flamel.		Nouveau.	Laforgue.
Agrippa.	Rabelais.	Huysmans.	Daudet.
Scève.	Ronsard	Caze.	
	Montaigne.	Jarry.	Gourmont.
Swift.	Molière.	Becque.	Verne.
Berkeley.		Allais.	Courteline.
	La Fontaine.	Th. Flournoy.	Mme de Noailles.
La Mettrie.		Hamsun.	Philippe.
Young.		Freud.	Bergson.
Rousseau.	Voltaire.	Lafargue.	Jaurès.
Diderot.			Durckheim.
Holbach.			Lévy-Brühl.
Kant.	Schiller.	Lénine.	Sorel.
Sade.	Mirabeau.	Synge.	Claudel.
Laclos.		Apollinaire.	Mistral.
Marat.	Bern. de St Pierre.	Roussel.	Péguy.
Babeuf.	Chénier.	Léautaud.	Proust
Fichte.	Mme de Staël.	Cravan.	d'Annunzio.
Hegel.		Picabia.	Rostand.
Lewis.		Reverdy.	Jacob.
Arnim.	Hoffmann.	Vaché.	Valéry.
Maturin.		Maïakovsky.	Barbusse.
Rabbe.	Schopenhauer.	Chirico.	Mauriac.
A. Bertrand.	Vigny.	Savinio.	Toulet.
Nerval.	Lamartine.	Neuberg.	Malraux.
Borel.	Balzac.		Kipling.
Feuerbach.	Renan.		Gandhi.
Marx.			Maurras.
Engels.	Comte.		Duhamel.
	Mérimée.		Benda.
	Fromentin.		Valois.
Baudelaire.	Leconte de Lisle.		Vautel.
Cros.	Banville.		Etc., etc., etc...

IMP. UNION, 13, RUE MÉCHAIN, PARIS

Les Livres Surréalistes ainsi que les Publications Surréalistes sont toujours en vente à la Librairie José Corti… Paris: Corti, [1931].

38 Rosa's Atelier Sale
1934 (1900)

Rosa Bonheur (1822–99) became one of the most celebrated artists of the nineteenth century, a time when women artists were seldom recognized on an international stage. She is known for her realistic portrayal of animals in her paintings, drawings, watercolors, and sculpture. Bonheur came from a family of artists including her father, who trained her, and three siblings. Throughout her career, she exhibited regularly and sold well at the Paris Salon.

Her fame enabled her to live openly with inventor Nathalie Micas (1824–89), and then with her assistant Anna Klumpke (1856–1942). In 1908, Klumpke, whose studio portrait is included in the Library's Stokes photographs collection, published a monograph on Bonheur.

Bonheur was a prolific artist, and at the time of her death in 1899, her studio contained thousands of works, many of them not seen before publicly. The French art dealer Georges Petit (1856–1920) held an auction of the property remaining in her studio. The atelier sale after the passing of an artist was common practice at the time. The auction of paintings took place 30 May to 2 June 1900, in Paris.

The Frick Art Reference Library holds the catalog for the atelier sale of Bonheur's paintings as well as the catalog for the subsequent sale of her watercolors, drawings, and engravings. Madame Clotilde Brière-Misme purchased both catalogs on behalf of the Frick in August 1934 for 250 francs. The paintings catalog contains 892 lot entries with brief descriptions. An extensive introduction by Léon Roger-Milès (1859–1928) praises the artist and her work. Taille-douce or copper-plate engravings illustrate several of the lots, which include lions, tigers, horses, goats, oxen, stags, dogs and other animals. The text is in French and English, reflecting the British—and American—interest in Bonheur's work: Henry Clay Frick acquired an engraving of *The Horsefair* (1852–55) from Knoedler in 1895.

The copy held by the Library includes price annotations.

—*Suz Massen*

CATALOGUE

DES

TABLEAUX

PAR

Rosa Bonheur

DONT LA VENTE AURA LIEU A PARIS

par suite de son décès

GALERIE GEORGES PETIT

8 — RUE DE SÈZE — 8

Les Mercredi 30, Jeudi 31 Mai, Vendredi 1ᵉʳ et Samedi 2 Juin 1900

A DEUX HEURES PRÉCISES

COMMISSAIRE-PRISEUR

Mᵉ PAUL CHEVALLIER, 10, rue Grange-Batelière, 10

EXPERTS

M. GEORGES PETIT | MM. TEDESCO FRÈRES
12, rue Godot-de-Mauroi, 12 | 33, avenue de l'Opéra, 33

EXPOSITIONS

PARTICULIÈRE : Le Lundi 28 Mai 1900, de une heure à cinq heures et demie.
PUBLIQUE : Le Mardi 29 Mai 1900, de dix heures à cinq heures et demie.

39 Under Construction
1934 (2010)

In 2010 in honor of the seventy-fifth anniversary of the 1935 opening of The Frick Collection and Frick Art Reference Library, the Museum's Director, Dr. Anne Poulet, and the Chief Curator, Dr. Colin Bailey, generously funded the purchase of this original drawing by the artist Vernon Howe Bailey (1874–1953) of the construction of the new Frick Art Reference Library in 1934. While the Frick archives hold countless primary, original documents, there are far fewer original works of art in the archival holdings and the Library is very grateful to have been given this lovely rendering of a truly exciting moment in its history.

The Library, designed by John Russell Pope to harmonize with his new additions to The Frick Collection, replaced a smaller library completed in 1924. Helen Clay Frick, the daughter of Henry Clay Frick and founder of the library, underwrote the costs associated with the construction. While we have photographs of all phases of the library's construction, this drawing is unique. Bailey, a talented and prolific painter, illustrator and print maker captured the excitement of a notable expansion in the life of the library.

It is not known how Vernon Howe Bailey determined to draw the Frick Art Reference Library under construction but his choice of subject fit well into his assignment with the *New York Sun* to document the architecture and street scenes in New York City as part of his 'Intimate Sketches of New York' column published in the 1930s. While the Frick's drawing was not included, Bailey published a selection of the New York sketches in the 1935 volume entitled *Magical City: Intimate Sketches of New York*. As Jeff Reuben noted in a 2018 article in *Dark Ink Magazine*, "Although little remembered today, Bailey's particular gift was in capturing both the details of stationary subjects and energy of urban landscapes with his pencil and pen strokes".

—*Sally Brazil*

Vernon Howe Bailey *The Addition to the Frick Museum under Construction*, 1934.

40 Construction 1933–35
1934 (1933, 2018)

The Cook collection of photographs documents architect John Russell Pope's conversion of the Frick family's New York residence into The Frick Collection, and the simultaneous construction of a new Frick Art Reference Library building during the years 1933–35. These photographs were taken at the request of Helen Clay Frick by the former Frick family footman, Alfred W. Cook (1902–58), who was then employed by the Frick Collection for miscellaneous duties.

The approximately 450 black and white photographs capture the construction process from demolition and foundation work to steel framing, stonework, and finished details. Alfred Cook carefully labeled each image, and often inscribed the date and his name on the negatives, allowing for identification and a clear chronological visual record of the project.

Before construction, Cook documented exterior and interior architectural details in the Frick residence, including stone carvings, woodwork, marble, fireplace mantels, and lighting fixtures that would be removed during construction. Rooms and outside areas that were to be demolished or completely altered were also captured.

Documenting the new Library construction began with the 26 June 1933 demolition of buildings on the site of 10–12 East 71st Street, both of which had been purchased by The Frick Collection for the site of the new library just a few months earlier. Images progress to the laying of the foundations and follow the Library's construction thirteen floors up to the Penthouse level, shown through both exterior and interior views. The photograph above shows the steel framing to the level of the Third Floor Reading Room on November 4, 1933. Pictured next to the construction site is the original Library building located at 6 East 71st Street.

Photographs of the construction of The Frick Collection, carried out at the same time, include the transformation of the exterior courtyard into the interior Garden Court; the former site of the original Library building into the East Gallery, Oval Room and Music Room; and the *porte-cochère*, or covered driveway, into the new Frick Collection Entrance Hall.

A recent graduate of the New York Institute of Photography, Alfred Cook worked under Library photographers Ira W. Martin and Thurman Rotan, observing and assisting with their work when possible. Cook went on to a successful career as an architectural photographer after he left The Frick Collection in 1936. Some of his work can be seen in *Cities in the Sand Leptis Magna and Sabratha in Roman Africa*, text by Kenneth D. Matthews, Jr., photographs by Alfred W. Cook, Philadelphia: Pennsylvania University Press (London: Oxford University Press), 1957.

While the historic and documentary aspect of these photographs is primary, many of the images also exhibit an eerie beauty, as shown in the 2018 publication *ASMR4, vol.5: Alfred Cook: Archival Photographs from The Frick Collection/Frick Art Reference Library*. The booklet was edited by Adam Putnam, a former Library staff member who worked on the conservation of the photographs in the 1990s, and photographers Katie Murray, Victoria Sambunaris, and Dan Torop.

The Cook series of photographs is part of a larger collection of images in the Archives that document all major construction projects for The Frick Collection and Frick Art Reference Library from 1913 to the present. Considered one of the Archives' most important photographic resources, these images are of special value during Frick construction projects, as each new architectural project team looks to the past for guidance. The Alfred W. Cook construction photographs have been digitized and can be viewed and downloaded on *digitalcollections.frick.org*.

—Susan Chore

41 Frick Art Reference Library Façade
1934 (1973)

The Frick Art Reference Library, designed by architect John Russell Pope (1873–1937) and built by general contractors Marc Eidlitz & Son, Inc. from 1932 to 1935, was part of a larger construction project to convert the Frick family's New York residence into a museum. The Library, which adjoins The Frick Collection to the east, was designed to blend harmoniously with the architecture of the new museum addition and the original 1913 Frick residence. John Russell Pope, Organizing Director Frederick Mortimer Clapp, and Library founder and director Helen Clay Frick were the key figures in shaping the building's design.

The Library is located on a lot 50 feet wide by 150 feet deep, the former site of townhouses owned by James B. Clemens (no.10) and Mrs. C. C. Auchincloss (no.12). These buildings were purchased and demolished by The Frick Collection in 1933 in order to provide a site for the new Library building.

Constructed of Indiana limestone in the French Renaissance style, the building's exterior features a grand arched entrance, decorative stonework panels and friezes, and arched niches. The thirteen-story building houses six main floors, four mezzanine floors, a basement, a sub-basement, and a penthouse floor. The new building, which quadrupled the space of the original Library building at 6 East 71st Street, was constructed at a cost of $850,000.

The central entryway arch, framed by two Ionic columns on either side, features a keystone depicting a human head. Decorative carvings line the underside of the arch. Stairs lead to the bronze day doors, above which is a decorative panel of leaves and ribbons, with a center medallion containing the "HCF" monogram. Above the entryway hangs a large lantern purchased from E. F. Caldwell & Company.

A most unusual feature of the Library's exterior is the unfinished lunette above the doorway. Three attempts were made at the lunette's design, initially based on a work by Pontormo. Because the source drawing required modification to fit in the unusual half-moon shape with a circular bull's eye, the result, according to Frederick Mortimer Clapp, was "a rather confused and wormy jumble". Once the Pontormo designs were abandoned, Helen Clay Frick made arrangements with sculptor Malvina Hoffman to redesign and carve the lunette, but the project was never completed, leaving the partially-modeled original stonework design in place.

To either side of the entranceway are arched niches containing empty pedestals. While Mr. Clapp lobbied against leaving the niches bare, Helen Clay Frick preferred to leave them "plain" and no statuary was ever considered for the niches. Two carved stonework panels, depicting urns and foliage, similar to panels on The Frick Collection's exterior, reside on either side of the top of the arch.

Just above the arch is the "Frick Art Reference Library" frieze inscription. Designed by Porter Garnett (1871-1951), the length of the inscription is 31 feet 6 inches. Mr. Garnett, head of the Laboratory Press at the Carnegie Institute of Technology in Pittsburgh, also designed the "HCF" monogram above the Library's bronze doors and worked on the design of The Frick Collection (folio) catalogue from 1928-32.

Above the inscription, three windows with triangular pediments fronted by stone balusters mark the location of the Library's third floor Reading Room. The top of the building is surrounded by a projecting cornice and a decorative frieze. Above the cornice, a stepped-back Penthouse floor includes an outdoor terrace that wraps around the north and east sides of the building.

In March 1973, both the exteriors of the Frick Art Reference Library and The Frick Collection were designated as landmarks by the New York City Landmarks Preservation Commission.

—*Susan Chore*

42 | A Model Reading Room*
1934

From the label: "¾ inch scale model / NE Corner of / The Principal Reading Room / The Frick / Art Reference Library".

Visitors to the main Reading Room of the Frick Art Reference Library are usually impressed by the large doors covered in red leather, the Lochoff fresco (a remnant of the former Library), the Formosa marble door surrounds, the Italian walnut paneling, or Helen Clay Frick's two dogs, Bob and Pat, staring from the East Wall frieze. But there are other features to investigate.

What to some may seem to be mundane floor tiles are the work of the Herman Carl Mueller (1854–1941) and Karl Langenbeck's Mueller Mosaic Co., founded in 1908 and based in Trenton, N.J., a pottery center with good railway and canal communications. The company was known for its Arts & Crafts designs.

The light fittings are by Caldwell & Co., who specialized in electrical rather than gas lamps—the founder Edward F. Caldwell (1851–1914) was a friend of and collaborator with Stanford White (1853–1906). Many public and private buildings in New York have Caldwell & Co.

light fittings—New York Public Library and the University Club are just two examples. Their business was so extensive that in 1901 they constructed a foundry at 36–40 West 15th Street.

Decorative details were provided by Angelo Magnanti (1879–1969), who has an artist's file in the Frick Photoarchive. A muralist, illustrator and decorator, Magnanti is now perhaps best remembered for his mural series in what was the Dollar Savings Bank in the Bronx. In the Frick Reading Room, besides Bob and Pat, he made an Italianate frieze that runs around the whole room, and added decoration to the supports/ties of the visible oak rafters.

The design of the Reading Room works well and the model shows how much preparation and testing took place before implementation, and the extensive discussions between Ethelwyn Manning, Helen Clay Frick, Frederick Mortimer Clapp, architect John Russell Pope and general contractor Marc Eidlitz & Son, Inc.

One fortunate omission was the open fire place on the East side of the Reading Room, which Helen Clay Frick had initially wanted, in which case Bob and Pat would have been elevated fire-dogs.

—*Stephen Bury*

The Italian Room
43
1934 (1924, 1999, 2021)

The first autonomous Frick Art Reference Library was housed in a single-story Indiana limestone structure designed by Thomas Hastings at 6 East 71st Street. Helen Clay Frick's original Library opened to the public in 1924, however plans for a larger and more permanent space began as early as 1922. Like her father, Helen oversaw nearly every aspect and detail to plan and construct the new building that would be home to her ever-growing collection of books and photographs for the scholars that visited.

Documented in the Library's archives, Helen's 1924 office was inspired by her love of Italian art that arose from her frequent visits overseas, which included trips to the Fondazione Horne and F. Quentin glass factory, Florence. Her office would embody the spirit and taste of a sixteenth-century Florentine palazzo and as requested by Helen, original architecture elements were to be used as much as possible. In a letter from the Durlacher Brothers of London, they agreed to furnish her office with a fifteenth-century Venetian mantelpiece with original hood, two doors composed of sixteenth-century linen-fold carved panels, and sixteenth-century carved wood panels that would make up a door  for a bathroom that was later converted into a closet. Other elements that add to this striking period room are hand-carved exposed ceiling beams, unglazed red tiles, large glass windows with wooden shutters and metal strapwork along said shutters.

In 1934, two adjoining houses, 8 and 10 East 70th Street, were purchased, demolished, and renovated into the Library Helen had been planning for over the last several years. Constructed by John Russell Pope, the new home for Helen's large collection opened to the public on 14 January 1935. Helen's Italian Room had been dismantled and moved to the sixth floor of the new building. With a new view of Central Park across Fifth Avenue, her 1924 office was rotated so that the large glass windows with heavy wooden shutters would face the spectacular sight. What was not retained was the original floor of plain, unglazed red tiles from Henry Mercer's Moravian Pottery and Tile Works, Doylestown, Pennsylvania, which were replaced by tiles from the Mueller Mosaic Co.: some tiles incorporate the prints of dog paws.

Helen used her Italian-inspired office for over fifty years until 1982 when she retired. It was largely untouched by the 1999 renovation of the sixth floor, although the bathroom door now opens onto a closet, and it will be little affected by the 2021 reconstruction, except that the fireplace mantle hood has undergone conservation for the first time by paintings conservator Soraya Alcala.

—*Payton Goad*

The Telautograph
1934

The Frick family loved new technologies. Not only was Henry Clay Frick's fortune indebted to the Bessemer steel process, but also the family embraced motorcars, cameras, movie cameras, travel by steamer and railway. It is perhaps no surprise that when it came to the building of a purpose-built reference library in 1934–35, that Helen Clay Frick decided to install a Telautograph system in conjunction with dumbwaiters, to request and move books and photographs. And it might have resonated with someone who had used the 1 East 70 Street mansion domestic servant call system.

The Telautograph was invented by the electrical engineer Elisha Gray (1835–1901). Gray had studied at Oberlin College, Ohio, where he also taught electricity despite having never graduated. He was a prolific inventor in the area of telegraph developments, and could reasonably claim that he invented the telephone in 1876, ahead of Bell, and anticipated the music synthesizer and close-circuit television. It was in 1887 that he invented the Telautograph, which enabled the transmission of handwriting remotely: "the act of writing the message at the sending station operates to produce it at the receiving station". He registered six patents in the U.S. for this invention 1888–93.

Demonstrated at the 1893 World Columbian Exposition, Chicago, it was used by banks for signing documents, steel plants, department stores and by train stations, such as Grand Central Station. In the 1990s Gray's Telautograph Company, in 1931 based at 16 West 61st Street, New York, was acquired by Xerox.

At the Library there were Telautographs on each operative floor. It is thought that the writing or "transmitting" station was on the Third Floor, where the Reading Room was, so that items could be located first in the card catalog before retrieval. The other machines were "receiving stations", so that the items could be located and sent to the Third Floor through the adjacent dumbwaiter. Staff who worked at the Library whilst the Telautograph and dumbwaiter system was in operation recall that the dumbwaiter system had a tendency to damage some of the books and photographs, and that the Telautograph was used to relay messages to staff from the one telephone line. A second theory is that the Telautograph was used to transfer "archival" data (made much of in the 1931 Telautograph manual) e.g. from Photoarchive researchers to the cataloguers or catalogue typists. This is unlikely given the location of the Telautographs next to the dumbwaiters.

The Telautograph at the Frick Art Reference Library is a cautionary tale on the benefits and disadvantages of technology.

—*Stephen Bury*

Pat and Bob
1934

Historically, dogs have always been a fixture in Frick family life. Favoring terriers and spaniels, the family owned a succession of animals whose images and antics are well documented within the Frick Family Papers. These include Brownie, a fox terrier from the 1890s who begged at the table and was professionally photographed on at least two occasions, and Fudgie (also called Fido), a small spaniel from the 1910s who spent time on the beach with the family and was permitted both on the velvet upholstery and in the Frick automobiles. This modern, indulgent approach to pet ownership has its origins in the Victorian era, when animals were welcomed into the home and treated as members of the family.

Helen Clay Frick continued this tradition as an adult, often keeping at least one or two dogs at her farm in Bedford, N.Y. Among her two favorites were Bob and Pat, variously referred to by a host of nicknames, or collectively known as "The Boys". Of the two, Pat, an Irish terrier, was slightly older than his canine compatriot. He joined the Frick household in June 1922, while Bob, a field spaniel, arrived in 1929. Both dogs lived to around the age of thirteen. There is abundant documentary evidence of Miss Frick's affection for these two animals. She photographed them at play and at rest around the farm, prepared specially prescribed meals, and ordered custom coats to keep them cozy. Near the end of his life, she had a special carriage built so that Pat could still enjoy walks around the farm. Bob later made use of the same carriage. The dogs are frequently mentioned in Miss Frick's diaries. A poignant entry dated 29 May 1941, the day of Bob's death, reads as follows: "My little darling is released from pain at 8 AM. I come home to a lonely house and nothing can ever be the same again."

So beloved were "The Boys" that Miss Frick elected to immortalize the dogs within the frieze on the east wall of the Frick Art Reference Library Reading Room, designed by John Russell Pope and completed in 1935. Painted by New York muralist, mosaicist, and illustrator Angelo Magnanti, the dogs are depicted in profile within two roundels high on the wall above the reference desk amid a border of scrolling acanthus leaves. The roundels flank an inscription reading *Nessuna cosa si vede sanza luce* (nothing is seen without light), which is taken from Renaissance sculptor Lorenzo Ghiberti's *Commentaries* from the late 1440s. Bob appears on the left with the word *lealtà* (loyalty

or faithfulness in Italian) inscribed above his portrait. Pat faces him on the right with *fedeltà* (fidelity or devotion in Italian) inscribed above his image. The model for the portrait of Pat is a photograph by J. O. Henschel, which is still in the Archives. Although both dogs were photographed by Henschel, most likely in the early 1930s, a photographic source for Bob's portrait has not been found. The dogs add a whimsical touch to the Reading Room, and are enjoyed by both staff and visitors alike.

—*Julie Ludwig*

46 *Dating Helen*
1935–45

By the time Helen Clay Frick had reached her early twenties, she had found outlets for her two principal interests: art and philanthropy. She established the Iron Rail Vacation Home in Wenham, Mass., in 1909, and that same year, she began creating a handwritten catalog of her father's art collection. With the onset of World War I in 1914, she added war relief to her activities, assisting the Red Cross both at home and later in France.

The death of her father in 1919 made her financially independent, and she broadened the scope of her philanthropic efforts to support the work of art historians. She established the Frick Art Reference Library in New York, and also began collaborating with the University of Pittsburgh to establish an art history department there. Per her father's will, she served as a founding trustee to The Frick Collection, and for the first time in her life, she established her own residence: a sprawling property in Bedford, N.Y., christened Westmoreland Farm. She also traveled extensively during the 1920s, spending time abroad every year of that decade with the exception of 1922, 1926, and 1929. By 1935, she had shepherded the Frick Art Reference Library into a much expanded building, and her father's principal legacy, The Frick Collection, had opened to the public. She continued to serve on the board of The Frick Collection until 1961, leaving a visible stamp on that institution through her work on the Art Acquisitions Committee.

As a professional woman, Helen Clay Frick sat for a photographer at least four times from the 1930s to the 1960s, though little is known about these images. The dates of the sittings are unclear, as are the circumstances that occasioned them. These four sets of portraits indicate a desire to formally capture her image, but to what end? As far as is known, they were not used as publicity photographs. They may have been distributed among family and friends, but that theory is unproven. What is well-known is that Helen Clay Frick did not like having her photograph taken, a fact that makes these images all the more perplexing.

In the portrait seen here, Helen Clay Frick is wearing a simple black dress and pearls, offering few sartorial clues to help date the image. Portraits of Miss Frick also tend to be retouched, especially as she aged, which makes dating them based on her appearance particularly difficult. The photographer is really our only clue to dating this image. Originally from England, The Misses Selby established a studio in New York just before the turn of the century, specializing in the

Portrait of Helen Clay Frick by The Misses Selby, *circa* late-1930s or early 1940s.

photography of women and children. One of the sisters, Emily, died around 1909, but her sister Lillian continued operating the studio for an uncertain amount of time. The studio was relocated several times, progressively moving uptown. At the time of this photograph, the Misses Selby were located at 64 East 55th Street, allowing us to date the image to approximately between 1935 and 1945.

    Although Helen Clay Frick disapproved of many images of herself (in some cases going so far as to ask that they be destroyed or even destroying them herself), this portrait apparently passed muster. It was later used as the model for a 1973 watercolor by Elizabeth Shoumatoff, now in the collection at The Frick Pittsburgh.

—*Julie Ludwig*

47 The Studios of Paris
1940

In 1940 the American artist and Arctic explorer, Frank Wilbert Stokes (1858–1955) gave the Library seventy-four albumen prints documenting artists in their Paris studios at the end of the nineteenth century. At the time, Paris was an attractive destination for American artists: art education there was (or at least was thought to be) more advanced than in the United States, and a burgeoning art market in the French capital made the city an ideal place to sell contemporary art. There was also an infrastructure of studios, art suppliers, and photographers, and the city was an inexpensive place to live.

Stokes is best known for his paintings of polar scenes inspired by expeditions he made to the Artic and Antarctic between 1886 and 1925. Born in Nashville in 1858, he studied under Thomas Eakins at the Pennsylvania Academy of the Fine Arts. In 1881 he enrolled in the École des Beaux-Arts in Paris under Jean-Léon Gérôme, who, Stokes noted on his copy of the photograph of Gérôme, was "a splendid draughtsman

Julius C. Rolshoven (1858–1930) in his Paris studio, 235 rue du Faubourg Saint-Honoré, c.1887–92. Gift of Frank W. Stokes, 1940.

and master. A noble and great character who would have been a great statesman if he had wished…" After participating as staff artist for the American explorer Robert Peary's expedition to Greenland in 1886, Stokes returned to Paris, where he continued to work until 1892. He exhibited two paintings, *Les Orphelines* and *Un bon sermon* at the Exposition Universelle in 1889. It is likely that the Frick's photographs date from this period, before Stokes joined the Peary Relief Expedition to Greenland in 1892.

There are twenty-one American artists documented in Stokes's collection, a third of whom are women—including Eliza Greatorex and her two artist daughters. Other photographs capture the Parisian *maîtres* who tutored many of them. They are identified by series number and name inscribed on the prints themselves, by Stokes's notes, or by the contents of their studios. Four are currently unidentified.

Studio visits were considered quite fashionable, prompted by a romantic interest in the creative process and an obsession with bohemian life. The photographs probably were created in response to a demand for souvenirs for those who had visited studios or as surrogates for those who were interested in the artists exhibiting at the Salons or the Exposition Universelle of 1889. At least two and possibly twenty-two others can be identified as the work of Édouard Fiorillo, who, beginning in 1881, was also involved in the documentation of state purchases from the Salons, particularly sculpture.

Stokes annotated some of the photographs retrospectively: "Rolshoven talented and returned to U.S. where he rather deliquesced into a semi-diligent attitude and died unappreciated." Julius C. Rolshoven's death in 1930 thus provides the earliest date for the annotation.

—*Stephen Bury*

48 A Gilded Age Home & Collection
1941 (1883–84, 1905)

William H. Vanderbilt (1821–1885) was the son of Cornelius Vanderbilt the steamboat and railroad magnate. William was the President of the New York Central and Hudson Railroad, and became President of the Lake Shore and Michigan Southern Railway, Canada Southern Railway, and Michigan Central Railroad after the death of Cornelius in 1877. At that time, he became the richest American with a worth of $232 million dollars (more than $6.6 billion dollars today). William's fortune doubled before his own death in 1885. William built a residence that was comprised of twin mansions connected by an atrium on Fifth Avenue between 51st Street and 52nd Street in New York City for his family. They were designed by John Butler Snook and Charles B. Atwood with interiors by the Herter Brothers, and completed in 1882. They were also connected to a third mansion located on 52nd Street at Fifth Avenue. Together they were known as the Triple Palace. Soon afterwards, a lavish privately printed set of volumes detailing the Fifth Avenue residence and its contents was published. Henry Clay Frick and

Mr. Vanderbilt's House and Collection, Edward Strahan. Boston: George Barrie, 1883–84. Gift of Helen Clay Frick, 1941.

his family rented one of the mansions from the Vanderbilt family, 640 Fifth Avenue, when he first arrived in New York City in 1905. He resided there until the completion of his residence on Fifth Avenue between 70th Street and 71st Street in 1912. The Vanderbilt mansion on the

Picture Gallery, Vanderbilt Residence, 640 Fifth Avenue, New York c.1884. Photograph by George Barrie.

southwest corner of 52nd Street was demolished in 1927. The one on the northwest corner of 51st Street was razed in 1947. The volumes documenting them are all that remain of these symbols of the Gilded Age past.

The Frick Art Reference Library holds a copy of the limited, numbered edition (no.279 out of 500), on Japan paper, oversized, four-volume catalog published by George Barrie of the Vanderbilt house and collection. The leather-bound volumes with gold leave edges take the reader on a journey from examining the exterior of the mansions to the drawing rooms to the private apartments of the family. Several different types of illustrations accompany the descriptive text written by Edward Strahan, the pseudonym for the art critic Earl Shinn (1838–86). Colored lithographs, photogravures, and photochrome prints bring the exteriors and interiors of the residence to life. Volume 1 and volume 2 of the set examines the interior spaces with mention of important works of decorative arts highlighted. There is even a section on the offices and stables, including a portrait of the horse Maud. Volume 3 and volume 4 focus on the works of art in the gallery of paintings in the mansions. Artists such as Giovanni Bodini, Jean-Baptiste-Camille Corot, Rosa Bonheur, Jean-Léon Gérôme, Jean-François Millet, and Joseph Mallord William Turner are in the collection. William had a taste for academic painting that can be seen throughout the collection documented in the catalog. Images of the paintings and decorative arts *in situ* show how the family lived with the works on a daily basis.

—*Suz Massen*

49 *Le Figurine*
1942 (1675–83)

The popularity of Salvatore Rosa (1615–73), poet, playwright, satirist, actor as well as printmaker and artist, has varied widely over time. In the eighteenth century no aspiring collector of the paintings of the Italian School could be without one. Horace Walpole in the introduction to *Aedes Walpolianae* (1752) waxed lyrical: "the greatest genius Naples ever produc'd resided generally at Rome; a Genius equal to any that City itself ever bore. This was the great Salvator Rosa. His Thought, his Expression, his Landscapes, his knowledge of the force of Shade, and his masterly management of Horror and Distress, have plac'd him in the first Class of Painters." In the Houghton sale, Rosa's *The Prodigal Son* sold for an astonishing £700. And in the 1775 Paris sale of drawings belonging to Pierre Jean Mariette (1694–1774) a Rosa drawing of *The Prodigal Son* attained the highest price. Towards the end of the

eighteenth century romantics such as Henry Fuseli (1741–1825) were captivated by Rosa's attitude to life and art—the fact that Rosa wanted to choose his own subjects, as well as his taste for the irrational. Despite championing Turner in *Modern Painters*, (whose landscapes were plainly influenced by Rosa), critic John Ruskin (1819–1900) assailed Rosa in the very same book: *Monks Fishing*, one of two Rosa paintings bequeathed to the Dulwich Picture Gallery by Sir Francis Bourgeois in 1811, was described as full of "unmitigated falsehoods". Although some nineteenth-century American landscape artists, such as Thomas Cole and Thomas Moran, were also influenced by Rosa, his value at auction rapidly diminished and works were consigned to the storerooms of museums. Only in the 1960s did interest revive.

The Library's *Studio dall'opere dell'eccellente pittore Salvatore Rosa* is a bibliographical nightmare: it is without a place of publication, publisher or printer, and date. There is no other recorded copy in WorldCat, though other copies might have been broken up, and sheets may survive in print cabinets. It consists of fifty-three engraved plates, after Rosa's Figurine or Diverse Figure series of etchings of mainly soldiers in various poses, *c.*1656–58.

The date is perhaps the easiest to determine. The book is dedicated to Monsignor Carlo Francesco Airoldi, who seems to have been born in Milan in 1637, and had an interest in art. He died on 5 April 1683 whilst Papal Nuncio to the Venetian Republic (since 29 November 1675), which gives us a publication range of November 1675 to April 1683 as the dedication in the publication refers to this title, and a possible/likely place of publication, Milan, given the Milanese connections of both Airoldi and the Santagostino families.

The engraver cannot be the Milanese painter Giacomo Antonio Santagostino (1588–1648) as Rosa executed his etchings, on which these are based, in the 1650s. It is likely to be the grandson, Giacomo Antonio Jr., an engraver, son of the painter Agostino Santagostino (1635–1706). He died at the age of twenty-four.

This book is one of the earliest copies of Rosa's Figurine series but the images are sometimes rather crudely executed and often reversed.

—*Stephen Bury*

50 Third Reich Sculpture
1942 (2017)

"Socialist Realism" dominated visual art in both the Soviet Union and the Third Reich. In Germany, Adolf Hitler promoted sculptors working in this vein and whom he personally liked, such as Arno Breker (1900–91) and Josef Thorak (1889–1952), both of whom in became in 1932 "official artists", and were provided with large studios and many assistants. Likewise the Olympic Games in 1936 generated state commissions for them and promulgated their iconography of strong, athletic figures which was meant to proclaim the Nazi racial ideal. In 1937, while the *Entartete Kunst* exhibition showed what the Nazis disliked in art and called degenerate, the *Grosse Deutsche Kunstaustellung* celebrated the Nazi program for art.

Kurt Tank's *Deutsche Plastik unserer Zeit* or 'German sculpture of our time' was published in 1942—a pivotal year in Nazi Germany's fortunes: whilst jet engines, rockets and nuclear fusion were in an advanced state, the first cracks in the Nazi edifice were beginning to show, with defeats of the 'invincible' German armies at El Alamein and Stalingrad. This would be the last time that such an expensive book, with Zeiss Jena lenses for its stereoscope viewer, would be produced.

It was published by Raumbild-Verlag Otto Schönstein, K.G. where *Raumbild* means stereoscopic or 3-D picture, manipulating left and right eye views of the same scene to make a three-dimensional image. Otto Wilhelm Schönstein (1891–1958), began as a textile merchant with an interest in stereoscopic photography, but made it his livelihood and registered Raumbild as a company in 1935 and started to focus on Germanic subjects. In effect, Raumbild became part of the Nazi party's propaganda wing, culminating in *Die Olympischen Spiele* for the 1936 Berlin Olympics. The success of this led Hitler's official photographer Heinrich Hoffmann (1885–1957) to acquire half the shares in the company, and become one of its main photographers. Hoffman had been put in charge by Hitler of the German Art exhibitions after 1937, was one of the commissioners for the confiscation of degenerate art, and after the war was accused of involvement in looting art from Jewish families.

Hoffmann was the photographer for Schönstein's 1937 *Tag der Deutschen Kunst* ('Day of German Art') which consisted of 100 stereoscopic cards. *Deutsche Plastik unserer Zeit* (1942) with 135 stereoscopic photographs continued this partnership with Hoffmann providing much, but not all, of the photography. It includes busts of Hitler,

Deutsche Plastik unserer Zeit / von Kurt Lothar Tank; herausgegeben von Ministerialrat Wilfrid Bade, Leiter der Abteilung ZP. Der Presseabteilung der Reichsregierung; Geleitwort von Reichsminister Albert Speer... München: Raumbild-Verlag Otto Schönstein K. G., [1942]. Purchased in honor of Ambassador Walter J. P. Curley, 2017.

Speer, Richard Wagner etc.; monumental figures for Göring's Luftwaffe Ministerium, the Reichschancellery, Berlin Olympic Stadium etc. But many of the photographs were taken at the House of German Art. Arno Breker, Georg Kolbe, Josef Thorak and Adolph Wamper are also shown working in their studios.

—Stephen Bury

51 Monuments Men
1943 (1944)

During the Second World War, the Frick Art Reference Library was instrumental in the development of resources to protect and preserve cultural and artistic heritage in active war zones throughout Europe. Through the direction of its founder, Helen Clay Frick, the Library became a headquarters for the American Council of Learned Societies' Committee on the Protection of Cultural Treasures in War Areas, and assisted its members in the creation of maps to locate cultural institutions, monuments, and other sites of artistic achievement for Allied military forces to avoid during air strikes. Bill Burke, Jane Mull, and Gladys Hamlin (pictured below), are three Committee members that engaged in this work. Although there is no photographer associated with the object, the verso includes a stamped credit line for the Commission for the Protection and Salvage of Artistic and Historical Monuments in War Areas, informally known as the "Second Roberts Commission". This indicates that the photograph may have been taken

Photograph of Bill Burke, Jane Mull, members of the Committee on the Protection of Cultural Treasures in War Areas of the American Council of Learned Societies (ACLS), with Gladys Hamlin, draftswoman, working on a map of Paris at the Frick Art Reference Library.

by the Office of War Information, a government agency that operated from June 1942 until September 1945 and was charged with bringing information on the war to civilian communities through different media.

Weeks after the attack on Pearl Harbor in 1941, Francis Henry Taylor, director of the Metropolitan Museum of Art, called a meeting of cultural institutions throughout the United States to convene at the New York Public Library with the goal to establish a local committee to protect cultural, scientific, and historical material of importance and national monuments from war destruction. Taylor, along with Sumner Crosby, president of the College Art Association, and David Finley, director of the National Gallery of Art, proposed to the Chief Justice of the Supreme Court that a governmental commission be established to this end. The Commission for the Protection and Salvage of Artistic and Historic Monuments in Europe was established in 1943.

To assist the Commission, William B. Dinsmoor, Chairman of the American Council of Learned Societies, established a local committee based in New York City, called the Committee on the Protection of Cultural Treasures in War Areas. The Committee was tasked with creating maps that identified the location of important monuments, landmarks, and cultural institutions, to distribute to Allied armed forces in occupied areas in Europe. At Miss Frick's suggestion, the Frick Art Reference Library closed its doors to the public between July 1943 and January 1944 during which the Committee headquartered there to devote its time to this initiative.

The Committee on the Protection of Cultural Treasures in War Areas was made up of thirty American and European scholars and volunteers. Bill Burke, Jane Mull, and Gladys Hamlin were among them and used Library collections to create a master index of important historic buildings and works of art in each occupied territory. Using maps provided by the Army Maps Service, American Geographical Society, and Library of Congress, Burke, Mull, Hamlin, and other members of the Committee worked with the Library's photographic department on a process in which gridded tracing paper was overlaid upon regional maps and marked numerically to designate cultural sites. In this photograph, Burke and Mull hold one of the master indexes compiled of the city of Paris and look on as Hamlin, a draftswomen, notates corresponding areas on the map.

—*Michelle McCarthy-Behler*

52 The First Jackson Pollock Show
1943

The abstract expressionist painter Jackson Pollock (1912–1956) was born in Cody, Wyoming, and spent time in Arizona and California while growing up. In 1930, he followed his brother Charles to New York City, where they both studied at the Art Students League under Thomas Hart Benton (1889–1975). Before his well-known drip paintings of the late 1940s, Pollock exhibited "abstract figurative" works in his first solo exhibition at Peggy Guggenheim's gallery, Art of This Century, 9–27 November 1943. Guggenheim, whose adviser was Marcel Duchamp, had given him a gallery contract in July 1943 and commissioned *Mural* (1943), painted on canvas rather than on the wall: in 1951 Guggenheim donated this work to the University of Iowa Stanley Museum of Art.

The Frick Art Reference Library holds a copy of the four-page exhibition checklist for Pollock's first solo exhibition. It is a folded sheet of paper with a list of the titles of the works included in the exhibition; a reproduction of one of the works exhibited, the painting *Male and Female* (1942–43), now in the Philadelphia Museum of Art; and a brief commentary on the artist by James Johnson Sweeney (1900–86), at the time a curator at The Museum of Modern Art, who described Pollock's talent as "volcanic. It has fire. It is unpredictable".

Two of the entries include the names of the collectors, mosaicist Jeanne Reynal (1903–83), who had bought the Pollock as early as 1941, and the photographer and graphic designer Herbert Matter (1907–84), who lent works to the exhibition. Other than that, no additional information is given about the gouaches and drawings exhibited.

The checklist is an example of the ephemera collected—often in person—by the staff of the Frick Art Reference Library. It was also catalogued whereas at other libraries this type of material was just put in vertical files and is not easily—if at all—discoverable in library catalogs. But this type of material provides important information about provenance and the milestones in the careers of artists before they were well known. These materials are important in the creation of in-depth publications such as a catalogue raisonné, which attempts to document all the works by a particular artist.

—*Suz Massen*

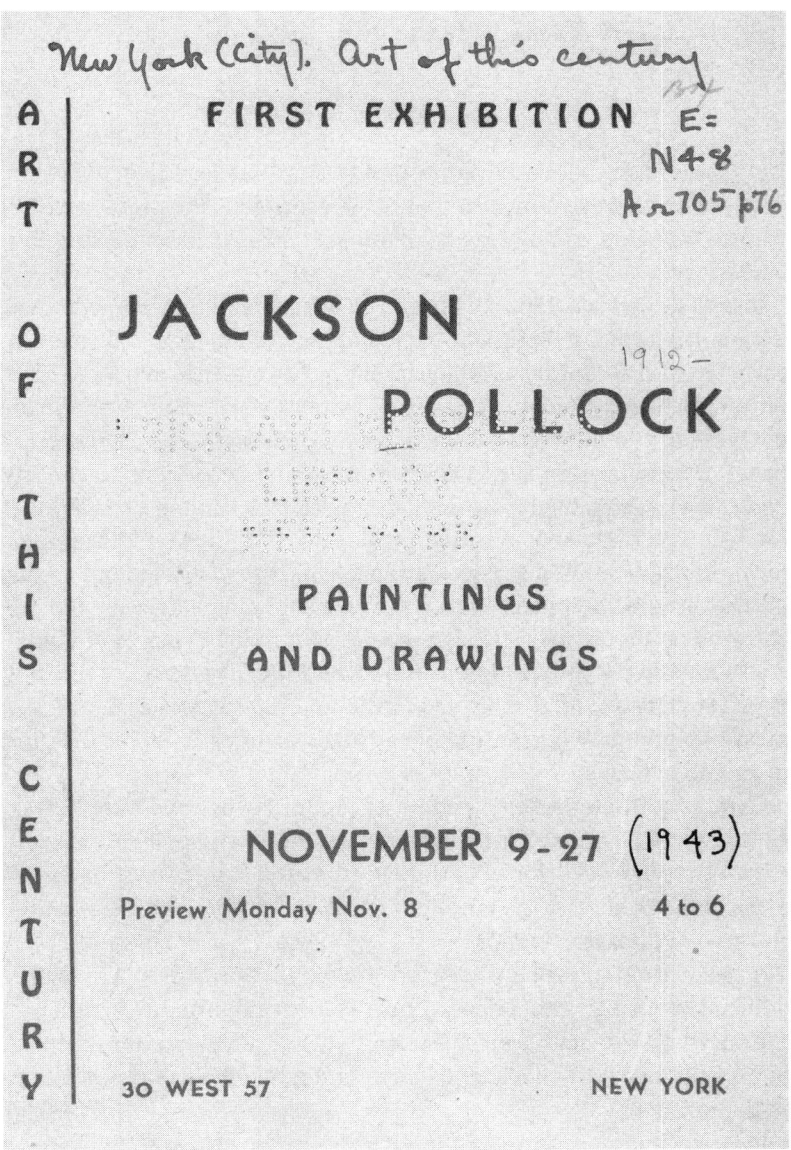

Jackson Pollock, Paintings and Drawings: First Exhibition. New York: Art of This Century, 1943.

53 Into the Wilderness
1944

The Library has collected original and facsimile artists' sketchbooks (along with their writings) so that researchers can investigate artists' private thoughts and ideas. One of our sketchbooks has an intriguing back story.

Joseph Knowles (c.1869–1942) was an artist and illustrator, who had a keen eye for nature, but who pulled off one of the biggest hoaxes in early twentieth-century journalism. With the freelance journalist and writer Michael McKeogh, Knowles, or rather Joe, came up with the idea of trying to test out survival skills in the wild. There was a general belief that civilization had made men weak and dependent on the city, and this also explained the fascination with Jack London's stories or the interest in Tarzan. At 10:40 am on 4 August 1913, the 5' 9" 180 pound Joe, initially wearing just a jock-strap (soon to be discarded out of view of the cameras), stepped out into the woods of Maine near Eustis, carrying no tool or aid. The idea was for him to light fires by rubbing sticks together, improvise shelters and clothing, live on berries, fish from the streams, or, if lucky and in the hunting season, deer, and leave messages and drawings, using burnt sticks on birch bark, for the press in agreed hideaways.

Two months later he emerged in Mégantic, Quebec, wearing bearskin clothing and no worse for the experience. On 9 October 1913 he had a hero's reception at North Station, Boston, and his ghosted memoir, *Alone in the Wilderness* (1914) sold 30,000 copies, and was made into a Hollywood film, starring Joe.

If this was all too good to be true, it was. *The Boston Post* had been fighting to keep its circulation against competition from Hearst, and the survival story had been the perfect vehicle. Rival journalists started to unpick the story—the bearskin had bullet holes, a cabin was found in the forest etc.

Joe's Hollywood career did not advance and he moved to Ilwaco, Washington State. In a one-person show at the Cowie Galleries, Los Angeles, 8–13 November 1948 he showed thirteen drawings of landscapes. The sketchbook that the Frick Art Reference Library acquired, alongside three others, for ten dollars in February 1944, obviously predates this exhibition.

—*Stephen Bury*

54 Civil Affairs Handbooks
1944 (1947)

These were published by the United States Army in 1944 to assist Civil Affairs personnel in occupied and formerly occupied territories in Europe and Japan. This particular copy was gifted to the Frick Art Reference Library by the Library of Congress on 21 March 1947. The

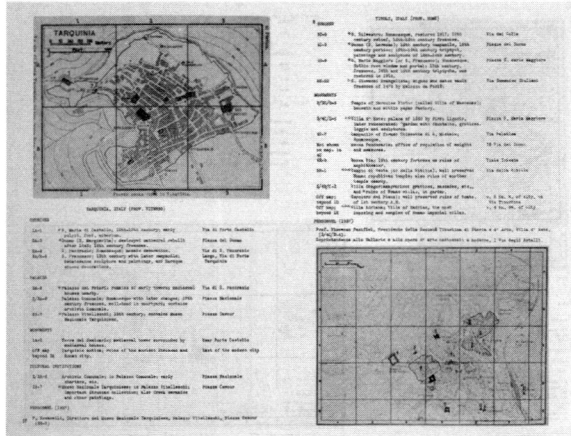

Civil Affairs Handbook, Italy. Section 17B, Cultural institutions. Washington, D.C.: The Army, 1944.

devastation incurred during the Second World War caused the United States government to institutionalize a Civil Affairs program in the Allied Armed Forces with the goal to salvage, preserve, and rebuild civil and cultural institutions in countries that had been directly affected by warfare. The Civil Affairs Handbooks, such as the one on Italy presented here, acted as field manuals for particular sections of civilian life to aid personnel in this recovery. Although the Handbooks did not deal with the creation of policies, they served as reference books that contained basic factual information related to the category or topic specified.

This Handbook was specifically designed to provide information for the recovery of Cultural Institutions and Works of Art for the country of Italy, as stipulated by the numerical code visible in the upper right-hand corner of the title page, 'M353-17'. This study was prepared under the direction of American Commission for the Protection and Salvage of Artistic and Historic Monuments in War Areas. The Commission, often referred to as The Second Roberts Commission, was established by President Franklin D. Roosevelt in June 1943 and chaired by the Associate Supreme Court Justice, Owen J. Roberts. It played a central role in the creation of the Monuments, Fine Arts, and Archives program of the U.S. Military's Civil Affairs section, and is described in this Handbook as the "concrete expression of the determination that… the culture of our time will be passed on, shall be preserved". The

Commission worked with local committees in the United States, such as the Committee on the Protection of Cultural Treasures in War Areas. This Committee, headquartered at the Frick Art Reference Library, created and prepared the maps included in the 'Civil Affairs Handbooks for Cultural Institutions and Works of Art in Italy'.

The Handbook includes an index and atlas for each country and comprises valuable maps of monuments and cultural heritage sites that were arranged by region, province, and town. The maps are divided into grids to which the first number and letter for each listed site location corresponds. The number after the dash refers to a specific monument listed and is superimposed on the map directly on the site location. Stars designate order of importance, with three stars given for cultural sites of the highest. A list of each type of monument is included in each regional map, as well as a list of Italian personnel contacts responsible for the buildings or collections whenever possible. If a personnel no longer works with the collections, the Handbook instructs that said persons be located to provide valuable assistance to preservation work.

Both the text and the atlas include a statement by the Commission for the Protection and Salvage of Artistic and Historic Monuments in Europe that describes the necessity of the Commission and its work in Europe, but particularly in Italy. This official statement divides the sites into the following categories: churches and religious structures, palaces and houses, monuments in the form of public structures and buildings, and cultural institutions such as art galleries, libraries, and archives. To assist Civil Affairs personnel in understanding a complicated system of Italian authorities, it provides a detailed account of each bureaucratic structure according to the type of cultural heritage it oversees for reparation and maintenance: Administration of Monuments, Fine Arts, and Antiquities; Administration of Libraries and Archives; Monuments Not Dependent on the State. A glossary of terms in Italian is also included as well as an alphabetical list of cities with superintendents and their operational organization for contact.

The Civil Affairs Handbook for Italy concludes with a bibliography of guide books and volumes related to Italian history, literature, and art for Civil Affairs personnel to review for each genre. It also includes a brief section entitled, 'Main Periods in History', that provides information on Italian cultural and political development from the eighth century B.C.E. through 1943 C.E.

—Michelle McCarthy-Behler

55 A Dadaist Doctor in New York*
1944 (1945, 1947)

The Library has exceptional holdings of twentieth-century catalogues of exhibitions taking place in New York since 1921. Staff went to galleries and collected any documentation that was available: price lists and press releases were often pasted into catalogs. If there was no catalog, the private view card, price list and reviews would be made into a stand-in one. These are very rich sources for provenance research.

One of the founders of Dada with Hugo Ball, Richard Huelsenbeck (1892–1974) took part in the activities of the Cabaret Voltaire, Zurich, including creating and performing the simultaneous Dada poem, *L'amiral cherche une maison a louer*, with Tristan Tzara and Marcel Janco. Huelsenbeck returned to Berlin in January 1917 and was closely involved with Berlin Dada.

Although the evidence is sketchy and largely dependent on Huelsenbeck's own account, it seems that he studied medicine in Berlin, Zurich and Greifswald. He worked as a military doctor in Fürstenwalde from April 1918, and then in Danzig with the neurologist Adolf Wallenberg. He worked with Karl Bonhoeffer at the Berlin Charité and as a doctor in ships voyaging to Africa, Asia, and the United States. As the situation in Germany deteriorated, he and his family moved to New York in 1936.

With the help of Albert Einstein he was able to have his Prussian doctor's license recognized in New York, and worked as an unpaid assistant psychiatrist at New York University Clinic. On 13 October 1939, he changed his name to Charles R. Hulbeck. In March 1942 he applied for membership in Karen Horney's American Institute for Psychoanalysis, where he became a lecturer. He credited Horney with sending him many patients and he built up a lucrative practice, enabling him to afford a suite at 88 Central Park West.

Despite conceptual differences—he eventually became interested in existential analysis (*Daseinanalyse*)—Hulbeck remained on good terms with Horney, who took painting lessons from him. She also owned his watercolor *Winterlandscape*, no.16 in the list of twenty-eight items in the catalog of his January 1945 exhibition at Feigl Gallery, 601 Madison Avenue, New York. This gallery had been founded by Hugo Feigl (1889–1961), a Prague dealer specializing in contemporary European artists, including Oskar Kokoschka. The Frick Art Reference Library holds two other exhibition catalogs of Hulbeck's work: that of his first one-man show at the Bonestell Gallery on 18 East 57th Street, 17–29 January 1944, where he showed fourteen landscapes and portraits in oil and

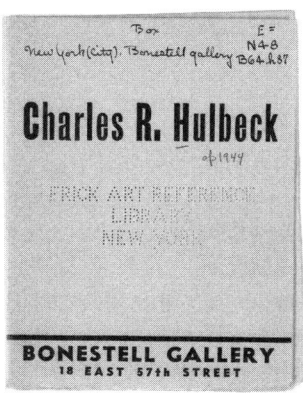
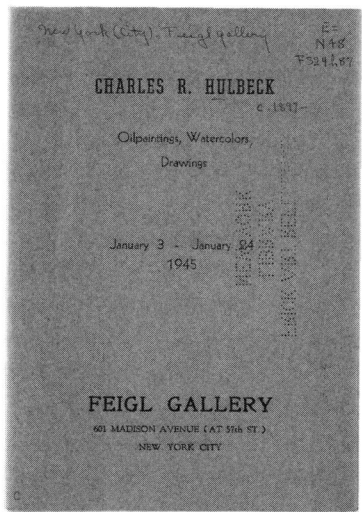

eight watercolors and ink drawings, as well as that of a second show at the Feigl Gallery, from 15 April to 7 May 1947, which presented fourteen gouaches and four drawings.

After Horney's death, Hulbeck became an adjunct staff member at the Karen Horney Clinic, which had been founded in 1955 at 329 East 62nd Street, and which followed the Berlin Psychoanalytic Institute (BPI) polyclinic model.

In 1969 he retired from practice and returned to Switzerland. In his 1969 essay 'On leaving America for Good', (the now again) Huelsenbeck maintained his case for this return to Switzerland: in America "as a doctor I was a success and as a Dadaist (the thing closest to my heart) I was a failure".

—*Stephen Bury*

Aedes Walpolianae
1947 (1752)

Sir Robert Walpole (1675–1745), created Earl of Orford in 1742, was the most prominent British politician of the eighteenth century, effectively running the government 1721–42. He has been called the first prime minister.

He built up his art collection from 1718: by 1736 there were some four hundred pictures. It was mainly housed in the Palladian-style Houghton Hall, Norfolk, built by Colen Campbell (1676–1729) and James Gibbs, (1682–1754), with interiors and the picture hanging by William Kent (c.1685–1748).

Walpole profited from the South Sea Bubble, buying the stock very cheaply and selling at the top price. This gave him the funds to expand his collection when others had lost heavily: Philip Wharton, the first Duke of Wharton (1698–1731) was badly burnt by the Bubble, and in 1725 sold Walpole the Wharton collection, which included works that Philip Wharton, fourth Baron Wharton (1613–96) had commissioned from Van Dyck, portraits of King Charles I in armor and Henrietta-Maria by Van Dyck, probably given to Wharton by the King himself. And there were gifts to Walpole—for favors wanted or granted: the Ambassador to Paris, James, Earl Waldegrave gave a Giacomo Bassano *Christ*, whilst the Ambassador to Lisbon, James O'Hara, second Baron Tyrawley, managed to find a Holbein portrait of Edward VI, which had been in the Royal Collection before its dispersal in the Interregnum. Walpole's three sons, Robert, Edward and Horace assisted their father in discovering or assessing works for possible acquisition.

It is the youngest son, Horace Walpole (1717–97), author of *The Castle of Otranto* (1764), letter-writer extraordinary, and impresario of the neo-Gothic Strawberry Hill, Twickenham, who compiled *Aedes Walpolianae*, an inventory of the contents of Houghton Hall. This was in manuscript form in 1736, and in 1748 (although the title page bears the date of 1747) was published in an edition of one hundred, intended primarily as gifts. The second edition of 1752 was printed for Walpole by John Hughs, London and distributed by Robert Dodsley. The third edition, unaltered, was published in 1767.

The Frick Art Reference Library has two copies of the second edition. After the catalogue of pictures, which had been re-measured since the first edition, there is 'A Sermon on Painting' by Horace Walpole, dated 1742, followed by Walpole's former tutor John Whaley's 'A Journey to Houghton'. There are two folding engraved elevations of the east and west fronts, and two folding engraved ground or room plans.

> PICTURES *at* Houghton-Hall. 51
>
> Over the Chimney is a genteel Buft of a *Madonna* in Marble, by *Camillo Rufconi*.
>
> Above, is Carving by *Gibbins*, gilt, and within it a fine Picture by *Vandyke*, of two Daughters of Lord *Wharton*, out of whofe Collection thefe came, with all the other *Vandykes* in this Room, and fome others at Lord *Walpole*'s at the Exchequer. Five Feet four Inches high, by four Feet three wide. £200.
>
> The Judgment of *Paris*, by *Luca Jordano*. There is an odd Diffufion of Light all over this Picture: The *Pallas* is a remarkably fine Figure. Eight Feet high, by ten Feet eight and a quarter wide.
> A fleeping *Bacchus*, with Nymphs, Boys, and Animals; its Companion. £500.
>
> King *Charles* I. a whole Length, in Armour, by *Vandyke*. By a Miftake, both the Gauntlets are drawn for the Right-Hand. *
> *Henrietta Maria* of *France*, his Queen, by ditto. £400.
>
> Archbifhop *Laud*, the Original Portrait of him; three Quarters, by *Vandyke*. The Univerfity of *Oxford* once offered the *Wharton* Family Four Hundred Pounds for this Picture.
>
> G 2 *Philip*
>
> * When this Picture was in the *Wharton* Collection, old *Jacob Tonfon*, who had remarkably ugly Legs, was finding Fault with the two Gauntlets; Lady *Wharton* faid, Mr. *Tonfon*, why might not one Man have two Right Hands, as well as another two Left Legs?

Horace Walpole *Aedes Walpolianae, or, A description of the collection of pictures at Houghton Hall, the seat of the Right Honourable Sir Robert Walpole, Earl of Orford.* 2nd ed. London: Printed by John Hughs, near Lincoln's Inn-Fields, 1752. Annotated copy acquired in 1947, from Stevens & Brown, Library and Fine Arts Agent, London.

The Frick's second copy contains the valuations of the sale of most of the collection (204 works)—some had already been sold by the third Earl in 1751 and others like Gainsborough's family portrait were not sold—to Catherine II. This was negotiated by the Russian envoy, A. S. Musin-Pushkin for £40,550 in 1779. Currently, the Hermitage has 126 Houghton paintings, while other museums in Russia have thirty-six. The works at the Hermitage include Giordano *Vulcan's Forge*, Rosa *The Prodigal Son*, Rembrandt *Sacrifice of Isaac*, Snyders *Bird Concert* and Poussin *Moses Striking the Rock*. It is a pity that John Wilkes's 1777 proposal to buy the collection for the nation was rejected by the House of Commons.

Our priced catalogue is another example of a collection catalogue becoming a sales catalogue.

—Stephen Bury

57 *Stieglitz Photographs from O'Keefe*
1947

On November 9, 1946, The Frick Art Reference Library's Ethelwyn Manning, its Chief Librarian from 1924–47, wrote to the artist Georgia O'Keeffe asking to purchase a photograph of her 1943 painting *Pelvis with the Moon*. O'Keeffe replied in the affirmative and on 19 April 1947 she sent the photograph along with a letter. On 20 May 1947, the library then received a gift of sixty-eight photographs from O'Keeffe of paintings and sculptures by French artists, such as Vincent van Gogh (1853–90), Henri Matisse (1869–1954), Pablo Picasso (1881–1973), Paul Signac (1863–1935), Henri Rousseau (1844–1910), and Paul Cézanne (1839–1906). Two of the photographs in the gift, Matisse's *Blue Nude* (1907) and Cézanne's *Le Sentier de la ravine, vu de l'Hermitage, Pontoise*, were marked as being taken by her husband, the photographer Alfred Stieglitz (1864–1946).

Frick Art Reference Library Photoarchive files, Henri Matisse, 'Blue Nude', and Paul Cézanne, 'Le Sentier de la ravine, vu de l'Hermitage, Pontoise'.

From 1905 until 1917, Stieglitz operated a gallery at 291 Fifth Avenue, New York; although the title of the business was "The Little Galleries of the Photo-Secession", it quickly became known as simply "291". In 1909 Stieglitz and Edward Steichen planned a second exhibition for Henri Matisse showcasing drawings to run from 23 February–8 March 1910.

No catalog or checklist was published for the exhibition, but scholars have determined approximately twenty-four drawings, of mostly female nudes, were included in the exhibition along with a few black-and-white photographs of paintings, including a photograph of the Matisse's *Blue Nude*. Matisse often allowed photographs of his works to be exhibited alongside original pieces allowing visitors and potential collectors a chance to view more works than could otherwise be accommodated in a gallery such as 291. Stieglitz also included a plate of *Blue Nude* in his publication *Camera Work* in August 1912.

291 continued to include photographs of paintings in their exhibitions. In the November 1910 a group exhibition entitled *A Loaned Collection of Some Lithographs by Manet, Cézanne, Renoir, and Toulouse Lautrec: A Few Drawings by Rodin: And Smaller Paintings and Drawings by Henri Rousseau* was held. The exhibition included approximately twelve photographs by the photographer Antoine Druet of Cézanne's paintings, which were exhibited alongside Cézanne's lithographs.

There is no indication that the photographic prints of *Blue Nude* and *Le Sentier de la ravine, vu de l'Hermitage, Pontoise* housed in the Frick Art Reference Library, are the actual prints exhibited at 291, but they may be copies of such photographic prints. In 1947 O'Keeffe wrote in a letter to Margaret Kiskadden that she had made an effort to make a small photograph of everything Stieglitz photographed, our prints might have come out of that effort.

—*Kerri A. Pfister*

58 An Anti-Slave Trader's Collection
1948 (1816)

William Roscoe (1753–1831) as a Member of Parliament for Liverpool in 1806 voted for the act abolishing the slave trade (1807). He had already published the two-part poem *The Wrongs of Africa* (1787, 1788) and a pamphlet *A General View of the African Slave Trade* (1788). These were brave actions in the then largest slave-trade port in England.

Roscoe was a true polymath: botanist, gardener, agronomist, linguist, bibliographer, historian, a founder of the Liverpool Athenaeum and the Liverpool Royal Institution. He learned Italian and published the *Life of Lorenzo de' Medici* in 1796: he was an early English collector of early Italian art with the assistance of the Liverpool dealer Thomas Winstanley (1768–1845), primarily from London sales, such as the Christie's sale of 12 May 1804 of what is thought to be the collection of Colonel Matthew Smith, Fellow of the Royal Society of Antiquaries, who had built up a substantial collection of early Italian paintings by the 1780s. Henry Fuseli was a friend since 1779 and stayed with Roscoe at his Allerton residence and so would have known his collection well. The money to collect art came from Roscoe's involvement in banking, which was his undoing in the commercial crisis of 1816: he was forced to sell his books and art.

The sale of the pictures and drawings took place in Liverpool with Thomas Winstanley as auctioneer, 23–28 September 1816. The books had already been sold in a two-week sale beginning 19 August 1816, which realized £5,150—more than the art would raise. Perhaps with the intention of keeping some of the collection together the first sixty-two lots (most, not all, of the Italian schools) and lots 78–122 (mainly the Flemish, Dutch and German schools) were unsuccessfully offered as groups at £1,000 and £500 retrospectively. The auction then went ahead but the paintings raised just £3,084 and the drawings £738. This might have been because of the specialist nature of the art or because of the difficult economic climate.

The Frick copy of the catalog, acquired in 1948, has price notations but no buyers. Comparison with other partially annotated catalogues reveal another buyer, Roscoe's friend Thomas William Coke of Holkham Hall, where Roscoe was later employed to catalogue the library. Coke used Thomas Stewart Traill (1781–1862), a Scottish doctor, polymath and a founder of the Royal Institution of Liverpool, as his agent in the sale. Traill was also involved in securing some of the unsold items for the Liverpool Royal Institution, and these works eventually became part of the Walker Art Gallery. This means that we can identify some of

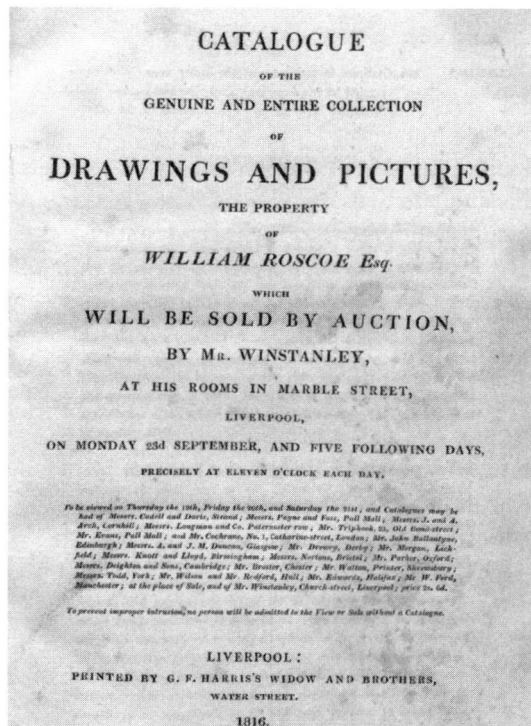

Catalogue of the genuine and entire collection of drawings and pictures, the property of William Roscoe, Esq: which will be sold be auction, by Mr. Winstanley, at his rooms in Marble Street, Liverpool, on Monday 23rd September, and five following days, precisely at eleven o'clock each day. Liverpool: Printed by G. F. Harris's widow and Brothers, Water Street, 1816.

the works in the sale. Roscoe had bought what the Smith sale (item 42) had attributed to Masaccio for nine guineas; it became a Fra Angelico (item 11 on the fifth day of the sale) in Roscoe's sale; it's now Perugino *The Birth of the Virgin* in the Walker. Again, Simone Martini's *Holy Family*, bought by Roscoe for five guineas at the 1804 Smith sale, was unsold at ten guineas in Roscoe's sale: that too eventually entered the Walker, with the same attribution but with the title *Christ Discovered in the Temple*.

The correlation of multiple sales, collectors and gifts to institutions and finally museums, enables us to learn more about the lives (and deaths) of paintings. The Frick's Photoarchive and its collection of sales catalogs, many annotated, are crucial to the telling of these stories.

—Stephen Bury

Prop Art
1948

The painter Robert Brackman (1898–1980) was known for his portraits as well as figurative works and still lives. He was born in Odessa, Russian Empire (Ukraine), and immigrated to the United States in the early 1900s. He studied at the National Academy of Design in New York City and the Ferrer School in San Francisco. Besides being an artist, he was also a teacher at the Art Students League, American Art School, Lyme Academy College of Fine Arts as well as other institutions. Some of his noted portraits are the likenesses of John D. and Abby Aldrich Rockefeller, and Charles A. and Anne Spencer Lindberg.

In 1948, Brackman painted the portrait of the actress Jennifer Jones (1919–2009) in character as the main prop in the Hollywood film *Portrait of Jennie*. The Frick Art Reference Library holds a promotional brochure published by Max Grumbacher, an art supply company, promoting the use of its products in the painting of the portrait of Jennie Appleton (Jennifer Jones) for the film. Its plot centers on the struggling artist Eben Adams (played by the actor Joseph Cotten), who meets the haunting Jennie and paints her portrait, which is celebrated as a masterpiece. The  text of the brochure outlines the making of the titular prop, showing photographs of the painting in different phases of completion, the artist in his studio with Jones and Cotten, stills from the film, and advertisements for Grumbacher products.

The brochure is a good example of the ephemera held by the Library that might have been otherwise lost. Later, art-collector Norton Simon (1907–93) acquired the portrait of Jones as Jennie for his personal

Gerry A. Turner
Robert Brackman, N.A., paints Jennifer Jones Portrait, 'Portrait of Jennie', as main prop in the latest Selznick film production. New York: M. Grumbacher, [n.d.].

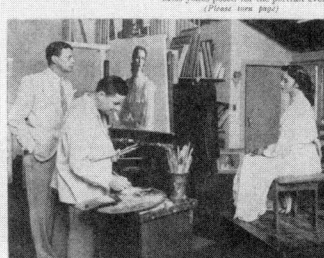

collection after their marriage in 1971—she had been married to the producer of *Portrait of Jennie*, David O. Selznick (1902–65) before his death.

The prop for the film continued to have a life after the silver screen as a real-world, art object. And this cutting too has now become part of the history of collecting.

—*Suz Massen*

60 *Le Da Costa*
1948 (1947, 2012)

Surrealism, official and unofficial, generated many periodicals, often referencing, in their appearance at least, mainline scientific or literary ones. With two possible titles—*Da Costa Encyclopédique or Le memento universal da Costa* (1947–48)—*Le Da Costa* is already a bibliographic conundrum, and, with scant publishing details, it was difficult to subscribe to, perhaps explaining why it lasted for just three issues. It also imitated a part-issued encyclopedia, though in differently-sized and numbered fascicles. Those asking for earlier numbered issues were told they were sold out, whilst in fact they had never existed.

The origins of *Le Da Costa* began to emerge in the 1990s. It might have been intended to coincide with the exhibition *Le surrealism en 1947*, at the Galerie Maeght, Paris, 1947, but publication was delayed. As there was already an exhibition catalog (with the famous foam-rubber

[Marcel Duchamp]: 'Permis de vivre valuable un an', *Le memento universal Da Costa*. [Paris]: [s.n.], [1947–48]. Purchased through The Heinemann Fund, in memory of Dr. Rudolf J. Heinemann, 2012.

breast cover, designed by Duchamp and Enrico Donati), the connection to the exhibition may be spurious. Its editors were the Swiss sculptress Isabelle Waldberg (1911–90), wife of the American art critic Patrick Waldberg (1913–85), whom André Breton later excluded from the surrealists in 1951 over the Pastoureau affair, and the writer, Robert Lebel (1901–86). The latter had met Marcel Duchamp in New York in 1936, and later, in 1959, published the first Duchamp catalogue raisonné. It is possible that Duchamp advised on the design of *Le Da Costa*, and he probably contributed perhaps two articles—'sens' and, more speculatively, 'permis de vivre valuable un an'. He might also have suggested the title as he had met already in New York the Morgan Librarian, Belle Da Costa Greene, but the London surrealists claimed they had intended to publish an encyclopedia, edited by the Portuguese painter António Pedro da Costa (1909–66).

Le Da Costa has been seen as aligned with the Acéphale wing of surrealism, associated with Georges Bataille (1897–1962) and Roger Caillois (1913–78), with interests in the sacred, ritual, the formless and scatology. And it does have some parallels with Bataille's fifteen-issue magazine, *Documents* (1929–30), not least in the entries in the 'Critical Dictionary' sections. Both Waldbergs had close connections to Bataille. But playing with definitions of words was a wider and earlier surrealist interest, as in Michel Leiris's 'Glossaire' in *La Révolution surréaliste*, no.3, April 1925. It could go back further—to Diderot's *Encyclopédie* (1751–72), which had pseudo-entries to avoid censorship, so that the Pope appears in Japanese guise in the article, Siako.

The first issue is confusingly labeled Fascicle VII, Volume II. It has a *faux* publishers device on the cover. The text begins mid-word ("-festations"), mid-sentence. The entries range from "échecs" to "extasiée" (and thus includes an entry for "encyclopédie", which is strangely about neologism), implying entries before them. And its contributors are anonymous. This ceases with the following two smaller-format issues: some of the contributors are Maurice Baskine, Francis Bouvet, Marcel Duchamp (MD), Marcel Jean, Pierre Mabille, Henri Pastoureau, Isabelle Waldberg and Jindrich Heisler.

—*Stephen Bury*

The Folio Catalog
1949 (1928, 1941)

This monumental catalogue raisonné describes the works Henry Clay Frick collected during his lifetime along with those purchased after his death, as part of his bequest, through 1955. The project was fully funded by Helen Clay Frick and published by the Frick Art Reference Library with the first three volumes completed and distributed in 1949, the centenary of the birth of Mr. Frick, Helen's father. This work is notable not only as one of the earliest attempts to catalog The Frick Collection but also as a significant object in the history of hand-press printing and book production.

The completed work comprises twelve volumes, all bound in rust-colored buckram. The paper used for printing the text is handmade Kelmscott paper from the Joseph Batchelor & Son mill in Kent, England. The reproductions are printed on rag paper, also handmade, from fine Italian linen. Special molds were commissioned that embedded both papers with a unique watermark bearing a variation of The Frick Collection monogram held within a round medallion. Jan van Krimpen (1892–1958), of the Dutch foundry, Enschedé en Zonen, was hired to redesign a modified version of his typeface, Lutetia, for the printing. The reproductions were printed using the collotype method—a variation of lithography—by Arthur Jaffé in New York City.

Volumes 1 through 3 describe the paintings held within The Frick Collection. The entries, all printed in volume 1, are organized first by country and then artist. After biographical sketches, works are then listed by title with a full description and plate numbers to cross-reference to the reproductions held in volumes 2 and 3. Critical and historical write-ups relating to the pieces subject matter and authenticity are then presented. These were written by expert scholars in the field commissioned by Dr. Frederic Mortimer Clapp, whom Ms. Frick tasked with overseeing the project. Later volumes contain both the printed entries and plates within their respective issues.

Dr. Clapp began working on the catalog in 1928, while he was head of Pittsburgh University's Fine Arts Department. At that time, he hired Porter Garnett (1871–1951), Head of Laboratory Press (1922–35) at the Carnegie Institute of Technology, to design the catalog's layout and style. Porter commissioned the typeface and paper and purchased the presses for printing the text. These were set up in two rooms of the Frick Fine Arts Building at the University of Pittsburgh. The rag paper stayed in Europe with the intention of having the reproductions printed there.

The Frick Collection : an illustrated catalogue of the works of art in the collection of Henry Clay Frick, with an introduction by Sir Osbert Sitwell. Pittsburgh: Printed at the University; New York: Frick Art Reference Library, 1949–56.

The project was put on hold in 1932, with the reproductions remaining unprinted, when Dr. Clapp became the Organizing Director of The Frick Collection, managing the transition of the collection and house into a public museum. Helen Clay Frick revived the project in 1941 but the ten-year interregnum meant much of the earlier research needed to be re-evaluated. However, World War II affected communications with the European scholars who wrote many of the entries, further slowing progress. Furthermore, the rag paper to be used for the reproductions was still held in a London storage facility and in danger of being bombed. The bespoke Frick Collection watermark prevented the paper from being salvaged for a third party. Eventually the entire tonnage was brought to the United States, at a high cost, to complete the project.

In 1948, Ms. Frick hired renowned book designer Bruce Rogers (1870–1957) to take over the work started by Garnett Porter who, by now, had retired. Rogers's embellishments can be seen in the design of the title pages, chapter openings, front matter, and binding, though he maintained the layout set by Porter.

Only 175 sets were printed, and none were ever intended for sale. Instead, the catalog was distributed throughout the United States and Europe as gifts to various museums, libraries, and universities.

—*Ralph Baylor*

Lenox Library
1950 (1879)

James Lenox (1800–80) founded the Lenox Library in 1870 to house his collections of books, manuscripts, maps, paintings, sculptures, drawings, and other works of art. His inheritance from his merchant father supported his love of collecting. Lenox's book collection included a Gutenberg Bible and by 1894 had grown to more than 80,000 volumes. His art collection expanded over the years receiving a major donation in 1887 from Mary McCrea Stuart, who was the widow of the sugar magnate Robert L. Stuart.

'Back of the Lenox Library, showing the "million dollar" hay field.' Gelatin silver print. c.1885. With permission of the Museum of the City of New York.

Lenox chose a lot located on Fifth Avenue between 70th and 71st Streets to build his library and hired the architect Richard Morris Hunt (1827–95) to design it. Construction was completed in 1875, and the galleries opened in 1877 to visitors with the exhibition of paintings and sculptures on 15 January, and exhibition of rare books and manuscripts on 1 December. The reading rooms opened to researchers a few years later in 1880. The farm surrounding the Lenox Library continued to operate after its opening. Admission to the reading rooms and galleries was free. In 1895, the Lenox Library along with the Astor Library and Tilden Trust became the foundation for The New York Public Library. Henry Clay Frick in 1906 purchased the Lenox Library lot to build his future New York City home. In 1912, the collections of the Lenox Library moved to the New York Public Library building on Fifth Avenue between 41st and 42nd Streets, and the Lenox Library was demolished to make way for the construction of the Frick mansion, which later became The Frick Collection.

Beginning in 1877, the Lenox Library annually published by the order of its trustees guides to its art galleries. The Frick Art Reference Library holds the 1879, 1885, 1892, and 1893 editions. The guides published before 1893 include notices of entrance on the versos of their front covers. The Lenox Library was open to the public at no cost, but it required gallery goers to secure tickets in advance of their visits by application to its superintendent. Initially only open on Mondays and Fridays, the Lenox Library expanded its hours to six days a week by its dissolution in 1895. The earliest guide in the collections of the Frick includes an index of artists and most entries include artist, title, date, and how Lenox acquired the works.

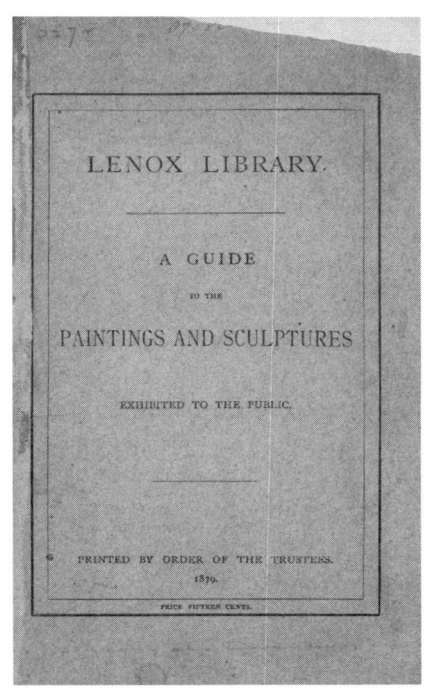

Lenox Library: A Guide to the Paintings and Sculptures Exhibited to the Public [New York]: Printed by Order of the Trustees, 1879.

Notations about copies and correspondence appear in some entries. Many of the works were commissioned, purchased directly from the artists, or bought at auction or through private sales. The acquisitions information gives insight into Lenox as a collector as well as where he traveled. Names of his trusted art advisors such as the artists Ferdinand de Braekeleer, Sr. and Charles Robert Leslie can be found throughout the list of works, and auctions important to his collecting such as the 21 June 1850, sale of the collection of Charles Meigh, Esq., who was a pottery manufacturer with a well-known art collection at Grove House his home in Shelton, Staffordshire, England. The majority of the works in the Lenox Library were produced in the nineteenth century by European, mainly English, and American artists. The recognizable names of Albert Bierstadt, Frederic Edwin Church, John Constable, Thomas Gainsborough, Jacob Ruysdael, Gilbert Stuart, J. M. W. Turner and others can be found in the pages of the guide to the galleries.

—*Suz Massen*

Costume Cards
1950 (1968)

The delicately detailed costume drawings of Library staffer and costume expert Doriece B. Colle (1904–99) are one of the treasures of The Frick Collection/Frick Art Reference Library Archives. Drawn in black ink on blue or pink 3 x 5 inch index cards, the drawings depict various aspects of men's and women's fashion from the late seventeenth century to the early twentieth century, including collars, hair styles, hats and facial hair. There are over 2,500 cards which include information identifying the portrait in the Library's Photoarchive from which the drawing was derived, as well as any other photographs that contain the same style. The drawings represent costumes from primarily American portraits. The cards are organized first by division into men's and women's styles, and then by specific categories. Ms. Colle's handwritten notes indicate the colors of the costume elements when known.

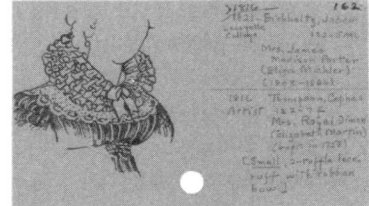

Ms. Colle began this project in about 1950, realizing that by extracting elements of costume from portraits that were dated, the visual information created could help to date other portraits about which little was known. It is believed that she worked on these costume cards until about 1968. While her project was pursued to create a useful resource for Library staffers in their work documenting photographs of portraits, her research culminated in her 1972 publication, *Collars… Stocks… Cravats: A History and Costume Dating Guide to Civilian Men's Neckpieces, 1655–1900*. The book includes photographs of portraits and Ms. Colle's own drawings to illustrate the neckwear.

According to the publication's acknowledgements, "the vast reference material of the Frick Art Reference Library… supplied the major contents of this book". The book can be used not only as a reference tool to help date portraits, but also as a resource for costume designers of theatrical and film productions to create authentic period costumes.

The cards also provide an overview of American fashion history, often revealing elaborate and sometimes surprising hat, hair, and clothing styles. The costume cards cannot be viewed without an appreciation for Ms. Colle's artistic talent. Browsing through the cards reveals a variety of drawing styles ranging from simple line drawings to finely detailed illustrations.

Doriece Colle compiled additional costume data during her tenure at the Library, including lists, indexes, and bibliographies. Her entire collection of costume research is now part of the Frick Art Reference Library—Staff Research series in the Archives. She also donated costume photographs, engravings and postcards, as well as printed material, to the Library.

Ms. Colle worked at the Library from 1948 until her retirement in September 1977 in what is now known as the Photoarchive Department; her primary job responsibility over those years was to research and prepare photo mounts for American paintings. She held B.A. and M.A. degrees in Art and Theatre from the University of Washington in Seattle. Ms. Colle taught dance, designed costumes for theatrical productions, and worked at the Costume Institute of the Metropolitan Museum of Art prior to her tenure at the Library.

The costume cards, housed in six card file boxes, are in the process of being scanned and cataloged to be made available digitally. Six volumes of bound photocopies of the cards are available for consultation in the Library's Reading Room.

—Susan Chore

64 Vienna Museum
1952 (1860, 1999)

The Vienna Museum could well have been called the Prague Museum. Holy Roman Emperor (1576–1612), Rudolf II built up a systematic cabinet of curiosities or *Kunstkammer* in rooms on the north side of Prague Castle. Known for his interest in alchemy and the occult, the collection was much wider, covering natural history, painting and prints, manuscripts and the decorative arts. Unusually, it had a curator 1587–1612 in the polymath, Anselmus de Boodt (1550–1632), who issued his definitive work on mineralogy, *Gemmarum et Lapidum* in 1609. An inventory of the *Prager Schatz und Kunstkammer* (Prague Treasury and Cabinet of Curiosities), completed on 6 December 1621 lists 1,428 items, although this understates the number of items as some are treated in aggregation.

As the space was required by Emperor Joseph II (1741–90) for military preparations against Prussia, the decision was made to move 573 paintings to Vienna, and sell what was left at an auction 13–14 May 1782. Most of it was bought by the Prague printer, Johann Ferdinand Ritter von Schönfeld, who added further pieces from dissolved monasteries after Joseph's Secularization Decree in the same year. He moved to Vienna and opened Schönfeld's Technological Museum in 1799 on Preßgasse (later Sterngasse) and Wollzeile by 1812. The museum was divided into fifty-one 'rubrics', beginning with writing and printing. After his death, his son sold the museum to Josef Freiherr von Dietrich in 1822/3, who built an exhibition hall in the Wieden area (now Technickerstraße) to house it and issued a catalogue by Joseph Scheiger in 1824. In the 1850s the exhibits were divided between his house on Hauptstrasse and Feistritz Castle (weapons). *Bradshaw's illustrated handbook to Germany* describes the contents: "50,000 copper and wood engravings, coins, pictures, books, and manuscripts, many of them first collected by the Emperor Rudolf at Prague. Here are a set of Chessmen, tuned by Rudolf himself; Wallenstein's Crucifix in ebony; and Adam and Eve carved in wood, both by Dürer; the parabolical burning glass of Regiomontanus (who died 1476); a gold Death's Head, about the size of a nut..." But this was published in 1879, well after the collection had been dispersed, for after Dietrich's death in 1855, the collection had been sold to the dealers Abraham and Markus Löwenstein of Frankfurt am Main, who sold 1,291 pieces at Christie's 21–23 March 1860.

The Frick's second copy of this auction catalogue was owned and annotated in his trademark spidery handwriting by Winthrop Kellogg Edey, interested in the clocks and automata in the sale. Edey indexed

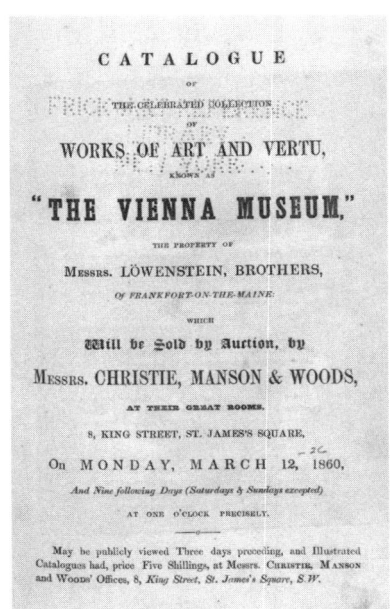

Celebrated collection of works of art and vertu known as "The Vienna Museum": property of Messers. Löwenstein, brothers, of Frankfort-on-the-Maine. London: Christie's, 1860. Copy 1: (with frontispiece of a portrait of Rudolph II), purchased through Baer, 1952. Copy 2: (with frontispiece of Plates 1–4), gift of Winthrop Kellogg Edey, 1999.

the clock entries, which include clocks by Johan Henner of Wurtzburg and Johan Sayher of Ulm: but the more renowned timepieces, commissioned by Rudolf II, by Jobst Burgi, Christoph Margraf, Georg Roll, Martin Schmidt and Georg Schneeberger must have been sold earlier.

Interestingly, this is also one of the earliest sales catalogues with photographic illustrations—by H. Emden of Frankfurt am Main—of the items for sale.

—Stephen Bury

65 A L'Etoile scellée
1952 (1953–56, 2018–21)

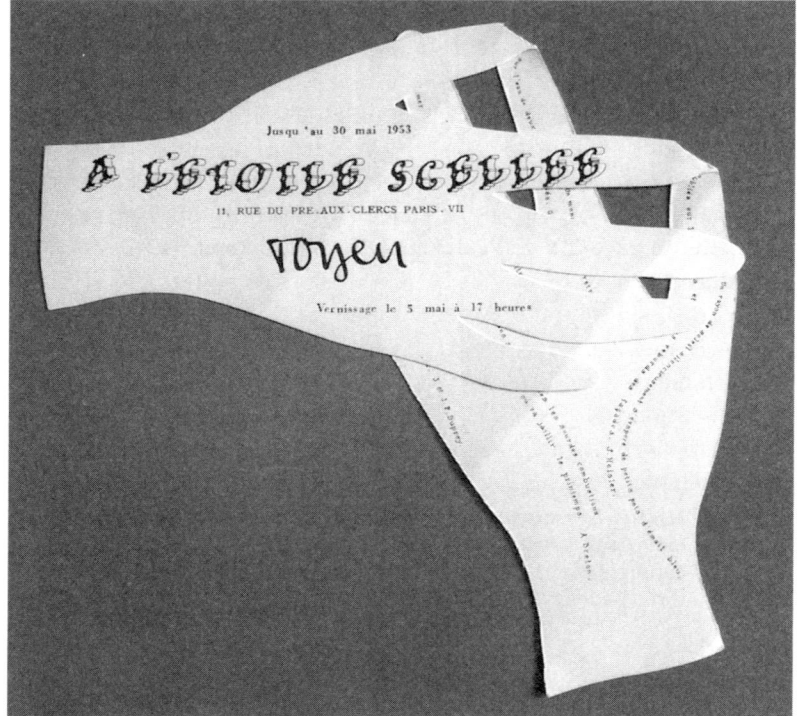

Founder of surrealism, André Breton (1896–1966) had roles as an advisor to three Parisian galleries: La galerie Surréaliste, 16 rue Jacques Callot, 1926–28; La galerie Gradiva, 31 rue de Seine, 1937–38; and A L'Etoile scellée, 11 rue du Pré aux Clercs, 1952–56. The name of the third gallery, A L'Etoile scellée, can be translated as "At the Sealed Star" and was suggested by René Alleau. This appealed to the interest in alchemy that Breton shared with other surrealists. As the gallery name could be read phonetically as "ah les toiles c'est laid"—"ah the canvases are rude"—it also appealed to their love of word games. But A L'Etoile was also a type of paper.

The gallery seems to have been financed by Sophie Babet, who closed it abruptly in June 1956.

The first two group shows, in December 1952 and February 1953, included surrealists—Ernst, Tanguy, Brauner, Lam, Paalen, Man Ray and Toyen. There was a further surrealist group show in April–May 1954 of work by Dominguez, Labisse and Magritte, and in July 1954 the gallery was involved in the *Pinturas surrealistas* exhibition shown at the Galeria de Lima. There were one-person shows for the surrealists Toyen (1953 and 1955), Man Ray (1956), and Meret Oppenheim (1956). Some of the artists provided images for the short-lived surrealist magazine, *Medium: communication surréaliste*, published in an edition of three thousand by Eric Losfeld's Editions Arcanes: Hantai (November 1953 issue), Paalen (February 1954), Svanberg (for the May 1953 launch of no.3 at A L'Etoile scellée and the May 1954 issue), and Lam (January 1955).

But the bulk of the shows were by younger or less well-known artists, and those associated with *tachisme*, championed by Charles Estienne, who was also an advisor to the gallery; art brut/primitivism; or eroticism. Breton gave the first Paris show to Slavko Kopac (1913–1995) who introduced himself by leaving a painting outside Breton's door. Realism, championed by communists, was not represented by any of the artists. The inclusion of abstract artists in the gallery's program was not popular with many surrealists. And Man Ray pointedly sub-titled his show 'non-abstractions'.

The Frick Art Reference Library has sixteen (out of a possible total of twenty-six) of the gallery catalogues, early ones acquired by Madame Brière, the Library's agent in Paris, at the time, and later acquisitions from European and US dealers retrospectively. Some are small single sheets with distinctive folding and cut-outs: Toyen (1953), in the shape of two connected hands; Kopac (1953), in the form of a bird; and the Galeria di Lima show, in the shape of a moth, perhaps also made by Kopac.

—*Stephen Bury*

Lettre-océan
1954 (1914)

Les soirées de Paris was set up in 1912 by four friends of the cubist and futurist poet, Guillaume Apollinaire (1880–1918) in order to improve his morale (and finances) after his arrest in the aftermath of the theft of the *Mona Lisa* from the Louvre. Using the same format as the *Mercure de France*, with chocolate-brown covers and mustard-colored paper, production costs were kept to a minimum—around 200 francs an issue. By the double issue no.12/13 André Billy had become the sole owner and editor (with Apollinaire), as André Salmon, Réné Dalize and André Tudesq struggled with their monthly 20 francs contributions. Friends of Apollinaire, the Russian painter Serge Férat and, supposedly his father's mistress, baroness (Hélène) d'Oettingen, who later wrote for the magazine under the pseudonyms, Léonard Pieux and Roch Grey, bought it for 200 francs. As an editorial team they created another pseudonym, Jean Cérusse, a play on "C'est russe"—it's Russian. And with their Russian money, they could afford illustrations, and the first of the new series, no.18 (15 November), included five photographs of still-lives by Picasso, though he was not mentioned anywhere in the texts.

Apollinaire's calligramme or visual poem, 'Lettre-océan', in issue 25 (15 June 1914) created a sensation. It obviously was influenced by Marinetti's words-in-liberty proposed in his manifesto 'The Destruction of Syntax' of May 1913, and put into practice by Francesco Cangiullo's 'Fumatori' in the January 1914 issue of *Lacerba*, and by Marinetti's own *Zang Tumb Tumb* of February 1914.

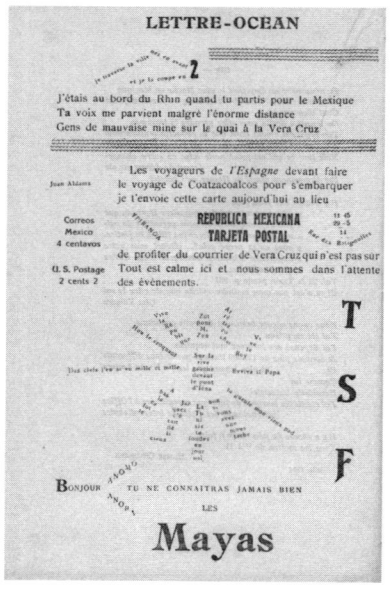

But there is another influence or at least context—the poetic rivalry between Apollinaire and Blaise Cendrars (1887–1961). The modernity of the latter's *Easter in New York* (1912) had led Apollinaire to make changes in the galley-proofs of his 1913 book of poems: it was originally titled *Eau de vie*—it now became *Alcools*. In 1913 Cendrars had published *La Prose du Transsiberien*, with pochoirs by Sonia Delaunay. Cendrars's Trans

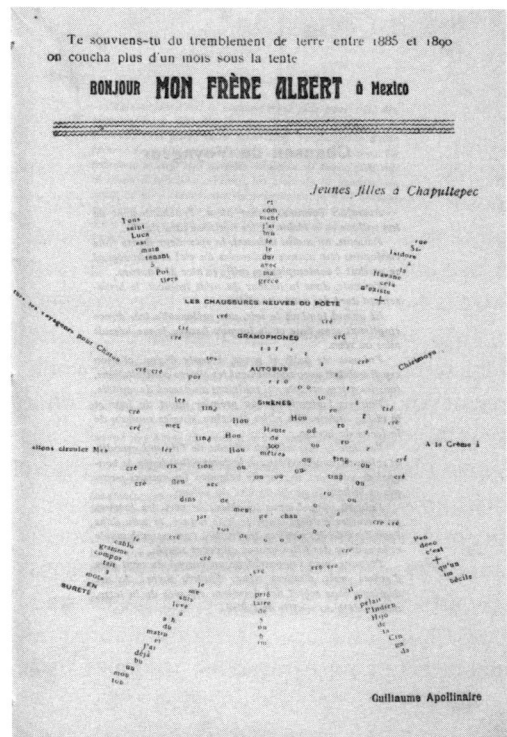

Guillaume Apollinaire, 'Lettre-océan', *Les soirées de Paris*, no.25 (15 June 1914). Acquired with four other issues through Madame Brière, 1954.

Siberian journey from Paris to Harbin (and back) along the telegraph-flanked railroad becomes in Apollinaire's *Lettre-océan* a journey to Vera Cruz, Mexico with letters with postmarks and possibly telegrams. Both converge on Paris: Delaunay's Eiffel Tower (the edition—spread out—was meant to be the height of the Tower), becomes in *Lettre-océan* two wheel-and-spoke aerial diagrams, smaller on the left-hand page and almost taking up the whole page on the right, where the top of the hub has "haute de 300 metres". And in Apollinaire the vertical "TSF" on the left page fetishes the wireless, supplanting other modes of communication. Apollinaire has challenged Cendrars's conversion of poetry into prose, by converting both into image. And not far away, on pages 345–46 of the same issue of *Les soirées de Paris* Cendrars contributed three prose poems, entitled 'Amours'. Nobody remembers these—they are not even included in Cendrars's complete poems.

—Stephen Bury

67 A Gilded Age Woman Collector
1956 (1884, 1886)

In March of 1886, Mary Jane Morgan's (1823–85) art collection was sold off by the auctioneer Thomas E. Kirby (1837–1905) by the American Art Association. The auction took place over thirteen days and raised approximately $1.2 million, setting a personal best for the firm. This record would not be surpassed in the United States for another twenty-four years when, in 1910, the Chicago financier Charles Yerkes's (1837–1905) paintings sold for roughly $1.7 million. Morgan was one of New York City's wealthiest women, and she amassed her art holdings in the seven years succeeding the death of her husband, the iron, shipping, and railroad magnate Charles Morgan (1795–1878). Morgan's collection included American and European nineteenth-century paintings, prints from two continents created over four centuries—Martin Schongauer, Alsatian, c.1450–53 to Joseph Pennell, American, c.1860–1926—and decorative arts—carvings, pottery, sculpture, and silver—from America, Europe, China, and Japan. A widow without any children of her own, she died intestate on 7 July 1885. Morgan's sister Emily (1837–1905) and brother-in-law William Moir (1837–1905) served as executors of her estate. In addition to selling the art collection, they liquidated all of Morgan's assets—her brownstone, furnishings, jewelry and orchid collections—then divided the proceeds accordingly among her less fortunate heirs.

Mrs. Morgan's Collection of Paintings provides valuable insights into her methods of collecting and display, mainly because very few of Morgan's papers—correspondence, receipts—have survived. However, by indicating where each painting was hanging in Morgan's home in 1884, it provides a glimpse into her aesthetic choices. Comparing her publication against the 1886 auction catalog, one can surmise the paintings Morgan purchased after 1884 and those disbursed—either sold or traded in for other pictures—before the 1886 auction and presents an understanding of how she operated as a collector. Commissioned by Morgan, the book was printed by the American

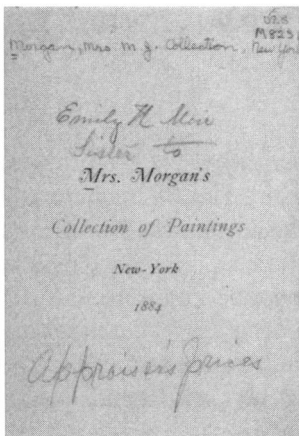

Mrs. Morgan's Collection of Paintings, New-York, 1884. New York: Theo L. de Vinne, 1884. Includes appraiser's price annotations. Gift of Mrs. Wilhelmina Waller, 1956.

printer and typography scholar Theodore Low De Vinne (1828–1914) at his publishing house. It was created to serve as a guide for those visiting her home and private galleries.

The first page of the catalog is annotated in pencil above the first two words of the title *Mrs. Morgan's*, with "Emily H. Moir" and "sister to". Below the full title is another annotation, "Appraiser's prices". All but twelve of the 207 entries are annotated with prices. The faux leather cover is embossed with a simple design and Morgan's initials "M.J.M.", in gold. The initials resemble her collector's mark, also "M.J.M.", which is stamped in blue ink on the back of several of the prints once owned by Morgan. She did not shy from burnishing her treasures with her brand. A set of custom-made porcelain plates and silver pieces from Tiffany & Co.—plateaus, wine coolers, and more—also bear her initials. These markings now serve as breadcrumbs in establishing the provenance for works once owned by her. The catalog measures almost six inches in length, three and a half inches wide, and is seventy-eight pages long. It fits ergonomically into the palm, and it is easy to imagine flipping through the pages while wandering through the rooms of Morgan's Madison Square brownstone musing about her collection.

The Library owns one of the few known remaining physical copies of the book, but unique in that it is the appraiser's copy. However, it has been digitized and is accessible via the Library's online catalog. It was given to the Frick Art Reference Library in 1956 by Mrs. Wilhelmina Waller, a granddaughter of the auctioneer Thomas Kirby.

—*Samantha Deutch*

68 Collecting Your Former Collection
1956 (1957)

Edward G. Robinson (1893–1973) is primarily known as an actor of the Hollywood Golden Era. He immigrated to New York City in 1904 and grew up on the Lower East Side. He married his first wife Gladys Lloyd, a stage actress, in 1927. The couple amassed an art collection that included many modern masterpieces. Their Tudor-style house in Beverly Hills, California, attracted thousands of visitors who wanted to see their art. Paintings by Degas, Van Gogh, Matisse, Modigliani, Picasso, Pissarro, Renoir, and Soutine could be found throughout the Robinsons' residence in very personal arrangements. For example, *The Willows* by Claude Monet could be found side-by-side with *Self-Portrait on a Bed* by Frida Kahlo. Edward purchased paintings from Kahlo in 1938 and was her first American collector. In 1941, the architect, designer, and interior decorator Samuel Marx designed a windowless, free standing art gallery on their property to show their collection. Twice a week the gallery was open to the general public.

In 1956, the divorce of Edward and Gladys forced the sale of their art collection. The Frick Art Reference Library holds the catalog for the exhibition of works they owned that were available for purchase. The exhibition traveled from the Los Angeles County Museum (Los Angeles County Museum of Art) to the California Palace of the Legion of Honor, San Francisco (Legion of Honor) from 1956 to 1957. The museum venues for the exhibition reflect the importance and fine quality of the Robinsons' collection. Artists such as Cézanne, Chagall, Degas, Van Gogh, Yasuo Kuniyoshi, Modigliani, Monet, Horace Pippin, Renoir, Soutine, and Grant Wood appeared in the exhibition. The Greek shipping magnate Stavros Niarchos purchased the collection in its entirety (fifty-eight canvases and one sculpture) for $3 million with the understanding that Edward could buy back works of art from his collection later. The Frick's copy of the exhibition catalog includes a tipped-in typewritten list from the dealer Knoedler & Co., which handled the sale of the collection, of the works purchased by Niarchos. The annotations on the sheet were done by Photoarchive staff.

Robinson was able to re-purchase fourteen of the works. With his second wife Jane Bodenheimer, Edward continued to collect art, eventually publish the book *Edward G. Robinson's World of Art* which is also held by the Frick. In addition to the published books, the Frick holds ephemera clippings of *Vogue* articles documenting the collection under both owners.

—*Suz Massen*

```
         GLADYS LLOYD ROBINSON - EDWARD G. ROBINSON COLLECTION
                        Schedule of 59 Items              Pictures here listed
                                                          were purchased by
  Cat. No.    Artist              Title                   Stavros Niarchos,
 Supply  2.   BONNARD     WOMAN SEATED IN STUDIO          Athens, Gr. per PWM.
    "    3.   BONNARD     NUDE (AFTER THE BATH)                   (1957)
    "    5.   BOUDIN      BEACH SCENE
    "    6.   BOUDIN      BEACH SCENE
 516h    7.   CEZANNE     THE BLACK CLOCK
 Supply  8.   CHAGALL     RABBI WITH TORAH
 522-7c  9.   COROT       L'ITALIENNE
 Supply 10.   DAUCHOT-GABRIEL  PARIS IN THE RAIN
 Supply 11.   DAUCHOT-GABRIEL  PORTRAIT OF A MAN WITH DOG
 556-3b 12.   DEGAS       DANCER LEAVING HER DRESSING ROOM
 Supply 13.   DEGAS       TWO DANCERS RESTING
 556-5a 14.   DEGAS       DANCERS IN PINK
 556-5d 15.   DEGAS       DANCERS IN GREEN
 Supply 16.   DEGAS       LA GRANDE DANSEUSE
 Supply 17.   DELACROIX   ODALISQUE
 Supply 18.   DERAIN      LA JOLIE MODELE
        19.   DUFRESNE C. STILL LIFE WITH CHRYSANTHEMUMS
 Supply 21.   FORAIN      COURT ROOM SCENE
 516-2c 22.   GAUGUIN     TAHITIAN FLOWERS
 518-8c 23.   GAUGUIN     HORSEMEN ON THE BEACH
 520-9d 24.   GERICAULT   MOUNTED TRUMPETER
 321-9c 25.   VAN GOGH    PORTRAIT OF PERE TANGUY
 317-19 26.   VAN GOGH    COUNTRY ROAD, ARLES
 Supply 27.   HOPPER, EDWARD  STREET SCENE - GLOUCESTER
 Supply 28.   KUNIYOSHI   DAILY NEWS
 520-2b 29.   MATISSE     DINNER TABLE (LA DESSERTE)
```

The Gladys Lloyd Robinson and Edward G. Robinson Collection. [Los Angeles]: [Anderson, Richie, and Simon], 1956.

69. From Medallions to Pop Art
1973

Robert C. Scull (1915–85) and his wife Ethel Scull (1921–2001) were fixtures in the New York City contemporary art scene from the 1950s through the 1970s. They married in 1944 and began building their wealth through an inherited share of a taxi fleet left to them after the retirement of Ethel's father. Robert grew the Super Operating Corporation, later known as the Scull's Angels, to include 130 taxis and 400 drivers. The couple started collecting Abstract Expressionism in the 1950s and held their first auction of works from their collection in 1965 to fund the Robert C. and Ethel Scull Foundation, which supported new artists by providing them with stipends, commissioning works, and paying for materials. Their focus moved from Abstract Expression to Pop and Minimal art.

On 18 October 1973, the Sculls sold fifty works at Sotheby Parke-Bernet to much fanfare. Ethel wore a Halston dress with the Scull's Angels logo emblazed across its front. A large crowd, and protests from the Taxi Rank and File Coalition, critical of Robert's treatment of workers, and Women in the Arts, critical of the fact that there was only one woman artist include in the auction, delayed its start. Other critics of the sale worried about contemporary American art being sold and exported to Europe instead of staying in its home country and the profits the Sculls were making from selling art they acquired at a low cost directly from the artists at high prices without benefiting the artists directly. The auction was such a spectacle that a film, conceptualized by E. J. Vaughn and John Schott, was produced and screened at the Whitney Museum of American Art in 1974. In the film the artist Robert Rauschenberg confronts Robert C. Scull about the profit he is making on the secondary market sale of his work and at the same time, he acknowledges that the Sculls gave support to artists when there was not much available. All fifty lots were sold with many garnering record-breaking prices. Lot 15 *Double White Map* (1965) by the artist Jasper Johns sold for $240,000, the highest amount paid at the time for a work by Johns, a work by an American living artist, a work of Pop Art, and a work of twentieth-century American art.

The Frick Art Reference Library holds a copy of the catalog that documents this historically significant sale that pushed the prices paid for contemporary American art to new levels. It has yellow covers that echo the checkered taxis that brought the Sculls their wealth.

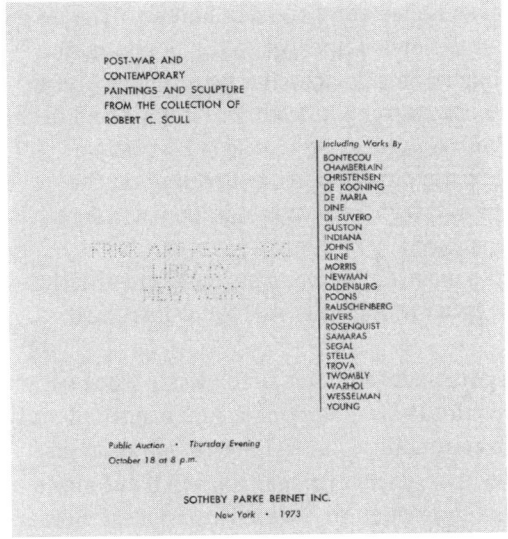

A Selection of Fifty Works from the Collection of Robert C. Scull. New York: Sotheby Parke Bernet, Inc., 1973.

The dust jacket that is missing from the Frick copy has an image of a bronze sculpture of two beer cans by Johns. The glossy pages of the catalog include entries with descriptive information about the works for sale as well as provenance, exhibition, and literature histories. Each lot is accompanied by a reproduction of the work it describes, with most in color and some fold-outs. The original estimates and pricelist accompany the copy at the Frick. The auction brought in $2,242,900.

—*Suz Massen*

70 The Exquisite Corpse
1976 (1948)

The *cadavre exquis*/exquisite corpse is the surrealist game involving folding a sheet of paper and each, usually of four, participant drawing four segments of the body, without the other participants seeing the previous contribution.

It initially started as literary game, based on the French game of *petits papiers*, related to the English game of consequences: the first two lines of the first instance of the game at Jacques Prévert, Yves Tanguy and Marcel Duhamel's house at 54 rue de Château, "The exquisite—corpse—shall drink—the new—wine", gave the phenomenon its name. The other participants on this occasion were André Breton and Benjamin Perét. This was sometime in 1925 and it appeared in the December 1931 issue of *Le Surréalisme au service de la Révolution*.

The game soon took an artistic direction, as, depending on the numbers, a head, torso, legs and feet were drawn in pencil, ink or crayon and even collage was used.

The visual exquisite corpse is posed between automatism and the entry of the psychographic into art, and this was what intrigued Breton.

The rules governing the game evolved over time, firstly black paper was introduced and then the fold was abandoned. And eventually it entered the art market as a commodity: in 1931 Breton would re-use his contribution to a 1927 corpse, *Silence* (cils, anse), as an autonomous work of art. It was also a medium open to the participation of women surrealists, such as Valentine Hugo.

This catalogue for the exhibition at the Galerie Nina Dausset, 19 rue du Dragon, Paris, 7–30 October 1948, has a preface by Breton which includes his definition of the exquisite corpse from the *Dictionnaire abrégé du surréalisme* (1938). It reflects the interest of the market in these surrealist artifacts by artists who were now becoming well known and commercially successful.

Simply produced with a card wrapper, pink endpapers and a simple red thread sewn binding, it recalls the exquisite corpse: the detachable outer card is folded in four.

—*Stephen Bury*

André Breton *Le cadavre exquis, son exaltation*. Paris: Galerie Nina Dausset, [1948]. Edition of 515 copies. Purchased through The Patrick A. Gerschel Fund, in memory of André Meyer, 1976.

71 Frick Art Reference Library Periodicals Index
1983 (1923, 1928, 1939, 2014)

Original index to art periodicals, the Frick Art Reference Library. Boston, Mass.: G. K. Hall, 1983.

In November 1923, the Library began indexing periodicals with the objective to create a comprehensive card catalog of English and French articles related to artists, artwork, art history and criticism. The selected publications focused on Western European and American painting, sculpture, drawing, and decorative arts from the fourth century C.E. through 1860. This first comprehensive index listed imprints from 1850 through the 1960s of important publications as *Gazette des Beaux-Arts* from 1859–1959, *L'Arte* from 1899–1952, and *The Burlington Magazine* from 1903–59. Imprints of Gazette des Beaux-Arts include detailed information on the Paris Salons in which the names of each participating artist are listed with the respective exhibitions. By 1928, the initiative expanded to articles from Italian publications that included *La Diana*, *Rassegna d'Arte Senese*, *Rivista d'Arte* etc.

In 1939 Catherine Sullivan began a second card catalog index that included articles in Eastern European languages. Both indices were added to until 1969. According to the Annual Reports of the Frick Art Reference Library for the years 1928–69, as many as ten librarians, library consultants, and assistants worked to compile the indices: they analyzed articles related to painting, sculpture, etchings, drawings, illuminated manuscripts, and mosaics, and more generally, those related to church architecture, iconography, and tapestry. In 1983, the Library with G. K. Hall, Boston, compiled the card catalog of the first index into a twelve-volume publication.

Both indices were arranged alphabetically with entries listed under the name of the article's author as well as under the name of the artist or other subject. Each entry card contains the author's name, the title of the article, the name of the journal, the volume, date, year, and pagination within the publication, as well as whether or not the article was illustrated. Exhibitions of a specific artist are often listed chronologically under the artist name followed by the term "exhibition", and then alphabetically by the city, gallery or museum, or author of the article in question. Articles on museum collections were filed under "Collections, Public", while those related to individual works in a public collection were filed by the city and collection followed by the artist's name. Similarly, articles on private collections were filed by "Collections, Private" and location, then alphabetically by the name of the collector. Individual works in a private collection that related to a specific artist were usually filed under the collection and then by the artist's name. The cards also provided information on exhibitions, provenance, and location of individual works at the time of the indexing.

In 2014, the Library worked with EBSCO, who had merged in 2011 with the H. W. Wilson Company, the owners of *Art Index* (1933–), to create a database that combined the information of the two Frick indices into one searchable online resource.

—Michelle McCarthy-Behler

72 The Plum Pudding in Danger
1989 (1805)

James Gillray (1756/57–1815) remains the doyen of British caricature—political and social—with his mordant wit and sense of the ludicrous, accompanied by a brilliant technique. He influenced many subsequent cartoonists/caricaturists such as Martin Honeysett (1943–2015) and Steve Bell (1951–).

Gillray began as a letter-engraver and later studied at the Royal Academy schools. 'Paddy on Horseback' of 1779 is his first attributable caricature. His publisher and companion was Miss Hannah Humphrey, whose shop was first at 227 The Strand, New Bond Street, then Old Bond Street and finally St. James's Street, which appeared in the caricature 'Very Slippy-Weather' (1808). Many cartoons lampooned George III, his ministers and the opposition. He detested the French Revolution, opposing the Jacobin with John Bull, and then found Napoleon an attractive target. With failing eyesight from 1806 and taking to drink in compensation, Gillray's output and quality declined, though he still produced prints until 1811, when he became insane.

The hand-colored etching, 'The Plum Pudding in Danger' (published 26 February 1805) is perhaps his most famous caricature. It depicts William Pitt (1759–1806), in regimental garb, but with a long sailor's pigtail (ironically it was the French sailor who wore their pigtails long), sitting at a round, white-clothed, table with Napoleon, carving a large plum pudding, giving off a cloud of white steam, in the form of a world globe. Pitt and Napoleon are using swords and forks (Pitt's  in the shape of a nautical trident). Napoleon is slicing off the landmass of Europe, whilst Pitt is taking the oceans. Interestingly, this predates the decisive defeat of the French and Spanish navies at Trafalgar in October 1805, and Napoleon's crushing land victory at Austerlitz in December 1805.

The Frick Art Reference Library was given an eleven-volume unpublished compilation of Gillray's political and social caricatures 1779–1811 by Leanore and Andrew Lawrence in 1989. They also donated a two-volume elephant folio of the 1851 Henry George Bohn (1796–1884) restrike, consisting of 627 plates.

—*Stephen Bury*

73 *Bric à brac*
1993 (1888)

Lord Ronald Charles Sutherland Gower (1845–1916), was the grandson of George Leveson-Gower involved in the Orléans sale/s consortium, and the youngest of the four sons of George, 2nd Duke of Sutherland: naturally he rails against primogeniture in *Bric à brac* (1888). He was the Member of Parliament for Sutherland 1867–74. But he was a sculptor, known for his 1888 monument of Shakespeare and four of his characters (Hamlet, Lady Macbeth, Prince Hal and Falstaff) in Stratford-upon-Avon. He may have been the prototype for the character Lord Henry Wotton in his friend Oscar Wilde's only novel *The Picture of Dorian Gray* (1890 in serial form, 1891 as a book). Like Wilde, Gower was a homosexual, but, unlike Wilde, his aristocratic background and connections helped him to evade Victorian society's criminal pursuit of the homosexual, even the aftermath of the Cleveland Street Scandal of 1889.

Bric à brac, was occasioned by Gower having photographs taken of the interior of Gower Lodge, Kings Road, Windsor, purchased in 1876 and which included many of the artworks in his collection. The photographer was Edward Dossetter (1843–1919), who is known for his photographs of First Nation peoples in British Columbia, but was in London 1885–89. He also made a photographic study of the Bayeux Tapestry for the South Kensington Museum (Victoria and Albert Museum) in 1872 and was commissioned by the British Museum to photograph prints. For Gower, Dossetter made Woodbury-type photo plates of the saloon and sitting rooms of Gower Lodge.

Gower's collection is obviously not at the level of his paternal grandfather, but is still of interest: it has been argued that it constituted a "queer" taste. The collection of Marie-Antoinette miniatures, medals and other related materials, described by Gower as "relics", could be argued anticipated the "queer" icon that Marie-Antoinette became from the late twentieth century, but this would be anachronistic. Also Gower had an intellectual interest in her with more a focus on her death than her earlier life, publishing a biography three years before in 1885, *Last Days of Marie Antoinette, an historical sketch*. The portraits were also sold at Christie's, 2 July 1889.

Medals and drawings were often the focus of an artist's collection, particularly of a sculptor. The entry for a red chalk Cupid by Giorgione lists a storied provenance—Mariette, Count Moritz von Fries, and Edward Cheney, with Gower buying it from the dealer Alphonse Wyatt Thibaudeau (*c*.1840–92).

Lord Ronald Gower *"Bric à brac", or some photoprints illustrating art objects at Gower Lodge, Windsor.* London: Kegan Paul, Trench & Co., 1888. Purchased from Marlborough Rare Books, London, 1993.

    Some of the paintings, e.g. Reynolds's *Lady Georgiana Spencer, Afterwards Duchess of Devonshire, as a Child* (c.1761) could have been family heirlooms, as Gower was her great-grandson—it was given in 1896 to the National Portrait Gallery, where he was a trustee. Likewise Holbein's *Portrait of an English Lady* seems to have been in the family too—and now in the British Museum. There are also seven late Georgian portrait drawings/studies by John Downman (1750–1824), including one of Queen Charlotte and another of Georgiana, Duchess of Devonshire, which too could have been in the family collection. But Gower's championing of the obscure Downman might well be a personal taste. And Gower's provenance notes in *Bric à brac* reveal purchases from Christies, Mr. Mackay at Colnaghi's and from the Mayer Collection sale in 1886

    And, of course, Gower had another home, Hammersfield, Penshurst so this was only a subset of his collection. Defrauded of a considerable sum by Francis Shackleton, brother of the Antarctic explorer, he had to sell Hammersfield. And his collection there was sold at auction at Christie's 28 January 1911, but it also included some Gower Lodge items, such as the Bronzino *Cupid* and the Millais *Constance Gower*.

—*Stephen Bury*

74 *Clock Work**
1999

In addition to the generous gift of forty antique clocks and watches left to The Frick Collection in 1999 by Winthrop Kellogg Edey (1937–99), a renowned watch and clock collector, the Frick Art Reference Library received his extensive library and archives. Along with books on horology, automata, and decorative arts (over 1,400 were accessioned into the library's printed materials collections), which greatly enhanced the library's holdings in these subject areas, Edey's research archives and his diaries were also given to the Frick.

The *c*.1823 drawing of the mantel regulator clock movement by Charles Mugnier illustrated here was included in Edey's archive of over forty linear feet of research materials the Frick received related to his own collection as well as to the overall horological research he undertook over the decades. The Edey bequest to The Frick Collection also included a Mugnier clock (1823), Accession no.1999.5.153, with a movement that appears to be identical to the drawing

Winthrop Kellogg Edey formed one of the world's finest private collections of clocks and watches over the course of several decades, buying clocks in his youth and upgrading over the years. His particular interests lay with French and English clocks and their technical developments over the course of the sixteenth to nineteenth centuries. A press release accompanying the 2001 exhibition of his clocks and watches at the Frick *The Art of the Timekeeper: Masterpieces from the Winthrop Edey Bequest* noted "He kept his collection at his home in New York City, where he maintained an eccentric, private and somewhat nocturnal lifestyle, surrounded by his remarkable English and French long case clocks, mantel clocks, and stacks of books and catalogues".

The Frick also holds Edey's personal diaries, which he began to write at the age of twelve and continued to write until his death. Interspersing details of his clock and watch research interests, purchases and other scholarly pursuits within the broader narrative of his daily—or rather nightly—life, the diaries will one day be opened to researchers interested in his life which encompassed the fervent, exciting life of New York City and the world of art, celebrity, nightlife and his involvement in the gay world from the 1950s until his death.

—Sally Brazil

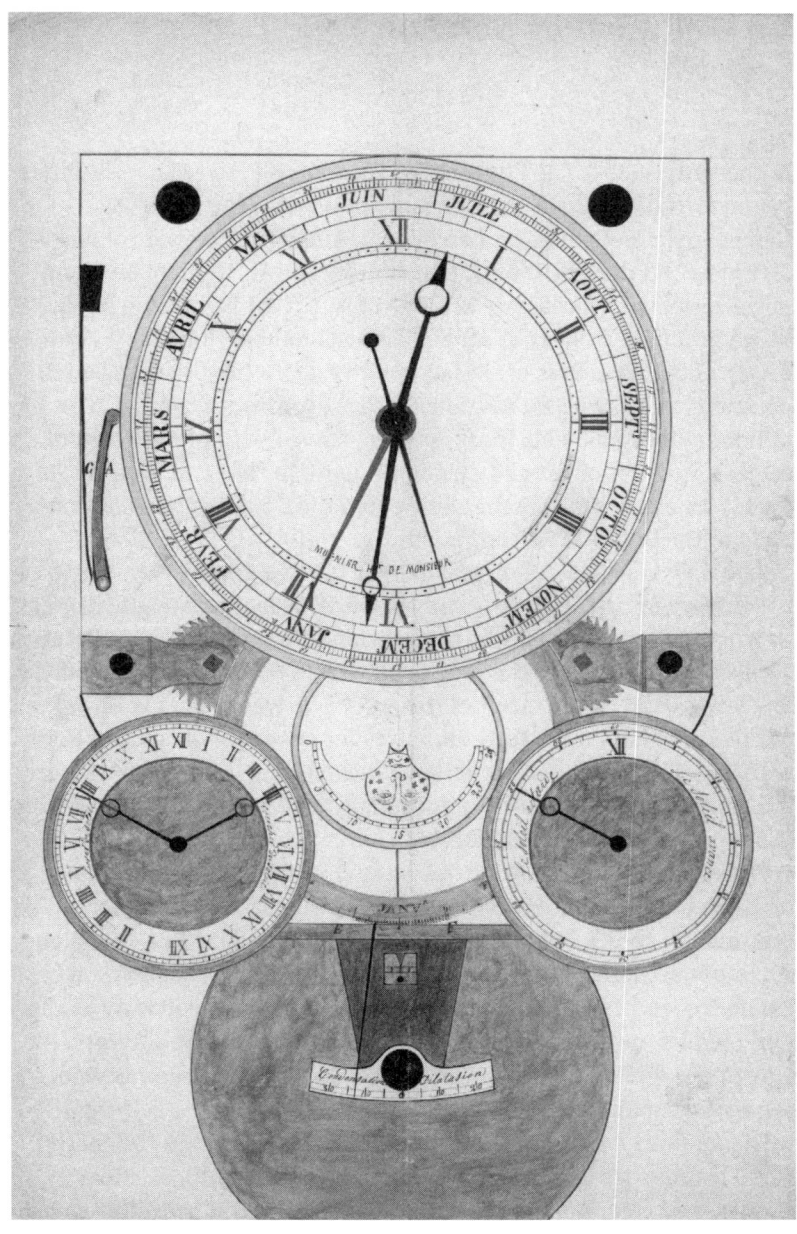

Drawing of Mantel Regulator Clock movement, *c.*1823. Movement by Charles Mugnier. Winthrop Kellogg Edey Bequest, 1999.

75 The Montias Database
2000

In the early 1980s, Yale Professor of Economics John Michael Montias began recording details of ownership of works of art from the Gemeentearchief (municipal archive) in Amsterdam as part of his own work on the prices of Dutch paintings at Amsterdam auctions in the seventeenth century. His love of Dutch art had begun when he was a graduate student of economics at Columbia University. For his dissertation, he at first proposed to write about the prices of Dutch paintings at Amsterdam auctions in the seventeenth century. This idea, although rejected by his thesis advisor, stayed with him throughout his career as an economist and during his work in the Delft archives. It was for his scholarly projects that he created the database installed since 2000 at the Frick Art Reference Library.

Originally, in 1986, Montias had been given a grant by the Getty Art History Information Program (now the Getty Research Institute) to work in conjunction with its Provenance Index. He was one of the earliest contributors to the Index, which had been established only a few years earlier. As a result of this grant, he was well in the forefront of the use of databases and computers for art history research. Not realizing their potential, especially for compiling the kind of detailed information that Montias was collecting, very few art historians were using personal computers in 1986.

When Montias formally parted ways with the Getty in the 1990s, he needed a home for his database. His first idea for a home, the Rijksbureau voor Kunsthistorische Documentatie (RKD) in The Hague, could not accommodate his technical needs. Happily, the Frick Art Reference Library was then using the same database software as the Getty, which meant that it could easily take in his valuable work. An agreement was made with the RKD that the two institutions would serve as co-sponsors.

The Montias database currently contains transcriptions of nearly 1,300 inventories drawn up between 1596 and 1681 for auctions, estates, and creditors in Amsterdam. They list a total of 51,071 works of art, including drawings, prints, paintings and sculpture. Although Montias did not have enough time to transcribe all seventeenth-century Amsterdam inventories, he chose an extremely useful cross-section.

The Montias database is a deep and valuable resource that can be used in a multitude of ways. For example, one can see if and when an artist's paintings were bought and sold, to or by whom, and often, their price. One could compare and assess the value of works by single artists over time, or compare the value of their works with that of other artists who executed works in the same genre. Charts could be made of the popularity of particular genres of painting over time, as measured by numbers in collections and by the value placed on them. Because the database indicates the room of a house where a work hung, one can determine the importance that seventeenth-century Amsterdammers assigned to particular genres or even particular artists.

Our 2021 digital art history fellow will be working on this dataset investigating the role of women as artists, collectors and dealers.

—*Louisa Wood Ruby*

Frick Family Papers
2001 (1913, 2015)

The Library is fortunate to hold an extraordinary archive of Frick family papers spanning the mid-nineteenth to the late twentieth centuries. This archive, a cornerstone of the collections under the care of the Frick's Archives Department, came to the Library on deposit in 2001 and was donated in 2015 by the Helen Clay Frick Foundation. The Foundation supported work on the project over many years and the Library and Collection are extremely grateful for the financial support that allowed the archive to be preserved, documented and made available to the public.

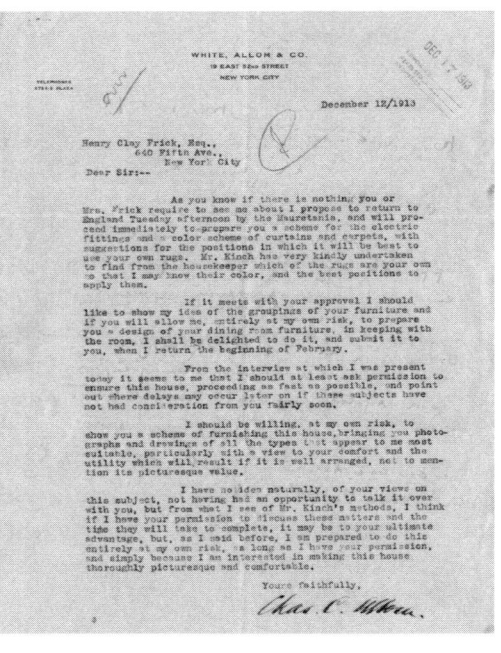

The letter illustrated here is part of a particularly rich series within these records that documents the real estate acquisition, building plans and construction of the Frick family home at One East 70th Street from 1907 to 1914 when Mr. and Mrs. Frick and their daughter, Helen, moved into the house and through the years until the house began the transition from house to museum in 1931.The letter draft, in Mr. Frick's hand, is written to Sir Charles Allom (1865–1947), who was responsible for the interior decoration of the downstairs rooms of the home as well as Mr. Frick's private rooms upstairs (Elsie de Wolfe (c.1859–1950) also decorated portions of the upstairs rooms). In it, Frick states "We desire a comfortable well arranged home, simple, in good taste, and not ostentatious".

Upon the death of Henry Clay Frick in 1919 the terms of his will stipulated that after his wife, Adelaide Frick, passed away, the house was to become a public museum. The Frick Collection opened in 1935, four years after the 1931 death of Mrs. Frick. This letter is one document in a records series containing architectural records, correspondence, accounts documentation, contracts, receipts and inventories to and from Frick, his representatives, architects, interior designers, engineers and tradespeople, amounting to nearly thirteen linear feet of materials.

The One East 70th Street Papers series constitute a small portion of the Frick Family papers, which are comprised of approximately 1,200 linear feet of materials. This archive is the essential starting place for researchers interested in the Frick family (especially Henry Clay Frick, his wife Adelaide and children Childs Frick and Helen Clay Frick), the construction and maintenance of other Frick properties in Pittsburgh

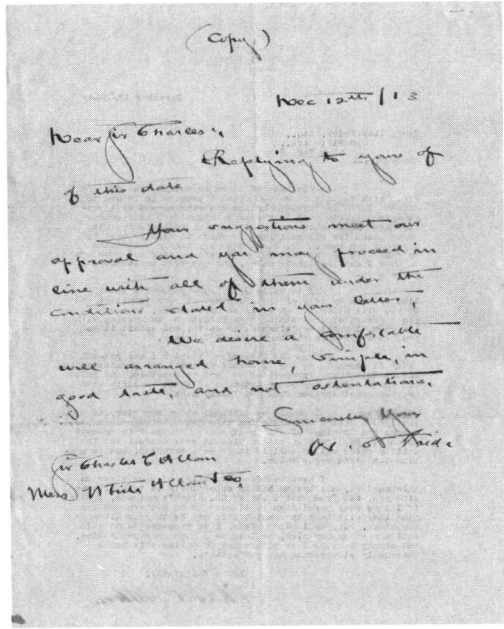

Letter from Henry Clay Frick to Sir Charles Allom, 12 December 1913.

and Massachusetts, the philanthropic and cultural activities the family supported and the day-to-day minutiae of their lives as Gilded Age representatives at the wealthiest end of the human spectrum. It is also of great utility to those studying material culture of this period.

—*Sally Brazil*

77 Helen Clay Frick debuts
2001 (1908–09, 2015)

Helen Clay Frick's early education took place at Clayton, the Frick family home in Pittsburgh. Under the tutelage of Swiss governess Marika Ogiz, she studied foreign languages, music, history, mythology, science, mathematics, and other subjects. In 1905, Henry Clay Frick relocated his family to the Vanderbilt mansion at 640 Fifth Avenue in New York, and Helen Clay Frick enrolled at Miss Spence's School for Girls in New York, graduating in 1908. Although Henry Clay Frick would have preferred his daughter's debut to take place in New York, Helen's allegiance was to Pittsburgh, and she was presented to society at Clayton on her mother's forty-ninth birthday: 16 December 1908.

Miss Frick assembled a scrapbook to commemorate the occasion, using a lilac-bound book bearing pages decorated by cherubs and garlands of roses. She ignored the book's suggestion to record guests' names, gown samples, and shopping trips, choosing instead to populate the volume mostly with clippings. One after another, these clippings document the receptions, dinners, bridge parties, teas, luncheons, theater parties, and dances that made up the Pittsburgh social season. The amount of press coverage given to these events is remarkable, exhaustively detailing décor and music, gowns and guest lists. Indeed, one account in the *Pittsburgh Index* makes a wry reference to the glut of entertainments, noting that there were invitations "two or three deep for every hour of every day for the last fortnight", and that "one could wish they might spread out a little more and give one a chance to rest up between times".

The scrapbook also holds the only two extant images of the reception at Clayton. The first of these is a view of the parlor bedecked with flowers for the occasion. Described as "a summer of bloom" in one clipping, this image only hints at the profusion of color in the hundreds of bouquets placed throughout the Frick residence. The second image is a portrait of Miss Frick with her mother and a small group of friends surrounded by flowers and greenery in the house's reception room. The photograph, however, is rather curious in its composition. Helen is seated at the far right, captured in profile while her mother is seated at the center of the group. The remaining women (counter-clockwise from back right) are Virginia Frew, Katharine McCook, Mary Painter, Renee Gourd, and Eleanor Whitney. Misses McCook, Gourd, and Whitney came from New York and assisted in receiving guests, while Misses Frew and Painter were daughters of prominent Pittsburgh families and were also aids at the event.

Clippings that appear later in the volume mark a more mature phase of life for Helen Clay Frick and her circle. Her childhood friend Virginia Frew was among the first of her friends to wed, marrying Thruston Wright about six months after the debut. Miss Frick kept numerous clippings recounting her friend's wedding in which she herself was maid of honor. Other friends seen in the debut photo would also marry, though none of those occasions are commemorated in the scrapbook. (Renee Gourd married in 1909; Katharine McCook in 1911, but divorced in 1916; Mary Painter in 1924, but a widow two years later; and Eleanor Whitney would marry her sister's widower in 1914.)

Helen Clay Frick chose not to marry, making philanthropy and family the focus of her adult life. In addition to requesting a park for the children of Pittsburgh as a debut present from her father, clippings here report the lease of a farm in Massachusetts in the summer of 1909. That summer marked the first of many offerings of respite to the overworked girls in the shoe factories and textile mills outside of Boston. The scrapbooks are part of the Frick Family Papers, deposited at the Library in 2001 and donated in 2015 by the Helen Clay Frick Foundation.

—*Julie Ludwig*

78 *The Heim Sale*
2005 (1861, 1897, 1954, 2012, 2019)

The Heim Gallery was founded in Paris by François Heim in 1954: it specialized in Old Masters. Heim was also a great collector of sales catalogs and amassed *c.*25,000 of them, with an ink stamp on the verso of each title page. The Bibliothèque Heim was housed in a Paris suburb and after many legal disputes most of it was sold, appropriately itself in an auction, conducted by Christophe Lucien at Nogent-sur-Marne 26–30 July 2005.

Heim had bought many of his catalogs from the Rouen-based widow of Marcel Noelle (1871–1934), a former curator at Lille and the Louvre, who helped found the dealership Trotti et Cie in 1901, initially at the rue Royale, Paris. Noelle himself had acquired the collections of the dealers and collectors, G. and [H]Enry Pannier, who had their own book plates—Enry's included a basket or pannier. And the collection of the Panniers included some twenty catalogues from the Goncourt collection of catalogs, known as the Bibliothèque d'Auteuil, annotated by Edmond de Goncourt (1822–96), and sold at auction in 1897.

At the Heim sale in 2005, the Frick Art Reference Library acquired 109 auction catalogs and three collection catalogs primarily from the eighteenth and early nineteenth centuries. Four have notations indicating that they belonged to Marcel Noelle, and one may be from the brothers Goncourt, though it lacks the red percaline cover distinctive of that collection. Twenty-five have the bookplate of G. Pannier and sixteen that of Enry Pannier. From 2012 the Library started to collect Heim items that came up on the market: forty more catalogs have been added, bringing items with G. Pannier bookplates to forty-two, and Enry Pannier bookplates to nineteen.

The initial purchase, made possible by the generous assistance of Melvin R. Seiden and Philip Anderegg, reinforced the very strong collection of sales catalogs, based on the early acquisition of the Anton Mensing Collection in 1921 and the gift by Daniel Fellows Platt in 1930. The Frick Art Reference Library has acquired and still acquires antiquarian, new and digital auction catalogs to support research into provenance and the history of collecting. Many of the earlier catalogs are digitized and freely available through the Library's catalog, the Internet Archive and the Getty Portal.

—*Stephen Bury*

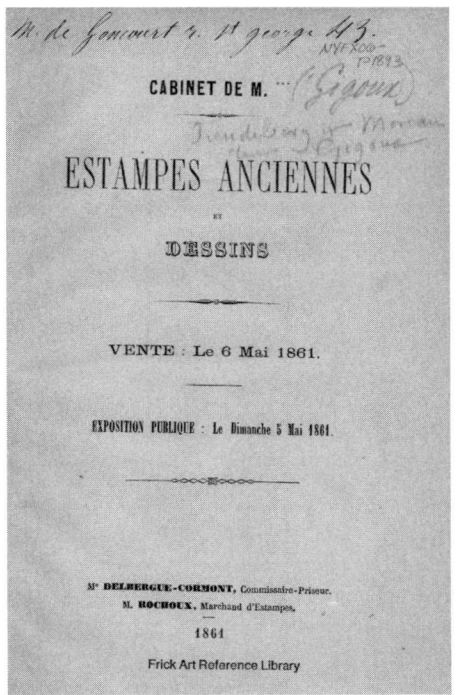

Estampes anciennes: pieces de diverses écoles, portraits, dessins, parmi lesquels plusiers des scenes de moeurs du XVIIIe siècle, par Moreau jeune et Freudeberg: un dessin par Charlet: cabinet de M***. Paris: [Hotel Drouot], 1861. Sale 6 May 1861.

With the annotation, opposite front cover, "exemplaire achat de la vente de Goncourt. Les dessins annoté 'a moi' se retrouvent dans sa collection". Purchase made possible through the generous assistance of Melvin E. Seiden and Philip Anderegg, 2005.

79 The History of Collecting Archives Directory
2010 (2007, 2011, 2017)

The Archives Directory for the History of Collecting is an online resource created to help researchers locate primary source material about American art collectors, dealers, advisors, etc. and the repositories that hold these records. The need for the Directory was first identified during the planning stages—meetings and colloquia—of the founding the Center for the History of Collecting at the Frick Art Reference Library. Hypothesized at the time that along with the Center's other programs—research fellowships, symposia, publications, oral histories, and book prizes—it would encourage new research. In 2007, Samantha Deutch was brought onboard to spearheaded the project, and by January of 2010 the first edition was published. Deutch won the Art Libraries Society of North America's Worldwide Books Award for Electronic Resources in 2011, for her work on the Directory. It serves an international community of museum, academic, and art professionals, most notably those seeking to chronicle the history of collecting in America.

The scope of the Directory goes beyond that of The Frick Collection and Frick Art Reference Library, including collectors and dealers of Ancient, African, Contemporary, and Indigenous Art. It includes more than 2,233 entries—collectors, dealers, etc.—pointing to approximately 8,885 archive collections. In addition to historical figures where the locations of their archives are known, it references information about those whose archives were deliberately destroyed or lost, such as the Massachusetts collector George W. V. Smith (1832–1923), who ordered the destruction of his correspondence upon his death. Entries feature a short biography, decades of activity, locations, and links to related entries. There are notes in the back end of the database, containing approximately 5,000 files documenting sources.

Most people find their way to the Archives Directory through an Internet search for a specific person or gallery: the Directory was the first database at the Frick Collection to be open to search engines. Once in the Directory, users can browse via a search bar, alphabetical list, or a map search interface. The map search application allows users to browse the Directory much as they might search Yelp or Google Maps for a restaurant. The dynamic search enables users to enter a "keyword" coupled with a specific "role", choose a date range with a sliding bar, and search by gender (assigned at birth). This type of searching facilitates connections which would be hidden in a single-person search. For example: if we add "Monet" as our keyword; "collector" for role, from the dropdown menu, select 1880–1960 as years active, and "F" for gender, we would get a map with a black dot to the far left in California, one in Chicago, many along the East Coast, and one in France. When we select the point in California, a window opens with an entry for the actress and collector Elizabeth Taylor. When viewing the full entry, we discover that her father, Francis Taylor (1897–1968), and uncle, Howard Young (1878–1972), were art dealers, at one time in business together. Whereas with the Pop Art collector Robert C. Scull (1917–86), in addition to his wife, Ethel, we are directed to the Green Gallery, where he was a financial backer. There are many more stories to be unearthed in the Directory and we are working on exploitation of the data for digital art history. Today, over 100,000 people use the Directory annually, and it is freely available over the Library's website.

The Directory has been generously supported by Melvin R. Seiden, Townsend I. Burden, Peter Blanchard, DeCourcy E. McIntosh, Juan Sabater, an anonymous donor, the Billy Rose Foundation and the Gladys Krieble Delmas Foundation.

—*Samantha Deutch*

Web Archiving*
2010 (2014)

Web archives were first added to the collections of the Frick Art Reference Library in 2010, as part of an investigation by the library to best address the shifting publication landscape of auction sale data being made available solely online in a web-based format, versus having been published in a print catalog format and historically collected by the library for scholarly reference. Web archiving is the process of collecting portions of the Web, preserving the collections in an ISO standard archival format, called a WARC file (or WebArchive file), and providing access to view and use the archived websites as they originally existed online at a specific point in time.

The Frick Art Reference library is a founding member of the New York Art Resources Consortium (NYARC), which was formed in 2006 and consists of the research libraries and archives of the Brooklyn Museum, The Frick Collection, and The Museum of Modern Art. NYARC formally established its consortial web archiving program in January 2014 in an effort to address the growing shift to web-based publishing of materials pertinent to the study of art and art history. A planning and an implementation grant were provided by the Andrew W. Mellon Foundation.

Given the impermanence of most web-based content, NYARC has continued to archive significant online art resources within the collecting scope of the three institutions. As of early 2021 the collections have amassed 8.5 terabytes of web archive data. These are also backed up in Duracloud. The web archive collections of NYARC include the archived websites of the Brooklyn Museum, The Frick Collection, and The Museum of Modern Art, the NYARC website and related born-digital project websites, art resources, auction house websites and their embedded auction catalogs, artists' websites, catalogues raisonnés, New York City gallery and art dealer websites, and websites related to the scholarship surrounding restitution efforts for lost and looted art. NYARC's rich web archives are publicly accessible and can be viewed and searched via the consortium's Archive-It collections page: *archive-it.org/organizations/484* and through its Primo discovery layer.

—*Sumitra Duncan*

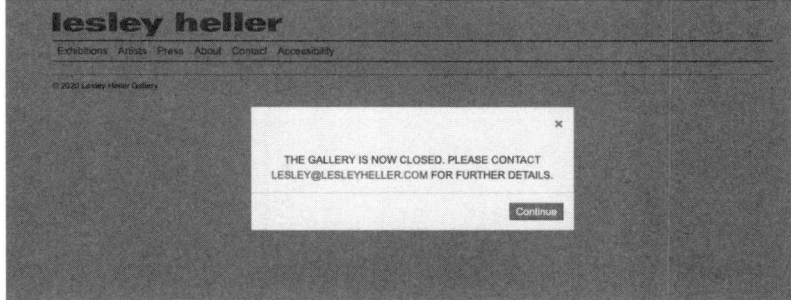

THE GALLERY IS NOW CLOSED. PLEASE CONTACT LESLEY@LESLEYHELLER.COM FOR FURTHER DETAILS.

81. Golden Age Spanish Art in the Gilded Age*
2012 (2008)

In the fall of 2008, the Frick Art Reference Library's Center for the History of Collecting, Centro de Estudios Europa Hispánica (CEEH), and the Center for Spain in America (CSA) organized and hosted a two-day symposium in honor of preeminent scholar Jonathan Brown, now the Carroll and Milton Petrie Professor Emeritus of Fine Arts at NYU, IFA. Jonathan Brown is known for his groundbreaking work in the history of collecting, Spanish and New Spanish painting, 1500–1800. The notion of a Center for the History of Collecting originated with Brown, and he was a guiding force in its development and success. Thus, the publication *Collecting Spanish Art: Spain's Golden Age and America's Gilded Age* is a fitting tribute to Jonathan Brown and his scholarly pursuits, from which we have all benefited. Brown also introduced Inge Reist, then Director of the Center for the History of Collecting, now Emerita, to the art historian José Luis Colomer the Director of CEEH and CSA. The symposium and subsequent publication marked the beginning of a fruitful relationship leading to another symposium (2015) and publication (2017) on collecting the artist El Greco; *El Greco Comes to America: The Discovery of a Modern Old Master*. More recently, the ongoing collaborative efforts have led to a volume with essays in honor of Inge Reist: *"What's Mine Is Yours": Private Collectors and Public Patronage in the United States* (2021).

Collecting Spanish Art: Spain's Golden Age and America's Gilded Age, edited by Inge Reist and José Luis Colomer. New York: Frick Collection in association with Centro de Estudios Europa Hispánica, Madrid, & Center for Spain in America, New York, 2012.

Many of the contributors to the volume *Collecting Spanish Art* were past students of Jonathan Brown's and represented major institutions across the United States and Spain: Museo del Prado, Madrid; National Gallery of Art, Washington, D.C.; Meadows Museum, Dallas; Museo de Bellas Artes de Sevilla, etc. The publication comprises three sections: the formation of the taste for Spain, great collectors of Spanish art, and the American taste for the great masters. The authors examine how the taste for Spanish art grew from travel and visits to world fairs, such as the Philadelphia Centennial and Chicago's World's Columbian Exposition, and the roles of contemporary artists, dealers, and advisors who were influential in importing Spanish works of art to the United States. The publication includes case studies examining how and why America's most well-known art collectors—Isabella Stewart Gardner, Henry Clay Frick, William Randolph Hearst, Archer Milton Huntington, and others—augmented and enriched their collections with the art of Spain.

From commissioning Walter W. S. Cook to collect photographs of Spanish works of art in 1922, to work on the print (1993–96) and later online *Spanish Artists from the Fourth to the Twentieth Century: A Critical Dictionary*, the hosting of the archives of Jonathan Brown, the prominent art historian specializing in Spanish art, to this symposium and its publication, the support for the study of Spanish Art has been a major *leitmotiv* of the Library's history.

—Samantha Deutch

The Artist as Tavern Keeper
2013 (1797)

Thomas Keyse (1721–1800) was a self-taught artist and a founder member of the Free Society of Artists with whom he exhibited 1761–73. He also exhibited at the Society of Arts 1765–68 and had two works—no.94, *Fruit Piece*, and no.545, *Flower Piece*—shown at the Royal Academy in 1799. In 1764 (1768 in some accounts), the Society of Arts awarded him thirty guineas for devising a method of fixing crayon drawings. Around 1765 Keyse became the tavern-keeper of the Waterman's Arms, Bermondsey, south of the River Thames: his homemade cherry-brandy was highly praised. Around 1770, a chalybeate spring was discovered, and Keyse decided to re-open the tavern as a pleasure ground called the Bermondsey Spa. In 1784, he obtained a music license from the Surrey magistrates and burlettas, musical interludes, solos, and duets were performed: the organist Jonas Blewitt composed some of the music. Poems were supplied by a Mr. J. Oakman and a Mr. Harriss. Copies of the words of the burlettas and the gallery catalog could be purchased for sixpence. A Gallery of Paintings included Keyse's representations of greengrocers, fishmongers, poulterers, and a famous butcher's shop.

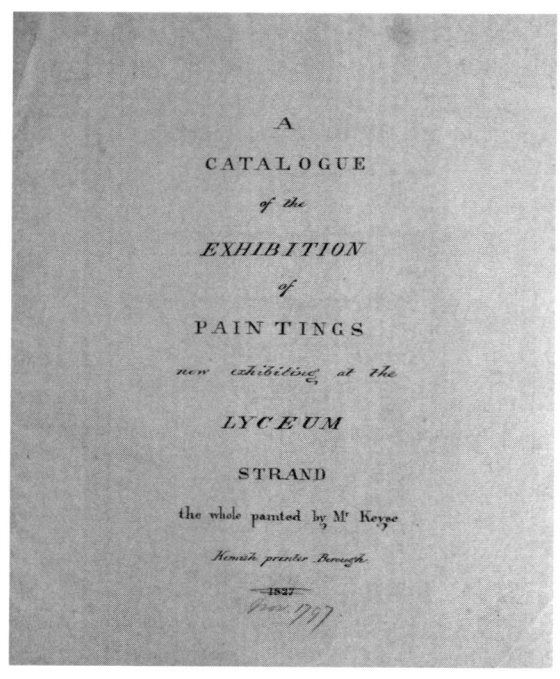

Catalogue of an exhibition of paintings now exhibiting at the Lyceum Strand the whole painted by Mr. Keyse is an eight-page manuscript in ink. It looks like a maquette for a printed catalog, as the manuscript hand imitates typography. And it has the imprint "Kemish printer Borough" on its cover. Intriguingly, there is a date of "1827", crossed out in pencil and "Nov 1797" inserted. There are seventy-two paintings of which seven are starred as for sale, mainly works not by Keyse. Painting no.51 is described as "lately painted by Mr. Keyse at the age of seventy-eight years". Keyse may have been born in 1721, which would give an approximate date of 1799 and most likely before Keyse died on 8 February 1800: otherwise it would have said "painted by the late Mr. Keyse". Many of the Keyse's paintings were auctioned by Peter Coxe, Burrell & Foster on Thursday 4 August 1803, which would thus make a date of 1827 extremely unlikely.

To add to the mystery, this manuscript was accompanied by a fragment of a printed catalog, which lacks a title page and the first four pages, so we do not know its title. There seem to be no other library holdings for comparison.

This is probably the Bermondsey Spa version of the printed catalog, perhaps entitled *Catalogue of an exhibition of paintings now exhibiting at Bermondsey Spa the whole painted by Mr. Keyse*, although this has not been found in any library holding. John Thomas Smith (1766–1833) in *A Book for a Rainy Day* (first and posthumous edition published in 1845) recorded under the year 1795 that the Spa was "most rapidly on the decline", and it is likely that from 1797 the collection was shown at the Lyceum, which had been built by the Society of Artists (of which Keyes was a member) in 1772 for exhibitions by their member artists. Whether this move was a seasonal one—perhaps just for the winter season—is not known. The entries for the paintings in the print catalogue are accompanied by poetry describing the works and almost giving it the feel of a live gallery tour, accompanying the visitors as they move through the gallery painting by painting.

So the manuscript copy may well be the maquette for a printed version of the catalogue of Keyse's works for the show at the Lyceum.

—*Stephen Bury*

83 *Independence*
2013 (1900)

Heriberto Frías's *Miguel Hidalgo y Costilla, padre de la Independencia* (1900) is a slight sixteen-page booklet less than five inches high. Part of the series 'Biblioteca del niño' (The Mexican boy's library), and published by the Spanish publisher, Maucci Hermanos, it is plainly intended to be a cheap and accessible means of mass education.

Hidalgo (1753–1811) was regarded the father of Mexican Independence from Spain, although it was Agustín de Iturbide (1783–1824) who finally achieved Mexican Independence in 1821. From a *criollo* family, Hidalgo was trained by the Jesuits before their expulsion in 1767 and became a priest in 1778. He was multi-lingual—with, besides Latin, Nahuatl, Otomi, Purépecha, Italian and French—the latter allowing him to read banned Enlightenment texts. He became rector of the Colegio de San Nicolás Obispo in Valladolid where he introduced novel teaching practices, which contributed to his dismissal in 1792. In 1802 he became the parish priest of Dolores, where he delegated most of his religious duties to a vicar, and instead encouraged the Indians, *mestizos* and *castas* to cultivate crops using the natural resources of the local area. This brought him into conflict with the mercantilist policies of the *Peninsulares*. He was also a member of the conspiratorial Querétaro group. On 16 September 1810, after Mass Hidalgo gave the *Grito de Dolores* (Cry of Dolores), calling on everyone to join him in a rebellion against the current government, ostensibly at this stage in the name of the king. At one point he had 80,000 in his army under the banner of the Virgin of Guadalupe. He defeated the government forces several times, sacked several towns, but inexplicably did not take the opportunity to attack Mexico City when he could have. His forces disintegrated and the government forces became more effective. Hidalgo was captured and executed on 30 July 1811. The father of eight illegitimate children with four partners despite the priest's vow of chastity, he was probably not the most perfect role model for young boys.

The cover of this booklet has a mechanically produced chromolithograph cover by José Guadalupe Posada (1852–1913), the Mexico City based political lithographer, who created over 20,000 images, with his signature skulls and skeletons, which inspired Diego Rivera and José Clemente Orozco.

—*Stephen Bury*

Heriberto Frías *Miguel Hidalgo y Costilla, padre de la Independencia*. México: Maucci Hermanos, 1900. Gift of Stephen J. Bury, 2013.

84 *Walter Gay Archive*
2014 (2017)

Helen Clay Frick and her mother, Adelaide Frick, commissioned Walter Gay (1856–1937) to paint three paintings, *The Fragonard Room*, *The Boucher Room* and *The Living Hall*, 1926–28, and they are all now at the Frick Pittsburgh. These empty interiors, where furniture and fittings reflect the makers', original and later owners' tastes, mark the change that had happened in Gay's work in 1902 and are very different to the paintings that were in the photograph of Gay in his Parisian studio in the Stokes collection at the Library.

Born in Hingham, Massachusetts in 1856, he moved to Paris, where he was a pupil of Léon Bonnat, who encouraged him to travel to Spain where he became familiar with the work of Velázquez and Fortuny. From around 1884 he began to paint peasant scenes e.g. *Étaples, Novembre* (1885). The 2017 gift by Peter Heydon of fourteen medals awarded to Gay, show how successful an artist he was: he won a gold painting medal (third class) at the 1888 salons, the Expositions Universelles of 1889 and 1900, with other prizes at international exhibitions at Vienna, Munich, Dresden. He helped many American artists navigate and exhibit in the Parisian art world. In 1894 he was made a chevalier of the Légion d'Honneur, an officer in 1906, and a commander in 1927. He bequeathed his substantial collection of artworks to the Louvre in 1937.

He met his wife, Matilda (*née* Travers), a rich expatriate New York heiress, in Paris, and they married (in London) in 1889: they had an apartment on the Left Bank, but in 1907 acquired the château Bréau, adjoining the Forest of Fontainebleau. From 28 February 1904 she kept a diary or record of travels until 1934. Friends and acquaintances mentioned included Bernard Berenson, Helen Clay Frick, Henry James, John Singer Sargent, Edith Wharton and the eccentric Comte de

Montesquiou-Fézensac, the model of Huysmans's Des Esseintes and Proust's Baron Charlus, and the subject of Whistler *Arrangement in Black and Gold* (1891–92) in The Frick Collection. Matilda records every dinner the Gays gave or attended, where the guests sat and what they said, and what she thought of their opinions.

The diaries—in manuscript and typescript—form part of an archive that the Library acquired in 2014. It had been assembled by Arthur T. Garrity, Jr., Hingham, Massachusetts—the Matilda Gay diaries acquired from the 1985 estate sale of Sophie Gay Griscom, niece of Walter and Matilda Gay. Together with the Peter Heydon gift of medals, and materials already in the Library e.g. the signed, limited edition and privately printed *The Memoirs of Walter Gay* (1930), this constitutes a considerable resource for the study of Walter Gay and his times.

—Stephen Bury

85. A Woman Artist at the Vienna Secession*
2014 (1902, 2014)

Just two women—interestingly both Russian—exhibited in the early years of the Vienna Secession: the sculptor Teresa Ries (1874–1956) and the painter, sculptor, printmaker and applied artist Elena Luksch-Makowsky (1878–1967), but only the latter took part in the Klinger Beethoven installation (Exhibition XIV) of 1902.

ORIG.-HOLZSCHNITT VON ELENA LUKSCH-MAKOVSKY.

Elena's father, Vladimir Makowsky (1846–1920), was a Russian court artist but in 1870 became a member of the *Peredvizhniki* or The Wanderers, an exhibiting organization of anti-academic and realist painters. Her uncle, Konstantin Makowsky (1839–1915) was also affiliated with this group. Elena trained with Ilya Repin (1844–1930) at the St. Petersburg Academy 1894-96, and won a scholarship to study in Munich with the Slovene realist painter, Anton Azbe (1862–1905). Two years later she returned to St. Petersburg to study sculpture under Vladimir Beklemischeff. She married the Austrian sculptor Richard Luksch (1872–1936) and moved to Vienna in 1900.

Luksch was a member of the Vienna Secession. As a woman, Elena could not be a member of the Secession, but as the wife of a member she could exhibit, and she did regularly from 1900 to 1903. She seems to have shared the Klimt Group's philosophy that artwork should be used to articulate space—*Raumkunst*—rather than the viewpoint of the rival Secession group, led by Josef Engelhart, who stressed the autonomy of individual works of art, and that Secession exhibitions should prioritize the sale of work. The twenty-one artists who took part in the Klinger Beethoven exhibition realized that the works they contributed were only temporary—only Gustav Klimt's *Beethovenfries* outlived, somewhat fortuitously, the exhibition.

Elena contributed two panel pieces, *Death and Time*, a painting on silicate with beaten copper, and *Sadko's Viewing of the Brides*, casein with metal inlay, which were set into the rough stucco walls of the

XIV. Ausstellung der Vereinigung bildender Künstler Österreichs Secession Wien: Klinger, Beethoven: April–Juni 1902. Wien: s.n., 1902.

right side room, located under Ferdinand Andri's frieze, *Man's Courage in Battle*, and opposite Josef Auchenthaler's frieze, *The Joy of Godliness*, and the cutaway windows through which could be seen Klinger's polychrome Beethoven statue.

The Sadko subject matter reflects Elena's increasing pre-occupation with Russian folk tales, proverbs and folk art. This is also evident in her color woodcuts in the Beethoven catalogue, and in the special issue of *Ver Sacrum*, v.6 n.8 (1903), commissioned by Leopold Bauer.

The Library took part in the Carnegie Hall 'Vienna: City of Dreams' season in 2014, digitizing all the Klimt-era Vienna Secession catalogues and creating a thematic website.

—Stephen Bury

86 The Digital Art History Lab
2014

In fall of 2014, the Frick Art Reference Library established a virtual Digital Art History Lab (DAHL), with a committee consisting of members from every department of the Library at the time: Archives, Public Services, Photoarchive, Books, Conservation, and the Center for the History of Collecting. Stimulated by the realization that a growing number of computer software programs that were proving fruitful in providing art historians with new and exciting research methodologies that traditional analog approaches could never hope to mimic, Andrew W. Mellon Chief Librarian Stephen J. Bury recognized that sharing these methodologies with the Library's audiences should be a top priority.

The full mission of the Frick's Digital Art History Lab is to provide art historians with the digital tools and data necessary to explore new research approaches and to stimulate collaborations between art historians and specialists from a variety of fields. The Lab aims to make the data sets amassed by the Library available to the public, so that developers, scholars and others can create tools that are freely available to the community and address a range of audiences, from general users to proficient researchers.

The DAHL began giving and hosting general workshops on digital art history in 2015. Workshop topics in the ensuing years have ranged from tutorials on how to use computer programs such as Cytoscape, Omeka, and Palladio demonstrations of visual recreations of lost spaces such as the old Lenox Library that used to stand on the current site of The Frick Collection.

The DAHL hosted its first lecture on digital art history in 2016, when Matthew Lincoln spoke on *Specialization and Diversity in Dutch and Flemish Printmaking: A Computational Approach*. Lecturers have included Rick Johnson on the use of computational weave maps to analyze the canvases of the Dutch artist Johannes Vermeer (1632–75) and Lindsay Cook on the possibility of using digital scans to help restore Notre Dame after the terrible fire of 2019.

In 2018, realizing that the growing field of computer vision technology could greatly benefit the research of art historians, the DAHL held a computer vision symposium that brought together professionals from the fields of computer science and art history to identify the precise technological needs for expanding image-based searching as a tool and a methodology with the ultimate aim of building a usable image-search platform with multiple applications in the arts. The Symposium also highlighted tools and projects that the Library itself had developed such as ARIES, an interactive image manipulation system that allows for the online exploration and organization of digital images in collaboration with the New York University Tandon School of Engineering, and a collaboration with Cornell and Stanford University researchers to use artificial intelligent to train computers to apply Frick subject headings to images in its photoarchive. In 2020–21, the Frick held a successful follow-up virtual symposium in four parts titled *Technological Revolutions and Art History*.

Screen shot of ARIES, showing Samantha Deutch's Mary Jane Morgan (1830–85) project, 2021.

Recently, the Library created a new staff position, Digital Art History Lead. Their role is to help answer digital art history questions, train and work with art historians, collaborate with university engineering departments and other technology partners to create new and vibrant tools, and help the Lab maintain a high profile in the ever-growing field of digital art history.

—*Louisa Wood Ruby*

ARIES: ARt Image Exploration Space*
2014

In 2014, two members of the Frick Art Reference Library's Digital Art History Lab, art historians Samantha Deutch and Louisa Wood Ruby, approached Claudio Silva and Juliana Freire of NYU's Tandon School of Engineering to see if they would be interested in collaborating to build a research tool that would assist art historians in their daily work with images. With the advent of digital photography, scholars lacked the technology capable of replacing what they had previously been able to accomplish in the real world. Deutch and Ruby imagined a virtual tool that would mimic and enhance methods employed when working with physical images: organizing and reorganizing photographs, slides, transparencies, Xeroxes, etc., making connections between them, finding similarities and differences, and visualizing stylistic changes over space and time.

Silva and Freire were excited about the idea and added three more members to the team: Lhaylla Chrissaff, Marcos Lage, and Joao Rulff of the Universidade Federal de Fluminense, Brazil. The result was ARIES—ARt Image Exploration Space, a free, cloud-based dynamic environment offering art historians and others an extensive array of practical tools for analyzing images. ARIES provides a novel, intuitive interface to explore, annotate, rearrange, and group art images in a single workspace environment, using organizational ontologies (collections, etc.) drawn from existing best practices in art history.

Investigating artists' workshop practices is one way in which ARIES can be particularly useful for art historians. The Flemish painter Sir Anthony van Dyck (Flemish, 1599–1641) is considered to have used repeated formulas when painting portraits, a practice which likely contributed to his prolific output. Using the Overlay and Relative Size applications available in ARIES, we tested this theory by examining five different portraits of women by Van Dyck from The Frick Collection. After bringing the images into the Image Menu and the Workspace, selecting Relative Size, and scaling up for close analysis (first screenshot), we stacked the images on top of one another and carefully lined up the features; in this case, the hairline, eyebrows, and nose of each of the sitters (second screenshot). The comparison is stunning; not only do these features line up nicely for each sitter, but their shoulders and clothing do as well. They also line up whether or not the sitters are wearing a collar, painted in full or three-quarter-length, sitting or standing.

ARIES is now in BETA and is available via the Internet using Google Chrome. More features for the tool, including working with images in

virtual three-dimensional space, will require more development and funding. In the meantime, we continue to work with our partners at New York University's Tandon School of Engineering and Brazil's Universidade Federal Fluminense with the future of ARIES in mind: enhancements and added functionalities that can answer the ever-changing research demands of the art library patron.

—*Louisa Wood Ruby / Samantha Deutch*

88 Leveson-Gower's Polite Repository
2015 (1785)

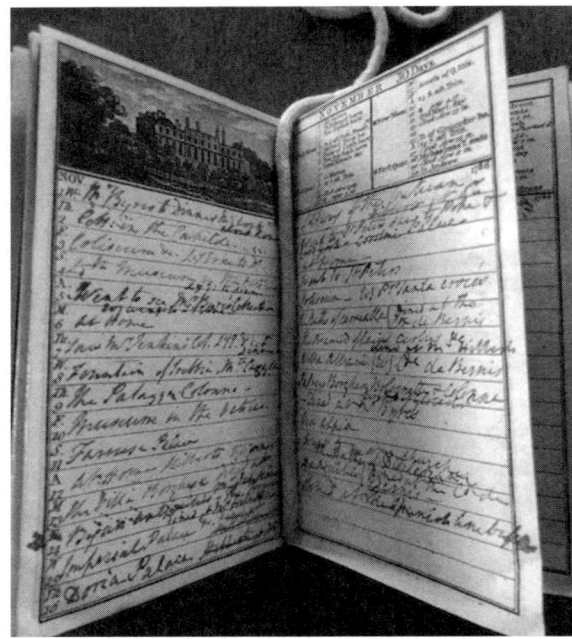

The Polite Repository, or Pocket Companion: containing an Almanack, the Births, Marriages, Etc. of the sovereign Princes of Europe, Lists of both Houses of Parliament [etc.]… and various other Articles of useful Information: ornamented with elegant Engravings… London: Printed [by T. Rickaby] for W. Peacock…, 1785.

Combining the taste for the miniature (the *Repository* is roughly 11 x 7cm), diarizing, and for viewing engravings of country-seats (by John Peltro (1760–1808) after Watts, Powell and Laporte), *Peacock's Polite Repository* sold well in the last two decades of the eighteenth century and the first decade of the nineteenth century. There were various bindings, and this copy is in red morocco leather. Many have survived but the English Short Title Catalogue (ESTC) only records a microform version for 1786. Our copy also includes diary entries by George Granville Leveson-Gower (1758–1833), known as Viscount Trentham until 1786. His mother was the sister of the heirless Duke of Bridgewater, known as the Canal Duke. In September 1785 Leveson-Gower married Elizabeth, Countess of Sutherland. With both huge estates in Scotland and a fortune from industrial ventures, later including railways, the family was one of the wealthiest in the British Empire. He could afford the red morocco!

Peacock's Polite Repository records two journeys: from 22 May to 9 June 1786 Leveson-Gower traveled to South West England, including Petworth, Arundel, Stourhead, Fonthill but also including Stonehenge; and from 14 September to the end of the year he traveled through

France (where from 1790–92 he would be the ambassador to France, despite no previous diplomatic experience apart from good French) and Italy. In Paris 21–27 September he attended the theatre, seeing performances of Molière's *Tartuffe* and *Les femmes savants*, before travelling to Turin via Lyons and Chambery for more opera. He arrived in Rome on 31 October, visiting major sites from the baths of Caracalla to the Villa Borghese. But he also dined with Cardinal Buoncompagni and Cardinal de Bernis. He also met the Jacobite antiquarian and collector, James Byres (1733–1817), who had sold the Portland Vase to Sir William Hamilton in 1770; and the art dealer, Thomas Jenkins (1722–98), also an unofficial banker and spy.

But Leveson-Gower has another interest to the Frick Art Reference Library, for he was one of the consortium/syndicate who acquired the collection of the former Duke of Orleans for £43,500 in 1798. Other members were Leveson-Gower's uncle, Francis Egerton, 3rd Duke of Bridgewater (5/8 shares), Frederick Howard, 5th Earl of Carlisle (2/8 shares). Leveson-Gower had just 1/8 share but with Bridgewater's death in 1803 he now had three quarters of the spoils. Of the 305 paintings the consortium had reserved ninety-four for themselves, with sales, exhibitions having offset much of the cost. What Leveson-Gower's precise role in this transaction is not yet clear, but his papers, recently acquired by the British Library, may illuminate this.

—*Stephen Bury*

89 Art Collecting Files of Henry Clay Frick
2016 (1881, 1925, 2001, 2015)

The study of collectors and collecting adds yet another facet to the discipline of art history. Records of collectors themselves, as well as galleries, dealers, and museums are essential for understanding the transfer of a work of art from one set of hands to another.

The Art Collecting Files of Henry Clay Frick, 1881–1925 is an artificial collection documenting his collecting career from its earliest days until his death and the years immediately thereafter. Through a generous grant in 2016 from the Carnegie Corporation of New York, archivists at The Frick Collection and Frick Art Reference Library were finally able to digitize and unite materials that were previously divided between the Frick Family Papers and the institutional records of The Frick Collection. Prior to digitization, researchers often had to check multiple places to get a full picture of a single artwork's history as it pertained to Henry Clay Frick. Uniting these records digitally adds to a growing number of collections available online that document collectors and collecting. These include the Knoedler Gallery Archive at the Getty and the Kress Collection Digital Archive at the National Gallery of Art, along with many others.

This collection contains correspondence, invoices and financial records, catalogs, inventories, registers, notes, narrative descriptions, and printed material largely documenting the selection and purchase of works of art in Frick's collection. Materials comprising acquisition files form the bulk of the collection, though the amount of documentation varies from one object to another. In the case of Fragonard *Progress of Love* series, for instance, the file runs to more than seventy pages, while the documentation for Bronzino *Lodovico Capponi* consists of little more than an invoice. Beyond simply recording purchases, though, these files also illuminate how the collection was refined over the years when works were returned, sold, or otherwise dispersed. Moreover, the collection documents works of art that were offered, considered, or pursued by Frick, but ultimately not acquired. Works by Holbein, Rembrandt, Van Dyck, Houdon, Memling, and others were rejected whether due to high cost, lack of quality, questions of authenticity, a lack of willingness on the part of the owner to sell, or sometimes for no apparent reason at all.

Other aspects of the Art Collecting Files document the day-to-day management of the collection, from insurance and transit to exhibition loans and catalogs. As documented here, the public relished seeing Frick's works on display at the Metropolitan Museum of Art, Boston's

```
POSTAL TELEGRAPH-CABLE COMPANY IN CONNECTION WITH THE COMMERCIAL CABLE COMPANY.
                CLARENCE H. MACKAY, President.              CLARENCE H. MACKAY, President.
            J. O. STEVENS, Sec'y.  WM. H. BAKER, V. P. & G. M.    ALBERT BECK, Sec'y.  GEO. G. WARD, V. P. & G. M.
                                    TELEGRAM
The Postal Telegraph-Cable Company transmits and delivers this message subject to the terms and conditions printed on the back of this blank.

COUNTER NUMBER.     TIME FILED.        CHECK.
                              M.
Send the following message, without repeating, subject to the terms and conditions printed on the back hereof, which are hereby agreed to-
                                    COPY IN LETTER BOOK.      Prides Crossing,
To     Fry.                                                                    190
                    Guildford,
        Enchanted,



                    Sent via Beverly Postal, July 22nd, 1910.

THE POSTAL COMPANY'S SYSTEM REACHES ALL IMPORTANT POINTS IN THE UNITED STATES AND BRITISH AMERICA, AND via COMMERCIAL CABLES, ALL THE WORLD.
                                                                        [T. 194, 074]
```

Museum of Fine Arts, and in the galleries of Knoedler and Duveen. Frick also welcomed visitors to his own galleries, especially at One East 70th Street, where a cross-section of scholars, society women, students, and civic organizations eagerly sought admission. Their letters are contained among these papers, as is the illustrated catalog Frick had privately printed in 1915, which through its small handbook size may have been prepared with these visitors in mind.

While this collection is extremely valuable for what it tells us about Frick's collecting activities, it raises questions through what it fails to tell us. Frick was famously reticent about his collection, leaving later generations to wonder about his motivation for collecting, his decision-making process, and his emotional attachment to his collection. In a rare departure from this silence, Frick cabled one word to Roger Fry upon the delivery of Rembrandt's *Polish Rider*: "Enchanted." Likewise, some of the works documented here have since been lost to time, such the Rubens purchased from Roger Fry in 1910 and known only as *Italian Prince in Armour*. It was given away in 1912 and remains unidentified.

—*Julie Ludwig*

90 Valadier's Shop Inventory
2016 (1810, 1827)

This 380-page manuscript, purchased in 2016 with the support of Marina Kellen French, was acquired in the years directly preceding The Frick Collection's monographic exhibition *Luigi Valadier: Splendor in Eighteenth-Century Rome* (2018–18). Its acquisition reflects the Library's expanded scope of collecting resources related to the decorative arts, which in turn supports The Frick Collection's exhibition program highlighting masters such as Pierre Gouthière and Valadier, as well as the Sèvres, Meissen, and Du Paquier porcelain manufactories.

The Valadier workshop originated with Giuseppe Valadier's grandfather, Andrea Valadier (1695–1759), who emigrated from France to Rome in 1714, establishing himself there as a prominent silversmith. Andrea's son Luigi (1726–85) took over the workshop in 1759, moving it in 1762 to a location on the Via del Babuino. Luigi's unique style and remarkable technical skill created great demand for his objects, requiring as many as eighty assistants to fulfill commissions from the Pope, noble families in Rome, and aristocrats and monarchs throughout Europe. His output of both secular and ecclesiastical works ranged from small objects such as cutlery and candlesticks to altars and large centerpieces, or desers, rendered in precious and semiprecious materials. Despite this success, however, Luigi was burdened by financial problems and drowned himself in the Tiber in 1785.

His son Giuseppe (1762–1839), already a successful architect, assumed control of the workshop after his father's death. This inventory is the principal documentary source for information on the family's eighteen-room workshop in Rome. Attesting to the multifaceted nature of the workshop, it itemizes tools and utensils used in a range of trades, particularly silversmiths, founders, gilders, bronze workers, ébénistes, and hardstone gem engravers. It also lists raw materials and completed works found in the workshop. Moreover, it inventories models and drawings essential to the workshop's output. These models included reproductions of works by prominent sculptors such as Gian Lorenzo Bernini, François Duquesnoy, Pierre Le Gros, and Luigi Valadier's father-in-law Filippo della Valle, and were either affixed to walls set on shelves or sideboards. References to drawings appear twice in the manuscript, these being stored in credenzas, or sideboards. Drawings such as these are essential to the study of works now lost. Fortunately, hundreds of drawings with provenance from the Valadier workshop survive, though many have been dispersed among museums and private collectors.

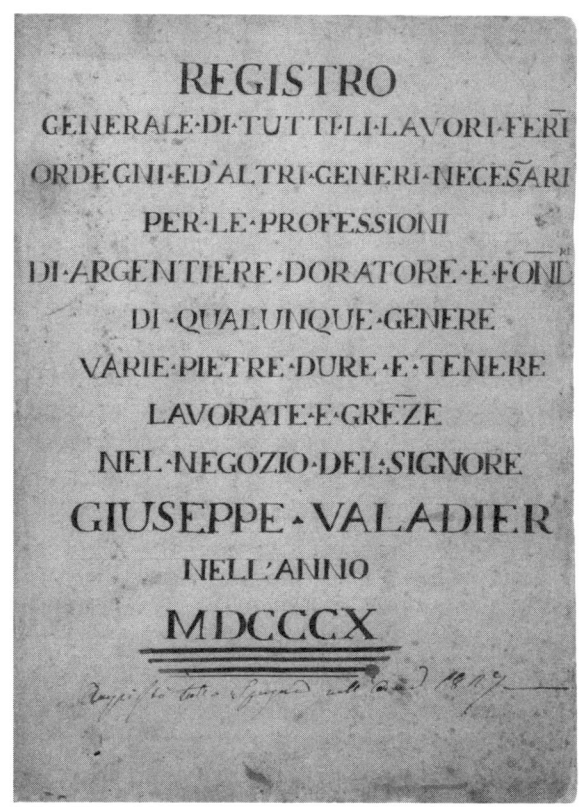

Registro Generale: Inventory of all the works, tools, utensils, and other articles necessary for the profession of silversmith, gilder, and caster of every sort, various stones, hard and soft, cut and uncut, in the shop of Signor Giuseppe Valadier in the year MDCCCX, 1810, 1827. Acquired with the support of Marina Kellen French, 2016.

The inventory was drawn up in 1810, perhaps as Giuseppe was contemplating transfer of the workshop to his brother-in-law, Giuseppe Spagna, in order to devote more time to architectural projects. Contents of the inventory are arranged by room, with ten rooms dedicated to various trades. Other rooms were mostly used for storage, while the remaining ones opened onto the street. At least one of street-level rooms was used for the display of completed items, where they might be seen by clients and visitors to the city and thereby suggesting a commercial aspect to the workshop's activity. After transferring the workshop and its contents to the Spagna family in 1827, Giuseppe continued to work as an architect, restorer, urban planner, and writer until his death in 1839.

—Julie Ludwig

91 French Fashion at the End of the Ancien Regime*
2016 (1778)

Gallerie des modes et costumes français, one of the first fashion magazines, was published at intervals between 1778–87 in sixty-six sets or *cahiers* of six hand-colored engravings by Jacques Esnault and Michel Rapilly, rue Saint-Jacques, Paris. The first *cahier* is without the abbreviation A.P.D.R.—*avec privilège du Roi*. The first six *cahiers* have no names of the draughtsman: for these, the artist was thought to be Claude-Louis Desrais (1746–1816), but no engraver is given. Later artists included François Louis Joseph Watteau (1758–1823) and Augustin de Saint-Aubin (1736–1807). We have no idea of the edition size. But we know each cahier sold for thirty-six livres—about sixteen dollars.

The first six cahiers concentrate on hairstyles (*coeffures*)—primarily of women—four to a leaf. This choice of topic suggests Esnaut and Rapilly were trying to emulate the success of the *Almanach nouveau ou recueil des plus jolies coeffures à la mode, dessiné et gravé par M. Davault, coiffeur* (1774).

The paucity of surviving copies renders it difficult to making a full collation of the work. Different images have the same signatures, and there is duplicate (and triplicate) numbering. Our set consists of 367 loose plates in three leather *coffrets*, and includes four extra plates, two of which are not in any other collection.

The top-left image of the first leaf (plate 31) of the sixth *cahier* is described as *Nouvelle coiffure dite la Frégate la Junon*, a hairstyle paying homage to the capture by the French frigate, the Junon, of the British Navy's *Fox* on 11 September 1778. The *coiffure* used the *pouf*, conceived by the *marchande de modes* and proprietor of the Grand Mogol shop, Rose Bertin, together with the hairdresser Monsieur Léonard, both of whom crafted Queen Marie-Antoinette's image. Built on a structure of wire and gauze, hair—including both the wearer's hair and supplemental human and horse hair, all heavily pomaded—was brushed back from the forehead to create a bed for an installation or still life, in this case a *Charmante*-class frigate, with the correct number of guns: thirty-two.

We know from the title page of the first composite volume that a Madame Le Beau colored them "with the greatest attention". It was also possible to buy them uncolored, and twenty-two of the Library's set are.

Gallerie claimed that the drawings were *après nature* and they might have been sketched in the Bois de Boulogne, Palais Royal, or Versailles. Some protagonists have first names—Arsène, Céphise, Elvire, Lisette etc. But there are also generic actors, cooks, opera singers, children, abbés and jeunes dames.

There are dresses *à la Polonaise* (the most represented), *à l'Anglaise* (despite the wars with England), *à la Turque*, *à la Sultane*, *à la Créole* etc.

One can almost sense the imminence of the French Revolution. After Louis XVI's and Marie Antoinette's executions, the house of the publishers was searched in January 1794 and a number of royal portraits were seized. To avoid being considered a royalist, copies of the Gallerie were destroyed by their owners—another reason so few survive.

The Library's set, a gift of Melinda Martin Sullivan in 2016, had formerly belonged to Charles-Gilbert Morel de Vindé (1759–1842), who technically could have collected the prints in Paris as they were published.

—*Stephen Bury*

92 A Bust Destroyed*
2016 (1919)

Most likely in Hoffman's hand, a written tag attached to the plaster version of the bust of Helen Clay Frick, painted to suggest terracotta, reads, "Carved in marble for Mr. Frick—destroyed by H. F. after her father's d[eath]". Archival evidence suggests that this destruction took place between 1956 and 1966, and not just after its completion after Henry's death.

Malvina Hoffman (1887–1966), whose date of birth is problematic as she claimed in her autobiography to be older than her mother remembered, trained at the Art Students League in New York, and with Gutzon Borglum of Mount Rushmore fame, and then in 1910 with Auguste Rodin in Paris: the latter suggested that she dissect cadavers on her return to New York. Her most famous work was the controversial Races of Mankind series (1930–33) for the Field Museum of Natural History, Chicago.

Malvina Hoffman and Helen Clay Frick may have known one another—perhaps through work with the Red Cross during World War I—before their correspondence in 1919, when the Frick family commissioned a death mask from her of Henry Clay Frick, subsequently used as the basis of the marble bust in The Frick Collection (1922). Helen also commissioned her in 1962 to make a stone bas-relief of her father for the Henry Clay Frick Fine Arts Building, University of Pittsburgh. So it would be unlikely that Helen would have destroyed her marble bust before this date. Helen and Malvina were good friends—Sir Robert Witt asked Malvina to intervene on his behalf in 1932, when Helen had fallen out with him.

According to Hoffman's autobiography, Henry Clay Frick commissioned her to make a portrait of his daughter: "Come and look at the Houdons in my collection: it might be suitable to do my daughter in the eighteenth century French manner." Hoffman's bust of Helen does seem to reference Houdon's *Comtesse du Cayla* (1777), which was in Henry Clay Frick's collection by 1916. But perhaps the Houdon references—the drilled irises of the eyes, the bacchante costume etc. recalled for Helen her Houdon studies—the only subject she had published on. Or perhaps, there was just too much flesh showing.

And how did Malvina know Helen had destroyed the marble? Was this a more personal quarrel?

—Stephen Bury

Malvina Cornell Hoffman (1887–1966) *Helen Clay Frick*, 1919, painted plaster. Gift of Lillian and Derek Ostergard, in honor of Margo Donahue dePeyster.

93 *Extra-Illustration*
2016 (1814)

Raphael Lamar West (1766–1850) was the eldest son of Benjamin West (1738–1820), President of the Royal Academy 1792–1805, 1806–20, whom he trained under and assisted in his studio. He exhibited at the Royal Academy 1781–82, but failed to be elected an associate member. He contributed Orlando and Oliver in 'As You Like It' to John Boydell's Shakespeare Gallery. In 1800–02 he was in Genesee County, New York, hoping to sell his father's land to William Beckford (1760–1844) but with no success. With his brother, Benjamin, he started West's New Gallery at 14 Newman Street, London, to display their father's works after his death in 1820. Despite inheriting much wealth and property, he applied to the Royal Academy for financial support in his later years. Many landscape and figure drawings, influenced by Salvator Rosa, and lithographs survive in major collections.

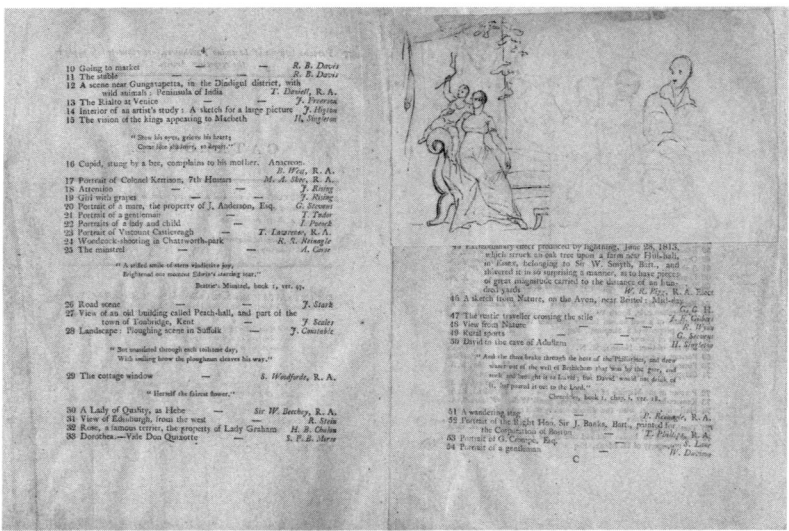

The Exhibition of the Royal Academy. The Forty-Sixth. London: Printed by B. McMillan, 1814. Contemporaneously extra-illustrated by Raphael Lamar West.

This object is the Forty-Sixth Royal Academy exhibition catalogue of 1814: the entries include Constable, Fuseli, Gainsborough, Lawrence, Northcote, Raeburn, Turner and Benjamin West himself. But this copy has a manuscript ownership inscription, "R. L. West" at the foot of the title page. It includes twenty-two pen and ink sketches by West, and one loosely inserted oil sketch of a man in formal dress: the paper of one of the sketch sheets has an 1813 watermark. It seems that West decided to focus on paintings and other artwork that caught his eye, and re-assembled/re-stitched them in the catalogue where cited, although, as West often used both sides of the sketch paper this was not always possible. He also graded sixty-eight of the works, mostly but not just paintings, in pencil.

As some of the works exhibited have not survived or no reproduction is now available, it is not possible to identify all the paintings etc. to which the sketch might relate. For example, the sketch sheet bound between pages four and five has two sketches on the recto and one on the verso. The first recto sketch has been identified as probably no.1 in the printed catalog, George Dawe's *Portraits of Mrs. S. N. Cowley and Son*: this is the only image of a painting that has disappeared, but the pose in the sketch is similar to Dawe's 1821 *Empress Alexandria and her Children* (Royal Collection Trust). The second sketch is probably no.23 in the printed catalog, Thomas Lawrence's *Portrait of Viscount Castlereagh* (copy in the Royal Collection Trust). On the verso is no.176, Henry Thomson's *Eurydice hurried back to the Infernal Regions*.

On acquisition in 2016, this item was not in good condition with soiling, tears, curling corners, creasing and two stitching regimes. It is testament to the professionalism of the Frick Art Reference Library's conservation staff that this item has been fully restored.

—*Stephen Bury*

94 *Bewick's Birds*
2017 (1804)

In December 2016 the Library was approached to see whether it would be interested in a collection of books by and about the wood-engraver Thomas Bewick.

This was the Thomas Bewick Library of Bernard ("Bud") Sherak (1919–2010), the former chair of Market Facts, New York, and offered to us by his wife, Gladys Sherak (1925–2018). In January 2017, the Library took possession of this collection consisting of twenty-four books by Bewick (seventeen of which are first editions), one "Proofs of vignettes" manuscript volume, one woodblock, and eight books about Bewick.

Thomas Bewick (1753–1828), the son of a collier, showed talent for drawing as a child, and was in 1767 apprenticed to an engraver of cutlery and jewelry, Richard Beilby (1744–1817), in Newcastle upon Tyne. He became a partner in 1777. Bewick's innovation in printmaking was the use of metal engraving tools to cut across the hard end-grain of boxwood. This allowed the blocks to be printed alongside metal type, thus dramatically reducing printing costs. But it also enabled much finer detail. Bewick's engravings are generally small in size and amazingly rich in detail, sometimes requiring the use of a magnifying glass. Bewick also used his fingerprint as a signature, but he also incorporated it into the images themselves—just as the painter, John Constable, also did but in paint.

The emerging Romantic movement had brought the appreciation of nature into focus and Bewick gained fame for his wood-engravings of birds and mammals in their natural surroundings in minutely and objectively observed and finely reproduced detail—especially in the uncaptioned tail-pieces. The Sherak gift contains the first edition of his most influential work *A History of British Birds* in two volumes—*Land Birds* (1797) with text by Beilby to which Bewick had contributed advice, and *Water Birds* (1804). The dispute about authorship of the text was reflected in the 1800 publication of just the plates, *Figures of British Land Birds*. Both *Land Birds* and *Water Birds* were very popular in the early nineteenth century: in the opening chapter of Charlotte Bronte's *Jane Eyre* (1847), Jane is looking at Bewick's *The History of Birds*—at one stage it is thrown at her, and in chapter XIII, Jane shows Rochester a watercolor of a cormorant.

—Stephen Bury

BRITISH BIRDS. 381

CORVORANT.

COLE GOOSE, OR GREAT BLACK CORMORANT,

(*Pelicanus Carbo*, Lin.—*Le Cormoran*, Buff.)

The weight of this species varies from four to seven pounds, and the size from thirty-two inches to three feet four or five in length, and from four feet to four feet six inches in breadth. The bill, to the corners of the mouth, measures four inches, and

Richard Beilby and Thomas Bewick *History of British Birds: II, Containing the History and Description of Water Birds*. Newcastle: Printed by Edward Walker, for T. Bewick: Sold by him, and Longman and Rees, London, 1804.

95 A Late Emblem Book
2017 (1789)

Emblem books developed in Europe in the sixteenth century and remained popular for over two hundred years. Most emblems found within these books consist of three elements: a motto or verse; an allegorical illustration; and several lines of explanatory prose or poetry. The reader is meant to reflect on the emblem, which elucidates a moral lesson.

Emblems of Mortality (1789) contains fifty-two woodcuts depicting the omnipresence of Death. The frontispiece and first print are by John Bewick (1760–95). The other illustrations are copied and recut by him from the Latin version of the emblem book *Imagines Mortis* first printed in French by Melchior and Gaspard Treschel as *Les Simulachres & Historiées de la Mort* (1538). It contains forty-one illustrations cut by Hans Lützelburger (1495–1526) after drawings by Hans Holbein the Younger (1497–1543). Another edition with fifty-eight cuts was published in 1562.

Emblems of Mortality follows the typical tripartite structure of the emblem book. Emblems begin with a Biblical verse, followed by an illustration, and ends with two to four verse quatrains, all thematically aligned. The quatrains are expanded English translations of the Latin versions, themselves translated from the French.

The first five emblems cover the creation of the world, the development of sin, and the end of the world as in Revelations. The following emblems can be understood as social commentary on the immoral behavior of the clerical and aristocratic orders. For example, the emblem on the Cardinal admonishes him for accepting indulgences against sin. It begins with a verse from Isaiah 5:23:

> *Which justify the wicked for Reward, and take*
> *Away the Righteousness of the Righteous from him.*

The accompanying illustration depicts the Cardinal accepting payment from a wealthy man while Death pulls back the Cardinal's hat to stare directly at him.

There is a change in tone for the emblems that cover the downtrodden and innocent, where Death is often shown as a release from pain.

By 1789 emblem books were no longer in vogue and their moralizing intent diminished in favor of reading them for historical purposes. On the title page we see that the book is printed for the "…Information of the Curious, as [well as] the Instruction and Entertainment of Youth".

Emblems of mortality: representing, in upwards of fifty cuts, Death seizing all ranks and degrees of people: imitated from a painting in the cemetery of the Dominican church at Basil, in Switzerland: with an apostrophe to each, translated from the Latin and French, intended as well for the information of the curious, as the instruction and entertainment of youth... London: Printed for T. Hodgson, in George's-Court, St. John's-Lane, Clerkenwell, [1789]. Thomas Bewick Library of Bernard Sherak, gift of Gladys Sherak, 2017.

Bewick's illustrations are built with strong vertical and horizontal lines cuts in the woodblock and display little or no cross-hatching, consistent with the techniques he would have learned during his apprenticeship from 1777–82 to his older brother, Thomas Bewick. After moving to London 1786, John found work under Thomas Hodgson, whose print shop published *Emblems of Mortality*. Death took him away at the age of thirty-five.

—*Ralph Baylor*

The Starr Wedgwood & Ceramics Library
2018

Bernard Starr's desire to create a Wedgwood library was influenced by the example Elizabeth Chellis of Boston who had built up from the 1940s the largest and most comprehensive Wedgwood library in the U.S. There are some differences between the Starr and Chellis libraries: Chellis is stronger on eighteenth- and nineteenth-century imprints, while Starr is better on the pre-1700 items and, surprisingly, on the 1900–50 books. The Wedgwood & Bentley Book List of 10 August 1770, listing thirty-two books used as source material, became for Starr a shopping list for potential designs for the Wedgwood pieces he collected: he had amassed twelve of these titles by his death. The 2018 Gift of the Starr Wolfe Family in honor of Bernard and Lydia Starr comprises 6,650 books and is the largest named library absorbed by the Frick Art Reference Library.

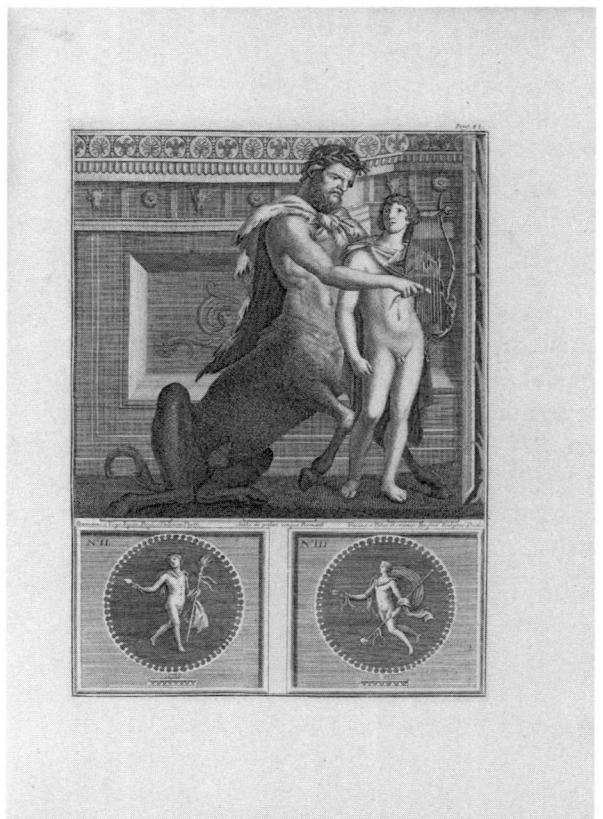

Le pitture antiche d'Ercolano: e contorni incise con qualche spiegazione = Antichità di Ercalano. Vol.1. Napoli: Regia Stamperia, 1757. Gift of the Starr Wolfe family in honor of Bernard and Lydia Starr, 2018.

Volume One of the large folio *Le pitture antiche d'Ercolano e contorni incise con qualche spiegazione*, published by Charles VII of Naples also Charles V of Sicily (1734–59), later Charles III of Spain (1759–88), covered the archaeological explorations at Herculaneum which had been rediscovered in 1738, to be followed by the easier to dig Pompeii (1748) and Stabiae (1749), all three towns destroyed by the eruption of Vesuvius in 79 C.E. and buried in tephra ash. It was edited by Ottavio Antonio Bayardi (1695–1764), whose text was ridiculed by the critic Johann Joachim Winckelmann (1717–68), whose *Monumenti antichi inediti* (Roma, 1821) is also in the Starr Library. The volume was the first of a series collectively known as *Le antichita di Ercolano esposte*, eight vols (1757–92), which, although in a very limited and expensive edition, had a profound impact on neo-classicism: the designs and motifs proved ideal for Wedgwood and Bentley's Etruria ceramics, whilst European porcelain could not surmount Rococo influence or was impacted by the Seven Years' War (1756–63).

Starr's copy contains eleven typed 3 x 5 inch catalog cards and a typed summary. Starr writes "this book is the source for a number of Herculaneum subjects used by Josiah Wedgwood for basalt and jasper plaques. These designs are nos.51 to 65 of Class II in the first Wedgwood Catalogue of 1773, and subsequent catalogues." The card at plate VIII page 43 comments "Lower two vignettes. Two Male Dancers. A black basalt plaque of the design on the left is in the Milestone Collection. A black basalt plaque of the one on the right is in the Wedgwood Museum at Barlaston."

—*Stephen Bury*

97 The Loewi-Robertson Archive*
2018

In 2018, the library acquired from the Gabriella Robertson Family Trust the remarkable decorative, fine arts and textile archive of Adolph Loewi, Inc. and Loewi-Robertson, Inc. It comprises a detailed record of business activities and client records of this renowned firm which operated out of locations in Venice, including from 1919 to 1939 the Palazzo Nani-Mocenigo. Adolph Loewi was the Honorary German Counsel in Venice from 1923–34, and when Hitler came to power, seeing the writing on the wall, he moved his family and business first to London, then New York and finally Los Angeles in 1939.

With this acquisition, made possible by David Robertson, the grandson of Adolph Loewi (1888–1977) and son of Gabriella Kay Loewi Robertson (1920–2020) and William Robertson, the Library has become the custodian of one of the great dealer archives of the twentieth century.

Comprised of over seventy linear feet of textiles, watercolors of interiors, photographs, stock books and other financial records and an enormous alphabetical correspondence series that documents sales to seemingly every major decorative arts and textile collector and museum in the United States and Europe from *c.*1939 through the early 2000s, this trove will offer scholars and other researchers expansive research opportunities.

The records include extensive correspondence with other dealers, notably Arnold Seligmann & Rey where Loewi shared New York office space in the 1930s, and with Alessandro Morandotti, who worked for Loewi in Venice and who assumed management of the gallery in Venice and in its later location in Rome where it operated as Antiquaria. In 1950, Morandotti bought the Rome business from Loewi. Correspondence to and from Morandotti and Loewi and family continued until 1981. Travel records, inventories, appraisals, sales records, architectural plans for rooms removed in their entirety from palazzos and other buildings, beautiful watercolors of interiors and furniture for sale as well as photographs, transparencies and slides give a complete picture of a vibrant, international business that lasted nearly a hundred years. Unfortunately, there are few business records from before *c.*1938 when Adolph Loewi began to plan his family and business move to the United States. The earliest records date to the 1880s and are primarily concerned with his family in Germany, notably the Bernheimer family who operated a noted art and textile gallery in Munich (Loewi's mother was Emma Bernheimer, daughter of Lehmann Bernheimer).

Adolph Loewi, Inc. Stock book 1939-56.

Most remarkable are the entire room interiors that were sold, disassembled and transported to the United States. In particular, the Studiolo from the Ducal Palace in Gubbio at the Metropolitan Museum of Art, and the Asolo Theatre now located in the Ringling Museum in Sarasota, as well as interiors at Caramoor, the former home in Katonah, New York of Mr. and Mrs. Walter Rosen provide ample evidence of the scope and influence of Adolph Loewi's gallery.

The stock books enumerate the many clients, both private—and as the business was based in Los Angeles, many Hollywood figures—and institutional, who patronized Adolph Loewi, Inc. and notes their purchases ranging from small textile samples to entire rooms and furniture suites.

Hand-made volumes of fabric swatches were compiled by Adolph Loewi for his daughter, Gabriella Kay Loewi (later Robertson), as she worked to master the artistic and business world of textile sales.

—Sally Brazil

Field Trips in the Digital Age
2018 (1922)

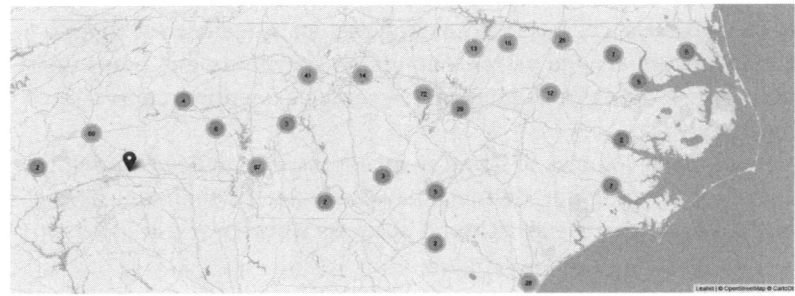

One of the first projects initiated by the Frick Art Reference Library was an ambitious photographic project to send Library staff up and down the East and Gulf coasts from Maine to Louisiana to photograph and obtain historical information about paintings and drawings in private and small private collections. These campaigns, taking place from 1922–67, resulted in over 35,000 photographic negatives that greatly enhanced the scholarly outreach of the Library's Photoarchive, documenting works of art that are still inaccessible to the public or have been lost or destroyed since they were photographed. While the campaigns ceased over fifty years ago, the images and documentation obtained from them are now being used in a manner that would not have been dreamed about while staff were driving across the hardly passable back roads. Beginning in 2018 the Digital Art History Lab at the Library, in collaboration with the Center for Advanced Research of Spatial Information at Hunter College, CUNY, has been developing an online tool that uses Geographic Information Systems (GIS) technologies to document these campaigns. This project has been accomplished with the work of several students who over the course of a school year or a summer term were able to combine their art history and computer science skills to augment the map. Currently, each year more individual photographic trips are researched and added to the map.

This interactive tool allows the interested researcher to easily see on a map of the United States where Library staff were active and how many photographs were taken at a specific location. The map is fully zoomable, so the viewer is able to see how the paintings are broken down by state, city, neighborhood and even to precise street address when available. This level of specificity was established by finding the latitude and longitude of the location and entering the coordinates into the map. The map does not only offer geographical information about the paintings and drawings. A researcher who is interested in works of art in a specific location will see a thumbnail image of the work or works along with a link to Library catalog record for the work. With one click the researcher is taken from the physical location of the work to the art historical record and digital images. Scholars interested in the history of collecting and provenance of works of art are now able to conduct interactive research on that level as opposed to the more common methods of looking at artist or subject.

The Photographic Campaign Map (*frick.org/map_photograph_campaigns*) truly showcases a century of art historical research. What began with index cards, fountain pens, and black and white photographs now continues with interactive zooming and geophysical coordinates. As more and more individual campaigns are added the map will present twentieth-century information in a new and interactive manner that researchers can utilize in our digital age.

—*John McQuaid*

99   *Painting Portraits from Photographs*
2018

The library acquired the Ulke family archive from descendants of Henry Ulke (1821-1910) in 2018. This portrait of Ulysses S. Grant was one of four painted by Henry Ulke, one of three brothers who immigrated to the United States from Prussia in the 1852 as part of a large wave of German immigration caused by political unrest after the 1848 German Revolution. After residing in New York for some years, Henry and his brother, Julius Ulke, moved to Washington, D.C. and in 1860 opened a painting and photography studio, where they pioneered the use of photographs as the bases for painted portraits. The brothers, Henry Ulke in particular, became sought after by politicians and other important Washington figures for formal portrait photographs as well as painted portraits.

Henry and Julius Ulke were boarders at Petersen House and became accidental witnesses to the death of President Abraham Lincoln in April 1865. After the President was shot at Ford's Theater he was brought to Petersen House where he died. The only existing photographic image of what is assumed to be the room where Lincoln died was taken by Julius Ulke.

The collections consist of Ulke family documentation dating from the eighteenth century to the early twentieth century with most of the early written materials in German. Primarily focused on Henry Ulke and his generation, the collection also houses records from his father, Carl Ulke (1791-1882), a publisher and botanical illustrator, as well as Henry Ulke's wife, Veronica Neumann Schultze (1843-93), a German actress and successful business woman. Henry and Veronica Ulke's children are also represented in the archive, notably Titus Ulke (1866-1961), a mineralogist.

In addition to his professional career as a photographer and painter, Henry Ulke was also a distinguished amateur entomologist who donated his collection of insects, primarily North American beetles, to the Carnegie Museum in Pittsburgh. A founding member of the Megatherium Club, named after an extinct giant sloth, he devoted considerable time to insect collection and study. The Megatherium Club, which operated out of the Smithsonian Castle initially, was evicted from that site due to the riotous nature of their activities when not discussing insects.

The collection contains over eight hundred photographs taken in the Ulke brothers' studio of noted Washington, D.C. statesmen and luminaries, two taken in the studio of Abraham Lincoln, as well as portrait

Henry Ulke
Portrait of Ulysses S. Grant, 1875.

paintings by both Henry and Julius Ulke, family memorabilia, botanical watercolors by both Carl and Henry Ulke, family diaries, correspondence and ephemera. Over 1,200 items have been translated into English and digitized. The collection documents the close Ulke family bonds and familial personal and professional interests over many years. It is an illuminating record of immigration and integration into the heart of American political, scientific and social circles as well as a vivid portrait of artistic endeavor.

—*Sally Brazil*

100 A Seventeenth-century Spanish Collector
2020 (1679)

This manuscript is the will of Don Juan Suárez de Toledo Gaitán, a Spanish nobleman who died around 1679. Though a seemingly mundane legal document, close inspection of it offers insights into seventeenth-century Spanish aristocratic collections and collecting practices.

Suárez de Toledo Gaitán's family history is well documented, being the direct descendant of Hernán Suárez de Toledo y Predraza (died 1570), the lawyer and private tutor to Prince Carlos of Asturias, the ill-fated heir of King Phillip II. Suárez de Toledo Gaitán also held several important posts during his life, including infantry captain and mayor of Talavera. We also know that his first marriage, to his niece, ended without an heir. He contracted a second marriage with Doña Inez Ceclia de Godoy Ponce de León of Cordoba with whom they had five children.

Written in various hands, on duty-paid legal stationary, the manuscript is divided into a will, inventory of objects, and partition of lands held by the testator. The inventory lists everyday household objects including candlesticks, curtains, and carpets but also lists properties such as a garden with fruit trees, all to be distributed among Suárez de Toledo Gaitán's beneficiaries. Personal lives of the family as they are related to inheritance are also revealed. For example, the manuscript records that the testator's daughter Antonia, renounced her inheritance in order to become a nun. But it is the documentation of paintings and sculptures that makes the manuscript a germane acquisition for the Frick Art Reference Library.

According to the inventory, Suárez de Toledo Gaitán's collection of art includes portraits of Prince Carlos of Asturias and the conquistador Hernán Cortés, not a surprise given ancestral relations to the Hapsburg dynasty. There are also several highly valued paintings described simply as being from Rome, demonstrating the vogue for Italian art. In addition, and of similar value as the Roman paintings, there are listed three works by Titian (1490–1576) and one by El Greco (1541–1614). The latter two artists were collected by Phillip II with El Greco being especially popular in Toledo after his move the city in 1577. Suárez de Toledo Gaitán's town of Talavera, only fifty miles from Toledo, would have been within the artist's orbit.

Authenticity of the works aside, the document shows the desire of Spanish nobility to follow the collecting model set in the sixteenth century by King Phillip II.

—Ralph Baylor

Nº 18
11 de Sep.e 1679

Este legajo contiene los papeles siguientes:

- El Testam.to del S.r D.n Ju.o Suarez de Toledo, otorgado en Talavera por Ant.o Gonzalez S.no en 20 de Mayo de 1663
- El Inventario que se hizo a la S.ra D.a Ines Leviña Ponce de Leon, muger del d.ho D.n Ju.o S.r Suarez de Toledo
- Las Particiones que de los Bienes que quedaron por muerte del d.ho D.n Ju.o entre la S.ra D.a Ines Zerda, y sus hijos de d.ho S.r D.n Juan que fueron los S.res D.n Fernando Suarez, D.a Gracia, D.a Theresa y D.a Marina hecha por Ju.o Martinez de la Cruz Contador nombrado, y las Reales
- Un Memor.l de los Bienes del Mayorazgo que antecede a d.ha partiz.on
- Otro Mem.l de Tercios incluso en el de arriba
- Otro Mem.l de deudas que quedaron por muerte de d.ho S.r D.n Ju.o Suarez
- Las Capitulaz.s matrim.s y dotacion al tiempo de Casarse d.hos Señores
- La Renuncia que hizo la S.ra D.a Ant.a que despues professó en el convento de S.n Bernardo
- Otro Mem.l de Tercios sobre los Bienes Libres

L.º 14. J.P. Talav.ra

4.

1679 - Testamento e inventario
J. Suarez Toledo

Index

291 Gallery 57

A L'Etoile scellée (gallery) 65
A. C. Cooper 3
Aedes Walpolianae 56
Allom, Charles 76
American Art Association 67
Anti-slave trade 58
Apollinaire, Guillaume 66
Aquatints 27
Architectural models 39
Archives Directory for the History of Collecting 79
ARIES (ARt Image Exploration Space) 86, 87
Art Collecting Files of Henry Clay Frick 89
Art Deco (exhibition) 26
Art of this Century (gallery) 52
artificial intelligence 7
artists' studios (Paris) 47

Bailey, Colin 42
Bailey, Vernon Howe 42
Baldwin, Muriel 18
Bataille, Georges 60
Bayardi, Ottavio Antonio 96
Beilby, Richard 94
Belle Da Costa Greene 60
Berenson, Bernard 31, 84
Berenson, Mary 31
Bermondsey Spa 82
Bewick, John 95
Bewick, Thomas 94
Bibliothèque d'Auteuil 78
blueprint (1923) 22
Bonaparte, Joseph 32
Bonestell Gallery, NYC 55
Bonheur, Rosa 38

bookplates 6, 15
Boston Post 53
Bowling alley 2
Braamcamp, Gerrit 9
Brakman, Robert 59
Breton, André 36, 60, 65, 70
Bridgewater syndicate 11, 88
Brière, Clotilde 3, 8, 38, 65, 66
Brière, Gaston 8
Bronte, Charlotte 94
Brunswick-Balke-Collender Co. 2
Bryan, Michael 11
Buchanan, William 11
Burke, Bill 51
Byres, James 88

cadavre exquis *see* exquisite corpse
Caldwell & Co. 39, 45
calligrammes 66
Canaletto 28
caricatures 72
Carnegie, Andrew 5
Carrère & Hastings 1, 22
Carriera, Rosalba 28
Cendrars, Blaise 66
Center for the History of Collecting 79
Chepstow Bridge 21
Chiesa, Achillito 24
Childs, Cephas Grier 32
Christina, Queen of Sweden 29
Civil Affairs Handbooks 51, 54
Clapp, Frederick Mortimer 45, 61
classification, photographs 7
Clayton (Pittsburgh), 77
Clerk, John (Lord Eldin) 12
Coke, Thomas William 58
Colle, Doriece B. 63

color reproduction 20, 27
Committee for the Protection of Cultural Treasures in War Areas 6, 23, 51, 54
Constable, John 34
Cook, Alfred W. 43
Cook, Walter W.S. 13
Corti, José 37
costume cards 63
Crozat, Pierre 29

d'Harnoncourt, René 35
D'Oelsnitz, Herman 19
Dada 55
De Boodt, Anselmus 64
de Braekeleer, Ferdinand 62
De Vinne, Theodore Low 67
Di Bartolo, Andrea 24
digital art history 86, 98
Dinsmoor, William B. 51
dogs 44
Dossetter, Edward 73
Duchamp, Marcel 60
Düsseldorf Galerie 15

EBSCO 71
Edey, Winthrop Kellogg 64, 74
Eidlitz, Mark 45
El Greco 100
emblem books 95
Esnaut, Jacques 91
Estienne, Charles 65
exquisite corpse 70
extra-illustration 93

fashion 63, 91
Feigl Gallery, NYC 55
Franco-Japan Fine Arts Company *see* Nichi futsu geijutsu-sha
Frick Art reference Library Periodicals Index 71
Frick Collection Catalog (Folio) 61

Frick Family Papers 76
Frick, Helen Clay 1, 2, 6, 14, 17, 22, 39, 41, 44, 45, 46, 51, 61, 76, 77, 84, 92
Frick, Henry Clay 1, 2, 5, 89
Frick Photoarchive classification headings 7
Fry, Roger 25
Fuseli, Henry 21, 49

G. K. Hall, Boston 71
Garnett, Porter 45, 61
Gay, Matilda 84
Gay, Walter 84
Gazette des Beaux-Arts 8
Gillis Press 5
Gillray, James 72
Goncourt, Edmund de 78
Gower Lodge 73
Grafton Galleries (London) 25
Graves, Algernon 15
Gray, Elisha 40
Grita de Dolores 83
Guggenheim, Peggy 52

Hamlin, Gladys 51
Hastings, Thomas 22, 41
Hazlitt, William 11
Heim, François 78
Hidalgo, Miguel 83
Hill, Gertrude 14
Hoffman, Malvina 45, 92
Hoffmann, Heinrich 50
Hope, Henry 16
Horney, Karen 55
Houghton Hall 56
Huelsenbeck, Richard 55
Hulbeck, Charles R. 55
Hunter College, CUNY 98

Iron Rail Vacation Home 46

Italian room 41

Jenkins, Thomas 88
Johns, Jasper 69
Jones, Jennifer 59
Joseph II, emperor 64
Josi, Christian 20
Junon (frigate) 91

Kahlo, Frida 68
Kelmscott paper 61
Keyse, Thomas 82
Kimbell, Sidney Fiske 14
Kleine Kabinett 27
Klimt, Gustav 85
Klumpke, Anna 38
Knoedler, Ronald 5
Knoeder & Co. 68
Knowles, Joseph 53
Knox, Katharine McCook 14, 23, 77
Kogan, Petr Semenovich 26
Kuroda, Hoshin 19

Lawrence, Leanore and Andrew 72
Le Brun, Elisabeth Vigée 10
Le Brun, Jean-Baptiste-Pierre 10
Le Da Costa 60
Le Gros the Younger, Pierre 29
Lenin, Vladimir Ilyich 31
Lenox Library 62
Leslie, Charles Robert 62
Leveson-Gower, George, first Duke of Sutherland 11, 73, 88
Leveson-Gower, Ronald Charles Sutherland, lord 73
Liverpool Royal Institution 58
Lochoff, Nicholas 31
Loewi-Robertson Archive 97
Löwenstein, Abraham 64
Löwenstein, Markus 64
Lunacharsky, Anatoly 36
Lutetia typeface 61
Lyceum (London) 11, 82

Magnanti, Angelo 39, 44
Makowsky, Elena 85
Makowsky, Vladimir 85
Malvasia, Carlo Cesare, count 30
Manning, Ethelwyn 23
Marie-Antoinette, queen of France 10, 73, 91
Marten, Mary Helene *see* Witt, Mary
Martin, Ira W. 18, 24, 43
Mathewson, Hope 18
Matisse, Henri 25
Matter, Herbert 52
Max Grumbacher Art Supply Co. 59
Mayakovsky, Vladimir 26, 33, 37
McKillop, William 14
Mechel, Christian von 15
Medici, Lorenzo de' 58
Megatherium Club 99
Mellon, Andrew W. 36
Mensing, Anton 8, 78
Mexican Independence 83
Misme, Clothilde *see* Brière, Clothilde
The Misses Selby 46
Montias, John Michael 75
Monuments Men 51, 54
Morgan, Mary Jane 67
Morrow, Elizabeth Cutter 35
Mortlake Terrace 1
Mueller Mosaic Co. 39, 41
Mugnier, Charles 74
Mull, Jane 51
Muller, Frederick 8
Musin-Pushkin, A.S. 56

Nedley, Grace 6, 18, 23
New Economic Policy (NEP) 26
New York Art Resources Consortium *see* NYARC
Niarchos, Stavros 68

Nichi futsu geijutsu-sha 19
Nina Dausset (gallery) 70
Noelle, Marcel 78
Northbrook, Lord 1
NYARC 80

O'Keefe, Georgia 57
Ogiz, Marika 1, 77
Orleans collection 11, 29
Orléans sale 11, 73, 88
Orozco, José Clemente 83
Overholt, Karl. F. 1

Paillet, Alexandre Joseph 10
Palais-Royal 29
Palatine, Electors 15
Pannier, Enry 78
Pannier, G. 78
Park, Lawrence 14
Pasquali Press, 28
Perkins, F. Mason 17
Peter Coxe, Burrell and Foster (auctioneers) 11, 82
photographic field trips 14, 98
Photosecession 57
Pigage, Nicolas de 15
Pittsburgh 77
Pittsburgh, University of 45, 61
Platt, Daniel Fellows 78
Ploos van Amstel, Cornelis 20
Point Breeze, N.J. 32
Polastron, Gabrielle-Yolande, comtesse then duchesse de Polignac 10
Pollock, Jackson 52
Pontormo 45
pop art 69
Pope, John Russell 2, 42, 43, 45
Posada, José Guadalupe 83
Post-impressionist exhibitions 25
Poulet, Anne 42

Prestel, Johann Gottlieb 27
Prestel, Maria Katharina 27

Rapilly, Michel 91
Raumbild-Verlag Otto Schönstein 50
Rauschenberg, Robert 69
Raynal, Jeanne 52
Red Cross 1, 14, 46, 92
Reni, Guido 30
Rivera, Diego 35, 83
Robertson, Gabriella Kay Loewi 97
Robinson, Edward G. 68
Rodchenko, Aleksandr 26
Rogers, Bruce 61
Rolshoven, Juilius C. 47
Rosa, Salvatore 49
Roscoe, William 58
Rotan, Thurman 43
Royal Academy 93
Rudolf II, emperor 29, 64

Salisbury Cathedral 1
Sansoni, Mario 17
Santagostino, Giacomo Antonio Jr. 49
Savord, Ruth 7, 18
Schönfeld's Technological Museum 64
Schönstein, Otto Wilhelm 50
Scull, Ethel 69, 79
Scull, Robert C. 69, 79
Selby, The Misses *see* (The) Misses Selby
Serov, Valentin 36
Simon, Norton 59
Sirani, Elisabetta 30
Slade, Thomas Moore 11
Smith, Joseph (Consul Smith) 28
Smith, Matthew 58
Soirées de Paris 66

Soviet Writers Federation 33
Spanish art 13, 81
Speer, Albert 50
Stieglitz, Alfred 57
Stokes, Frank Wilbert 38, 47
The Story of the Frick Art Reference Library 23
Strahan, Edward 48
Suárez de Toledo Gaitán, Juan 100
Sullivan, Catherine 71
Surrealism 37, 60, 65, 70

Tank, Kurt Lothar 50
telautograph 40
Third Reich sculpture 50
Titian 100
Toyen 65
Traill, Thomas Stewart 58
Turner, Joseph Mallord William 21, 48, 49

Ulke Family Archive 99

Valadier, Giuseppe 90
Valadier, Luigi 90
Van Delip, John R. 4
Van Dyck, Anthony 87
Van Krimpen, Jan 61
Vanderbilt Mansion 5, 48
Vaudreuil, Joseph-Hyacinthe-François de Paule de Rigaud, comte de 10
Vienna Museum 64
Vienna Secession 85
VKhUTEMAS 26

Waldberg, Isabel 60
Walker Art Gallery 58
Walker, John 21
Walpole, Horace 28, 29, 49, 56
Walpole, Robert 29, 56
web archiving 80
Wedgwood, Josiah 96
Wells, Pauline (Polly) 17, 18
West, Benjamin 93
West, Raphael Lamar 93
Wharton Collection 56
Winstanley, Thomas 12, 58
Witt, Mary 1, 4
Witt, Robert 1, 3, 4, 6, 7, 15, 16, 27, 92